Ex-centric Cinema

Thinking Cinema

Series Editors
David Martin-Jones, University of Glasgow, UK
Sarah Cooper, King's College, University of London, UK
Volume 10

Ex-centric Cinema

Giorgio Agamben and Film Archaeology

Janet Harbord

Bloomsbury Academic
An imprint of Bloomsbury Publishing Inc

B L O O M S B U R Y
NEW YORK · LONDON · OXFORD · NEW DELHI · SYDNEY

Bloomsbury Academic
An imprint of Bloomsbury Publishing Inc

1385 Broadway	50 Bedford Square
New York	London
NY 10018	WC1B 3DP
USA	UK

www.bloomsbury.com

BLOOMSBURY and the Diana logo are trademarks of Bloomsbury Publishing Plc

First published 2016

© Janet Harbord, 2016

All rights reserved. No part of this publication may be reproduced or transmitted in any form or by any means, electronic or mechanical, including photocopying, recording, or any information storage or retrieval system, without prior permission in writing from the publishers.

No responsibility for loss caused to any individual or organization acting on or refraining from action as a result of the material in this publication can be accepted by Bloomsbury or the author.

Library of Congress Cataloging-in-Publication Data
Names: Harbord, Janet, author.
Title: Ex-centric cinema : Giorgio Agamben and film archaeology / Janet Harbord.
Other titles: Excentric cinema
Description: New York : Bloomsbury Academic, an imprint of Bloomsbury Publishing, Inc., 2016. | Series: Thinking cinema | Includes bibliographical references and index.
Identifiers: LCCN 2016009710 (print) | LCCN 2016021676 (ebook) | ISBN 9781628922424 (hardback) | ISBN 9781628922417 (pb) | ISBN 9781628922387 (epdf) | ISBN 9781628922400 (epub) | ISBN 9781628922387 (ePDF) | ISBN 9781628922400 (ePub)
Subjects: LCSH: Motion pictures–Moral and ethical aspects. | Agamben, Giorgio, 1942–Criticism and interpretation. | Motion pictures–Philosophy. | Motion pictures–Aesthetics. | BISAC: PERFORMING ARTS / Film & Video / History & Criticism. | PHILOSOPHY / General.
Classification: LCC PN1995.5 .H365 2016 (print) | LCC PN1995.5 (ebook) | DDC 791.4301–dc23
LC record available at https://lccn.loc.gov/2016009710

ISBN: HB: 978-1-6289-2242-4
PB: 978-1-6289-2241-7
ePDF: 978-1-6289-2238-7
ePub: 978-1-6289-2240-0

Typeset by Integra Software Services Pvt. Ltd.

For Tara

Contents

Acknowledgements		x
Introduction		1
1	**Girls and Other Incomplete Things: On Archaeological Method**	**21**
	Archaeology at the end of the world	21
	Incomplete film	27
	A fragment of a ruin	30
	'The Six Most Beautiful Minutes in the History of Cinema'	32
	Philosophical archaeology	35
	Typographic man	41
	The incomplete girl	44
	On the (im)possibility of (in)completion	45
	The incomplete girl (ii)	48
	Notes	52
2	**Gesture: Cinema Muto Mutato**	**57**
	Testing	57
	Test results: Inner life	58
	Running man	60
	Engram: Encryptions and transmissions	67
	Cinema gives itself up to psychology	71
	Seeing inside: Cinematic X-ray machines	77
	Biopolitics versus the donkey that craps gold coins	80
	Gesture as potentiality	84
	Transmitting cinema	88
	Notes	94
3	**Dim Stockings and Pornography: Community, Spectacle and the Example**	**101**
	What is disappearing?	101
	Community to come	103
	Barely discernable: Dim Stockings	106

The spectacle and the mass ornament	109
Pornography	113
Making an example of Chloë des Lysses	118
The example of Soad Hosny	122
Notes	126

4 Cinema as Laboratory: On Insects and the Anthropological Machine — 131

Flight	131
Types of machine I: The lottery machine	133
Interval	135
Mon Maître Marey	137
Mon Maître La Grosse Mouche Bleue	138
Types of machine II: The animal machine	139
Insect temporality	141
Divine insects	143
Air	145
Accident	147
Carriers of significance	148
Stones	150
Muteness	152
Incubators	155
Teleporting the interval	157
Types of machine III: The anthropological machine	158
Animal. Mineral.	160
Worlds	163
The concealedness of cinema	164
Notes	165

5 When the Assistants Profane Cinema — 169

Do it yourself: Instruction or description?	169
Lively matter	171
Assistants assisting	174
Amateur practices: Birt Acres makes the Birtac in conditions of dissent	180
Parody: A literary digression	186
St Anthony patron of lost things	190

	Play and profanation	194
	When this becomes that	196
	Notes	200
6	**Ex-centric Cinema**	**205**
	Towards X	205
	Assembling the cinematic machine: Three scenes from the separation of life	206
	Selective exclusions	211
	The machine at work: Producing centric cinema	214
	A nameless science	217
	Ex-centric cinema as transmission	219
	Ex-centric cinema as aggregate	222
	Ex-centric cinema as impotentiality	225
	Are films dead letters?	229
	Playout	231
	Notes	232

Bibliography	235
Index	245

Acknowledgements

My engagement with film archaeology began long before I was aware of it. The year was 1976. My parents had just invested in a new piece of audiovisual equipment: the home video player. The brand that they had chosen was Sony's Betamax (adopted also by industry). It was duly unwrapped and installed in our living room beneath the television. In what has become marketing lore however, the Betamax was almost immediately outpaced by a technically inferior rival system, JVC's VHS. For my sister and me, the realization that there would be no films to hire from the newly opened video store was a slow one. We admired the machine that sat beneath our television gathering dust and gradually our expectations of it changed. In moments of boredom and misanthropy we would post paper clips and other small matter through its front loading tray. We told the time on its digital clock. But we never watched films on it. New and yet obsolete, obsolete and new, it became an enigmatic object of untold secrets and stories. This is perhaps where it all started.

This book has been enriched by many people in many different places. My colleagues at Queen Mary in the department of Film Studies have provided, in addition to their collegiality, insightful and provocative discussion: Lucy Bolton, Jenny Chamarette, Charles Drazin, Sue Harris, Nick Jones, Alasdair King, Ros Murray, Anat Pick, Libby Saxton, Pauline Small, Guy Westwell and, in the School of Languages, Linguistics and Film more broadly, Shirley Jordan and Adrian Armstrong. Film Studies doctoral students Tay Graiwoot Chulphongsathorn, Calvin Fagan and Jo Stephenson have enriched my thinking in various ways. In the School of English and Drama at Queen Mary, Maria Delgado, Nick Ridout, Bill Schwarz and Lois Weaver have enlivened my environment as well as my thoughts. My involvement with a project that overlapped with the writing of this book, 'Bazaar Cinema', brought friendship with Amitabh Rai, Gil Toffell, Nurull Islam, Ali Assan, Phakarma and, at the Tiss School of Social Sciences, Mumbai, Anjali Monteiro, K.P. Jayasankar, Faiz Ullah and Nikhil Titus and, in Bangladesh, Lawrence Liang. Rosa Ainley and Jo Henderson have been comrades sharing the trials and tribulations of writing, thinking and rewriting. I would also like to extend thanks to former colleagues at Goldsmiths who in various ways contributed to the ideas formed here: Chris Berry, Lisa Blackman, Angela McRobbie, Rachel Moore, David Morley, Richard MacDonald, Robert Smith and Pasi Valiaho.

I am grateful to those who gave me the opportunity to experiment with these ideas through invitation to speak on Agamben and cinema: Olga Smith, curator of the Digital Image series at the Photographer's Gallery (London) in September 2011, Dina Iordanova at the University of St Andrews, David Martin-Jones and the postgraduate committee at the University of Glasgow, Carol Mavor at the University of Manchester, Gabriel Menotti and Virginia Crisp for *Besides the Screen*, and Mads Anders Baggesgaard and the Aesthetics Seminar at the University of Aarhuss, and to co-panelists Cathy Fowler and Michael Pigott for sharing ideas in Lisbon. Thoughts on the assistants and film production were stimulated by a discussion with the artist Simon Starling at Tate Britain in May 2013. My ideas have also benefitted through discussion with the students who took the Film Archaeology course at Queen Mary in recent years to whom I am indebted. I would also like to extend my thanks to *NECSUS European Journal of Media Studies* in which a version of Chapter 2 was published in Autumn 2015 as 'Agamben's cinema: Psychology versus an ethical form of life'.

For their views on translations of some of Agamben's terms and passages, I thank Jill Harbord and Daniela Lupi. For archival support during the researching of the book, I thank Brian Liddy and Rebecca Smith at the National Media Museum, Bradford, for their detailed knowledge and tenacity when going through the stores, and at the Muybridge Collections, Kingston, Charlotte Samuels and Jill Lamb.

For the opportunity to publish a book in this exciting new series of Thinking Cinema, I would like to offer enormous thanks to the series editors, Sarah Cooper and David Martin-Jones, with whom an informal conversation in Gordon Square was the start of something. They have provided unrelenting support, feedback and encouragement on versions of the manuscript, which has improved it beyond measure. I also thank Katie Gallof, editor of the Film list at Bloomsbury Academic, and Mary Al-Sayed for their ongoing goodwill in the face of various requests.

There are two people who have lived with this book and met its many challenges with nothing but good spirits and verve. My son Emile who is inquisitive about all things mechanical, scientific and philosophical, and is perfectly captured by Agamben's description of humanity's little scrap dealers, has been a great companion and source of fun. My biggest thanks go to my wonderful partner Tara who has been my best interlocutor, and the most enthusiastic and insightful reader of the manuscript. During the time of writing this book she has become my wife and my being is all the better for it! I dedicate this book to her.

Introduction

When the artist Rachel Whiteread made one of her first sculptures, *Closet* (1988) as a student, she cast the space inside a wardrobe in an attempt to capture the air and the atmosphere of the enclosure. In using the sides, shelves, floor and ceiling of the piece of furniture as a mould, the space within it was rendered an object. One could say that Whiteread transformed one thing into another, translating the properties of air into the concrete features of a sculpture. This act of translation has the effect of shifting the register of what is visible by bringing into being qualities, such as an atmosphere, that would traditionally fall outside of current systems of representation. After *Closet*, Whiteread continued the experiment; amongst her next works was a cast of the area underneath the bed upon which she was born, *Shallow Breath* (1988) and then spaces beneath a staircase, behind a row of books, under a desk, giving life to a realm comprised of seemingly unproductive and inert space. It is as though once glimpsed, the world of unobjects starts to appear everywhere with the effect that a familiar environment is put into reverse, that things are turned inside out, that nothing is in fact something. In the book that follows, a similar impulse is at work in an attempt to get hold of what might be called an unlived history of cinema, a cinema that is not visible until its negative form is cast as a set of objects, networks, practices and iterations. It is this that I am referring to as an ex-centric cinema, a cinema that resides not only in the margins and ephemera of cinema, but in the direct light of the everyday as a negative form, as space as yet uncast.

This book adopts a philosophically driven archaeological approach to elicit the form, detail, trace and shadow of ex-centric cinema as it exists in the space around and within the cinema that we have, and it engages the work of the Italian political philosopher Giorgio Agamben to do so. Archaeology in Agamben's work has had a sustained and modest presence across his writings from the 1970s onwards, yet it is only with the publication of *The Signature of All Things: On Method*,[1] published in Italian in 2008 and translated into English a year later, that his practice of a philosophical archaeology is fully elaborated. Agamben renders this practice of casting an illegible substance in terms of experience. That is, in every living moment there are potential experiences that are unlived, possible iterations of a life that exists in a space around the life that we lead. Agamben describes it in this way:

> Every present thus contains a part of non-lived experience. Indeed, it is, at the limit, what remains non-lived in every life, that which, for its traumatic character or its excessive proximity remains unexperienced in every experience.[2]

The non-lived, however, is not without influence. Its negative presence-as-absence presses in on the contemporary and shapes its form. An unlived history, that is, is not confined to a parallel track or the discrete margins of existence but operates forcefully in giving contour to the life that is lived, to the cinema that has come to be. In this description there inheres a grain of the Foucauldian premise that the excluded (albeit of identity, of sexuality or of knowledge) reveals the foundations of a system of thought more properly than the positive presentation of what is. Yet, Agamben's archaeology is more profoundly influenced in the final instance by Benjamin's thesis that the profane is not simply excluded matter but rather is that which lies dormant within the overlooked detail of the life, or cinema, that we have. His description of the 'immense forces of "atmosphere" concealed in these things' might very well describe Whiteread's sculptural objects or cinema's overlooked details that threaten to explode what we commonly subscribe to as reality.[3]

If ex-centric cinema is a name for the matter around the cinema that we have, (with a relation to the Greek ἐξ, meaning out of or from), what form does this take and how might we come to know it? The answer to this question directs us towards numerous sites of investigation. The first and most obvious destination is the archive, the storehouse of obsolete media and technical forms that are piled high in rooms labelled 'large object store' and 'small object store', at least in the sites of my research. The categories thereafter are less assured in their descriptive capacity: an ornate art deco sideboard (revealing a television screen behind a wooden roller desktop) resides next to a life-size cardboard sign of a bikini-clad woman advertising Polaroid photography that stands adjacent to a collection of stainless steel studio lights. The gathering has no evident collective noun or system of classification and whoever toils here is destined to inhale the dust of decades far apart. This is of course the appeal to archaeologists in search of random connections across media forms and across time whose impulse is to find new genealogies, to write new family resemblances and patterns of kinship amongst things, in effect replacing a positivist discourse of lineage with an evolving symmetry of the fractal.

The sites of ex-centric cinema, however, cannot be delimited by the structure of the archive, nor aligned along the axis of an enquiring subject and compliant objects. External to the archive is the ebb and flow of the everyday and its jumble of things and connections that entice us to do, to think, to dream and to experiment. Increasingly, as media theorists have argued, we are amateur assemblers and enquirers, and what we discover is untold possibilities for a cinema not yet born, the location of which is hard to determine in spatial terms. The practice of contemporary amateurs is a subject rather than a location for enquiry, which in turn recalls and resonates the labour of unauthorized or economically unviable practitioners of the past. Yet whilst the ledger of patent law testifies to a history of unrealized ideas, it upholds a notion of agency-in-creation as the provenance of the subject, the inventor whose will shapes the object at its inception. This division between subject and object is put into dispute by the concept of ex-centric cinema through which the material forms of the non-human world are co-actors and evolvers in the web of things produced. It is perhaps pertinent to add that within this conceptualization of agency as a distributed form, the concept of cinema itself is written as one stage in a process of endless transformation of technics and desires, with economic motive largely determining the stabilization of its form at various junctures.

An example of the form that ex-centric cinema takes is the stereoscopic spark drum camera, an assemblage that stabilizes as an invention in 1904 and is attributed to Lucien Bull, the protégée of chronophotographer Étienne-Jules Marey. The camera, a multiple assemblage in itself, is the stable point in a series of collaborations involving flies, photographic emulsion, micro-rotating engines, a rotary contact drum, brushes, wood, a sparking system and a scientifically interested audience. Bull's machine was devised in response to an enquiry about how fast an insect's wings beat, a feature of creaturely movement that, like the hooves of a galloping horse, exceeds the perceptual capacity of the human subject. Operating without a shutter, the frames of the filmstrip are the registration of movement illuminated for a brief instant by a spark. Significantly for our understanding of distributed agency, the process of filming the short sequences of flight was triggered by the insect as it launched. Bringing into contact the differential between human time and insect time, the event of the spark drum camera is a form of knowledge produced through the intra-action, to use Karen

Barad's descriptor, of multiple systems brought into relation.[4] Beyond this demonstration of insect flight and its scientific value, the film sequences revealed the arresting affective power of slow motion. As an accidental by-product of an experiment, this affective capacity of cinema was to become harnessed to more human-centred requirements in the development of narrative cinema as emotion amplified. Yet its potential to facilitate a relational intra-action between animal forms, including the human animal and insects, remains intact as an ex-centric cinema.

As one final footnote to this event of the stereoscopic spark drum camera, it is possible to read a reversal of our mode of thinking about the history of cinema. The reversal runs thus: the laboratory conditions in which this cinema of insects co-evolved were not reserved for the study of these creatures but became the transferable technique configured on a larger scale as a laboratory for human subjects. Cinema, that is, may be regarded as the containment and control of human sensory capacities through types of privation: darkened auditoriums, fixed seating arrangements, bans on food and beverages all of which regulated and delimited corporal experience. The human creature who, seemingly, has presided at the centre of the system of moving images, appears as the insect-like creature caught in a web of sensory control, with his head fixed in a compulsory manner towards images of his free self on the screen before him. The demarcation between insect and human, between freedom and captivation and indeed between captivation and boredom is suddenly less than clear.

At this point it is possible to comprehend how an ex-centric cinema is a methodology, and not merely a set of possibilities running in parallel but an incision, a detail or a signature that allows entry to a new mode of reading the present and the past together. It is a method the contours of which Agamben sketches in his essay 'What Is the Contemporary?,' opening with the injunction that in reading past works (be that images, written texts or other objects) it is incumbent upon us to become their contemporary.[5] Drawing on Nietzsche's observation that 'the contemporary is the untimely',[6] those who have a relationship with the contemporary never perfectly coincide with their time but are disconnected through anachronism, a distancing measure or an out of time. Conversely, the archaic is present and appears to us in the detail of the current time, but not as an origin to which one may return as a site of authenticity or authority. The origin 'is contemporary with historical becoming and does not cease to operate within it, just as the embryo continues to be active in the tissues of the mature organism, and the child in the psychic life of the adult'.[7] In reading for the ex-centric, the movement is not one of back and forth across time, but of reading the past as effective in the present, ultimately erasing the distinction between then and now, dismantling the discourse of progress along the way.

One further attribute of the method of ex-centric reading that operates through a philosophical archaeology is the exertion of pressure upon systems of binary thought. In returning to moments of division, in which for example cinema becomes a mode of recording separated from acts of transmission, the fracture of this division becomes reworked and brought into question. The so-called official history of cinema accords it predominantly the capacity to witness and document rather than to disseminate. In classical film theory, cinema is valued for its revelatory potential and for its ability to preserve, thereby inculcating cinema in a process of securing the past as a record, contributing to what Nietzsche critically referred to as monumental history. Yet in reading the signature turns of cinema through acts of gesture (in the following pages), the image is seen to transmit variously across time, changing according to how the qualities and opacities of the image resonate with other features of its environment. Reworking the story of origins in effect wears away the seam of distinction, revealing recording and transmission to be two parts of the same activity. This is one of the crucial binary divisions to undergo treatment in this book, in addition to the separation between (the past and the present). We can add to this the division that cleaves cinema from other media as an autonomous and media-specific system rather than an aggregate form composed of multiple properties, and finally, the line that separates the actual from the potential. If, in his most famous work, *Homo Sacer*, Agamben sets out to combat 'the primacy of actuality' over potentiality in the domain of politics and ontology, the task of an ex-centric project is to dismantle the primacy of actuality over potentiality in the realm of cinema.[8]

If an ex-centric approach draws a philosophical archaeology into correspondence with film archaeology, there are questions of the strains and tensions between the two types of approaches and their fruitful dialogue. The following section provides an indication of how Agamben's work has been adopted by film scholarship before moving on to the limits between his philosophical archaeology and that of a media archaeology (within which film archaeology resides).

Giorgio Agamben: Philosophical archaeology into film archaeology

Whilst Agamben's practice as a philologist has produced a body of work across different loci and disciplinary fronts, he is best known for the ongoing project of books that comprise the *Homo Sacer* series.[9] He is highly influential in contemporary conceptualizations of political life, forcefully arguing that the suspension of law, far from being a temporary measure, constitutes the foundation of modern power as a state of permanent crisis and exception. Yet, as Leland de la Durantaye notes, the effect of the fame of the *Homo Sacer* series has been to focus critical attention on this select number of texts, obscuring the range, depth and dimensionality of a body of work produced over four and a half decades.[10] Such a selective focus has also restricted understanding of the term political as it is manifest variously across Agamben's work, reducing it to concepts that may be directly applied to current events to 'make sense' of the contemporary; the state of exception and its application to the suspension of rights at Guantanamo Bay is but one instance. As a result, some of the most finely grained readings and subtle inferences of Agamben's method, rooted in philology and characterized by a patient movement between the archaic past and the present, fall by the wayside. A further effect of Agamben's prominence as a political philosopher has been his assimilation by the disciplines of politics and law, whilst his relevance to the disciplines of film, visual culture, literature and history across subjects as weighty as eschatology, ethics, the biopolitical, anthropocentrism and time is only in the process of emerging.

A growing body of Agamben scholarship dedicated to film and visual culture has begun to move through the wider body of Agamben's work, generating a conversation that 'fundamentally rethinks the theory and praxis of film'.[11] This work, which Henrik Gustafsson and Asbjørn Grønstad situate within the emergence of film philosophy as a distinct research area within cinema studies, has responded to the select number of texts in which Agamben explicitly addresses cinema,[12] and more recently, moved beyond these to engage a wider number of concepts and ideas. Each of these essays is characterized by what Christian McCrea has aptly named Agamben's 'love for analysis-as-spectrum'.[13] Perhaps the most influential essay to have an impact on the study of film has been 'Notes on Gesture', a text that appeared in its earliest iteration in the book *Infancy and History: Essays on the Destruction of Experience*, published in

Italian in 1978 and in English in 1993.[14] Here, Agamben positions cinema at the forefront of a transition of biopolitical relating in which human communicability (an openness to communicating with others) as gesture is caught in the act of its own disappearance. That is, the human subject's capacity to communicate is, in the earliest manifestation of cinema, found to be waning, its residue form trapped within a pathologized form of gesture including the ticks and spasms of a body leaking communicative disorder.

Agamben's analysis of a catastrophe of gesture is read by Pasi Väliaho as the entry of the human body into a 'new system of sensation and reference ... so that it changes in function and in substance',[15] a moment that Deborah Levitt identifies as 'the joint production of modern biopolitics and new media technologies'.[16] The essay on gesture, despite its gnomic form, is the text in which Agamben flashes up a new history of the image, one in which cinema has a privileged place but is simultaneously rewritten from within. For Agamben, cinema facilitates a prolonged stare at the image as it mutates across time, a transformation that he takes up seventeen years later in a memorial lecture dedicated to Guy Debord, 'Difference and Repetition: On Guy Debord's Films'.[17] Here, he adopts Debord's diagnosis of a cinema that is at once part of the machine of separating our desires from us and playing them back in commodified form, and the retainer of a redemptive possibility. Benjamin Noys, whose engagements with Agamben's film essays have been seminal markers in the field, writes that for Agamben as for Debord, every image 'is a force field structured by a polarity between the deadly reification and obliteration of gesture ... and as the preservation of a dynamis intact'.[18] Cinema is both things, and in the vignette essay that describes cinema's destruction through Don Quixote's slashing at the screen,[19] 'The Six Most Beautiful Minutes in the History of Cinema', cinema's destruction bears as many fruits, if not more, than its positive manifestation.

There is also criticism of Agamben's engagement with cinema from film scholars for his selective practice of consistently drawing on avant-garde filmmakers such as Jean-Luc Godard and Debord, and ignoring the main substance of cinema as narrative form. Garrett Stewart comments that when Agamben writes about cinematic montage and its capacity to illuminate difference, 'his avant-garde preferences narrow the application of his vocabulary even as they may sharpen his aesthetic sights'.[20] Agamben's avoidance, if it may be called that, of narrative cinema marks for Stewart an unnecessary limit to the thesis on montage and repetition as the two transcendental features of cinema. Coming from another direction, James S. Williams finds in Agamben's 'small but urgent' body of work on cinema an unnecessary disregard of the aesthetic in favour of ethics.[21] Referencing Agamben's near dismissal of the aesthetic in the essay on gesture, which relocates cinema in the realm of ethics and politics, Williams suggests that ethics provides a safe option that pulls aesthetics back into its territory. In asking the question 'does the aesthetic have any real role or function now?', there is a sense that Agamben has effectively remaindered the category.[22] Yet in Alex Murray's critical introduction, we find a different reading of Agamben's engagement with aesthetics as the charting of a failure of the aesthetic. He writes, '*Gesture* is the name for the harnessing of the collapse of subjectivity and aesthetics, and cinema is the aesthetic space in which this is most possible.'[23] Cinematic aesthetics, viewed awry, present a form of ruin that can be grasped as a differential.

Film scholars have also engaged with Agamben's thought beyond the confines of the cinema essays. His work on the paradigm of the camp, elucidated in *Homo Sacer* (1995) as the generic 'nomos' of the modern and developed in *Remnants of Auschwitz* (1998) as a particular manifestation of the camp as Holocaust, has had resonance in various treatments of cinema. In film analysis, Agamben's reading of the camp as a pre-eminent figure of modernity is reinvested from the position of cinema as a medium with the capacity to record (or 'witness'), register and transmit. Libby Saxton's compelling discussion of the ethical relations pertaining to the idea of witnessing, and film's complex relation to this, both engages and critiques Agamben's account of *der Muselmann* (the figure of the starved and emaciated prisoner of the camps who is resigned to his own death) as a paradigmatic figure of suffering. This subject is revisited in Trond Lundemo's analysis of the archive as a site of death[24] and Henrik Gustafsson's application of the concept of 'remnant' to Palestine.[25] There is, in addition, an increasing trend to take a concept from Agamben's cache of ideas with which to read individual films, a practice evidenced by essays such as Carolyn Ownbey's analysis of bare life in *Hotel Rwanda*.[26] In terms of its provenance, it is also notable that Agamben's work is selectively being anthologized in edited collections dedicated to visual culture.[27]

Yet it is Agamben's philosophical archaeology that finds resonance with an interdisciplinary set of debates oriented by the term media archaeology that seeks to make correspondences between moments and events far apart and objects disparate in nature, illuminating the potential of a thing from the past in the now-time of the contemporary. This Benjaminian inflection in Agamben's archaeology finds a corresponding model of temporality in Siegfried Zielinski's work on the *deep time* of media. The descriptor is a phrase borrowed from geologist John McPhee, who uses it to distinguish the scale of cosmological time from the temporality of everyday life. Zielinski's archaeology brings to the study of media an account of tangentially related and bizarrely inspired inventors whose method is that of the polymath (such as the seventeenth-century German Jesuit scholar Athanasius Kircher), the importing of ideas from one domain into another ad infinitum. One of the aims of Zielinski's method is 'a reversal with respect to time', where the smooth narrative of technological progress is undone by the many dramatic and unruly events that multiply the potential of the past. He writes, 'The goal is to uncover dynamic moments in the media-archaeological record that abound and revel in heterogeneity and, in this way, to enter into a relationship of tension with various present-day moments, relativize them, and render them more decisive.'[28] The political implications of such an incisive reading of the past and present together can be found in Laura U. Marks's project to write a media archaeology through Arabic-Islamic arts and sciences in her recent *Enfoldment and Infinity* (2010), a work that locates Islamic thought in the midst of contemporary media practice. Conceptual workings of dimension, rhythm, the vector, aniconism and infinity find affinity between contemporary digital art and historical Islamic arts that practice the same understanding of virtual and actual levels. Her incision into Islamic art, demonstrating how the patterns of a Persian carpet prefigure the algorithmic aesthetics of the contemporary digital aesthetic, operates to make the relation between Islamic theology and the present, in Zielinski's terms, more decisive.[29]

The features of a media archaeological practice may be summarized in terms of the following: a disregard for traditional disciplinary boundaries across which correspondences are worked and reworked with the aim of their erasure, the embrace of a deep time model of temporality in which patterns of co-evolution and change are mapped on vastly different scales, a setting into motion of cross-interference of the past and present to create joins 'out of time' and a predilection for the marginal, the ephemeral and the barely legible. Whilst Agamben's archaeology exercises a more precise identification of 'cuts' and their treatment through the concepts of the signature and the paradigm (which we come to in Chapter 1), it shares a common goal with media archaeology of altering an experience of time, a goal with a political exigency.[30] William Watkins articulates the characteristics of Agamben's archaeology as 'a radical intent towards change in the present through a critical relationship to what is determined as "past" within contemporary structures of transmissible intelligibility'.[31] However, there are two further related aspects to media archaeology and the discourses that it draws from that are less compatible with Agamben's focus. The first of these is a radical critique of anthropocentrism as the dominant orientation of historical and philosophical accounts of media (which appears variously as accounts of the anthropocene, critical animal studies and posthumanism). The second related approach refuses both consciousness and the text as the site of enquiry for the study of media, embracing instead the challenge of an irreducible materialism, a set of approaches that are named variously as a material turn, a speculative turn and a continental realism. Clearly, both of these aspects of media archaeology problematize the centrality of the human in western metaphysics and point to its radical delimitation of the field of enquiry, that is, its bracketing of any concept of the 'real' that falls outside of the perceptual apparatus and sensible range of the human subject. There is, I will argue, a gulf between the approaches grouped together here and that of Agamben's philosophical enquiry, which returns repeatedly to and turns recursively upon the question of what it means to be human.

Agamben has of course addressed anthropocentrism directly. The question of the animal receives focused treatment as the anthropological machine in *The Open* (2004), where the arbitrary and unstable border between man and animal is redescribed as the marking of a separation that suspends their mutual animality or creatureliness. This division underpins Agamben's project more broadly as the political philosopher of the state of exception, famously elaborated in the *Homo Sacer* series. In his definition of life, taken from Aristotle, as a form split between *bios* (the life of the polis) and *zoe* (the body of bare life) life is more than one thing, both biological existence and the life of political speech and acts. As it is the right exercised by the sovereign to suspend the rules of the polis, effectively creating an exclusion of certain forms of life that are rendered devoid of humanity and situated outside of the political terrain in the space of the camp, the paradox arises that the sovereign authorizes the temporary suspension of a law that supports his power. In excluding certain forms of life, the state of exception effectively draws a distinction between bare life and the life of the citizen; the state of exception would seem to be another demonstration of the anthropological machine at work. Yet despite the analysis of the machine that permanently cleaves the critical distinction of human from non-human animal, the non-human animal persists as an aberration for the human within his account of the camp, for example. As John Mullarkey notes, 'Agamben is disingenuous when he argues that bare life is "neither an animal life nor a human life", for it is much closer to the former in value.'³² Non-human animals feature infrequently in Agamben's work, and when they do it is as a creature from fable or the Bible, such as the donkey that craps golden coins or the hen that speaks,³³ animals that have human or magical qualities. They are, therefore, the animal crossed out or under erasure. At the centre of Agamben's philosophy, it is the human who insinuates himself as the figure whose presence gives recourse to the (Heideggerian) question of what it means that the human has language, and furthermore in (Benjaminian) eschatological mode, the question of what form the salvation of humanity might take. It should, however, be noted that Benjamin's notion of the world as 'unsavable' and 'irreparable', that is, not in need of human redemption, provides for Agamben a possibility of 'letting beings be *outside of being*', in Matthew Calarco's summative description.³⁴

Zielinski's dictum that media are essentially inhuman strikes a markedly different chord for media archaeology, where humans are neither the origin nor the natural actants in an account of media, and unsurprisingly, in the background to many media archaeological works is Friedrich Nietzsche, whose critique of humanity and human consciousness appears as an inspiration for thinking otherwise. The media theorist Jussi Parikka is inspirational in this regard, with his work *Insect Media* (2010) a study of the transposition between insects and media technologies from the nineteenth century to the present. Insects, he writes, are implicit to the concept and design of various media as engineers, weavers and transmitters who systematize, collectivize and swarm, all without the influence or recognition of human worlds. Parikka avoids the deductive model of what can be learned from insects (as the US military has attempted to quantify), rather, insects are themselves media if we understand media (with a Deleuzian inflection) as the contraction of forces in the world to produce particular resonance. He writes:

> In other words, the fascination with simple forms of life such as insects, viruses, and the like has been interfaced with media design and theory for years now, but nineteenth century entomology, and various other cultural discourses and practices since then, have hailed the powers of insects as media in themselves, capable of weird affect worlds, strange sensations, and uncanny potentials that cannot immediately be pinpointed in terms of a register of known possibilities.³⁵

Insects provide models of social organization to be mimicked, strategies of sensory response to an environment composed of multiple forms of life and metaphors for the relationship of biology to technology, but they are also irreducibly creaturely others internal to a human media world.

Critical animal studies also attend to the crucial place of creatures in mediating the relationship between bodies and technologies, and the transitions marking a late nineteenth-century industrial culture and a twentieth-century modernism. Akira Lippit's historical analysis, *Electric Animal* (2000), returns to the horizon of modernism as the moment in which animals were evacuated from the rituals and patterns of urban life, causing their reappearance in psychoanalytic, biopolitical and technological discourses, and in particular the realm of cinema, as trace. The loss of (non-human) animals from everyday life in late nineteenth-century life, writes Lippit, invokes their reappearance elsewhere as figures of melancholic reflection. For the loss of the non-human animal is always also the loss of the human animal, a capacity that must at all cost be disavowed. The cinema is a crypt where the other than human resides spectacularly and into infinity (the cinema's embalming function), a deathly residence where the animal is endlessly animated by the new circuits of technology, electricity and biopolitical circulation.[36] The animal takes us to the centre of questions of mortality and realism, two complex and imbricated terms in cinema's history, which are reworked in Anat Pick's suggestive account of a creaturely cinema. By re-positioning cinematic realism within the domain of bodies and necessity, a creaturely cinema 'rejects in the name of realism the editorial constructions of humanism'.[37] The (often obsessive) concern with cinematic specificity across a century of writing on film is here brought into contact with its underbelly, that is with its implication in the production of species differentiation, or in Pick's terms speciation.

The concern to break with a human-centred epistemology characterizes another cluster of thinkers whose work is not explicitly addressed to cinema but nonetheless has relevance for thinking cinematically. The object-oriented philosophy of Graham Harman, Ray Brassier and Iain Hamilton Grant, in dialogue with Quentin Meillassoux's *After Finitude* (2008), challenges in very different ways the predominance of both post-Kantian and post-structural thought alike by reaching speculatively for a concept of realism that is not dependent on human consciousness nor reduced to textuality.[38] In this form of speculative realism, the world is constituted by things that are 'real' if we apply a definition of the term that does not limit reality to perception or consciousness. The non-human world, it is argued, is not dependent for its existence on a human capacity to know it, an approach that not only relegates the human, but reduces his involvement to that of an observer. Objects and non-human others have an allure for each other, and the equivocation that this brings about is described by Harman at the beginning of *The Quadruple Object* (2011) in this way when he writes 'the interaction between cotton and fire belongs on the same footing as human interaction between cotton and fire'.[39] It is a statement that contrasts strikingly with Heidegger's prosaic pronouncement on ontological registers in which the stone is world-less, the animal is world poor and only the human is world forming. And whilst Agamben makes some rapprochement between the categorical distinction of animal and man in Heidegger's account, he fails to attend to the relegation of the stone (as we find in Chapter 4).

The continental materialist approach has impacted on the field of film philosophy in dialogue with the renewed interest in André Bazin's writing on realism and cinema, of which John Mullarkey's writings are exemplary.[40] The return to the concept of realism, however, is of a markedly different order from its earlier iteration. Mullarkey schematically presents the difference in terms of ontology: 'Ontologically speaking, for materialist systems, there is no fundamentally different *kind* of being (substance, process, property) outside the system, and indeed both representation or biology here would be of the same ultimate stuff as matter.'[41] Speculative realism also lends itself to partnership with the processual thinking of Manuel DeLanda, whose archaeologies turn towards the most radical interdisciplinarity, interfacing in one book, *A Thousand Years of Nonlinear History*, geological, biological and linguistic history.[42] This analysis pursues the changing formation of matter and energy as it manifests variously as stones and water, corn farming and nitrogen, villages and high roads, in a dynamic model of stasis and flux written within the folds of a *deep time*. In the midst of these currents, human life is commensurate with other non-human forms, but not greater in importance. It is analogous to other forms of matter in its patterns of change over time, and yet its pace of transformation is subject to different rates. DeLanda's presentation of these various ontologies as systems in constant (but differentially charged) processes of transformation posits the gradual shifts in human language as akin to the changes in the composition of stone as it travels through a river.

The book that follows

Ex-centric Cinema joins these conversations by a reading that moves as two differently motivated currents. The first approaches the practices, objects and texts that constitute what we call cinema largely through and with Agamben's philosophy, although at times critical of its focus, whilst the second inverts the direction by moving from practices, objects and ideas about cinema towards Agamben's thought. Chapter 1 reads Agamben's method into cinema's shadows, finding in the incomplete film a version of cinema that exists at the edges, that proffers a glimpse of an unlived cinema and yet fails to fully disclose its form. The incomplete film, we could say, emerges in this chapter as an unthought cinematic paradigm that through archaeological method comes into view. The chapter works from the scene of Quixote's slashing of the cinema screen in Agamben's 'The Six Most Beautiful Minutes in the History of Cinema', to trace this image to a lost sequence from the unfinished film *Don Quixote*, by Orson Welles that appeared online as a film fragment in the same year as Agamben's publication of the essay. This enigmatic deconstruction of cinema enables Agamben to speculate on what 'supports' cinema, revealing the unthought cinema beneath or behind it, a cinema of materials, entities and substances, as well as the revenants of Orson Welles's cinema. In this chapter that aims to bring into view a theory of archaeology through both its discursive elaboration and its practice, we are offered cinema as one manifestation of a paradigm that emerges as both a repeatable example, a single case that through repetition has the ability to model behaviour and values, and a constellation of technologies and techniques whose relations were given coherence only under a paradigmatic logic.

The subject of the second chapter is gesture, an optic that Agamben uses to view cinema not as a series of moving images but as a mode of communication and historical transmission. Yet if gesture is the site of a potential within cinema to operate *historically*, it is also the locus of a biopolitical investiture in the human body that takes place towards the end of the nineteenth century. The human body, famously in Agamben's account, displays its failing capacity for gesture as communicability through an increasingly bizarre repertoire of bodily tics and spasms that are revealed in early cinema. This account of gesture has gained considerable traction in film scholarship, yet a particular line of the essay on gesture, I argue, has largely gone unnoticed, a line that marks the establishment of human identity as an interior modality: 'In this phase the bourgeoisie, which just a few decades earlier was still firmly in possession of its symbols, succumbs to interiority and gives itself up to psychology.'[43] This chapter pursues the various manifestations of a turn towards interiority as truth (and away from communicative interaction), suggesting that cinema comes into being as an apparatus tasked with articulating human truth through an array of affective presentations. Resonant with a new set of investigative procedures such as the X-ray, deployed to verify corporeal interiority, the cinema adjusts its reliance on gesture from 1927 onwards when speech may disclose the inside. The revelation of interiority as feeling and expression identifies the body-come-star as the site of an enigma that the film seeks to resolve, interpellating the film star as an autonomous entity, or an individual, to borrow Jodi Dean's formulation.[44] The transition from communicative gesture to enigmatic interiority invokes then the loss of a commons, a loss that has political dimensions.

The loss of a commons is taken up in the third chapter, where the question of cinema's relation to community and the possibility of a 'whatever being' is considered. The chapter begins with an engagement of the ideas Agamben presents in *The Coming Community* (1990), a collection of essays published shortly after the fall of the Berlin wall in 1989. 'Whatever being' is a term that Agamben uses to attempt to describe the possibility of a community that has no criteria for belonging. Cinema's part in this discussion is not as a producer of collectives (as workers or audiences), but as a cultural form implicated both in the endless reproduction of the spectacle, as Guy Debord named the relations mediated by the image, and as a practice able to suspend the spectacle's function. In an essay dedicated to Debord, Agamben names cinema once again as a medium of transformational potential. Citing cinema's 'transcendentals', as stoppage and repetition, there is the possibility, he argues, that cinema above other cultural forms can jam the system of commodity image flow. In a further and final development of the argument on the image as commodity, Agamben turns to the example of pornography and the porn star's clichéd return-look-to-camera as an example of a disruption and suspension of the spectacular system that separates our desires from us and replays them as images. It is in this interpretation of film solely as virtual image rather than as material event, I argue, that Agamben's argument fails to engage with the potential of cinema fully. A more effective example (as both exemplary instance and paradigmatic feature) of jamming the system is to be found in the irrepressible interference or 'noise' of a media system whose presence destroys the pretence of the image as a version of the real.

The potential manifest as interference in cinema continues in Chapter 4, with attention to the presence of flies, dragonflies, bluebottles in its early history and the development of a stereoscopic spark drum camera. A moment in cinema's emergence is recast as a creaturely driven assemblage that reverses the account of an inevitably anthropocentric cinema. Integral to the discussion is

Agamben's treatise on the subject of the human–animal distinction in his work *The Open* (2002), where his engagement with Heidegger's explication of *Dasein* in *Fundamental Concepts of Metaphysics* and *Parmenides* is somewhat equivocal. This chapter suggests that the concept of captivation that orients Heidegger's discussion can be fruitfully rethought through the figure of the fly, the scene of the experiment and cinema as a human laboratory. Chapter 5 threads together amateurism, assistants, hallways, minor characters and the Birtac box camera projector as an assemblage that exhibits its own quixotic functionality. Rereading the term 'parody' as a mode to the side of another, the chapter configures an ex-centric cinema practice in the minor space and activities of minor characters, namely those who are assistants to those in office. In a number of essays, Agamben renders Kafka's assistants and Benjamin's hunchback as figures whose ordinariness shines on judgment day, inverting the terms of success and productivity. This inversion is also a parody, a productive unproductivity (or in Agamben's terminology, inoperativity) that befits the amateur inventors and innovators of the late nineteenth century whose machinic enterprises unravel the structures that they create. A chapter punning on twins and twinning, official and unofficial accounts, and the sacred and profane, the border maintaining these divisions is on closer inspection less than secure.

The final chapter arrives at the topic of ex-centric cinema, which is manifest both as a name for the relationships that we have to cinema and as a name for what Agamben calls potentiality. Here, the question of what exactly archaeology can gain access to is examined. Does it work from phantasmatic ruins to build a fictional enterprise, in the spirit of Eric Kluitenberg's *The Book of Imaginary Media* (2007),[45] Christian Janicot's *Anthologie du Cinéma Invisible* (1995),[46] Lippit's shadow archive of destroyed Palestinian films[47] or the artist Sarah Wood's reconstruction of the Palestinian Film Archive through retellings and drawings of the films lost, *For Cultural Purposes Only* (2009)? Or is it the constellation of that which has never yet been aligned but lies dormant? The practice of archaeology as ex-centric cinema is read with Agamben's concept of potentiality. This is a complex concept derived from Agamben's reinterpretation of one line from Aristotle's Book Theta of *Metaphysics*, a rereading that displaces the traditional opposition between potentiality and actuality. In Agamben's sightline, potentiality is both the past form of actuality and also the ability to not bring (a thought, a concept) into practice; 'all potentiality is non-potentiality', he writes. Ex-centric cinema is read within this paradigm, emerging as a term in two parts, and this is the final designation of the book. It is the potential cinema that rests in its own impotentiality, recursively drawing us back to what remains in reserve. It is, in addition, the designation of non-cinema, of the materials, subjects, political situations and compromises that have foreclosed possibilities in many different contexts in many different times. In its double articulation, as a force that is felt more than seen, the ex-centric thus partly defines the cinema that we have.

Notes

1 Giorgio Agamben, *The Signature of All Things: On Method*, trans. Luca D'Isanto and Kevin Attell (New York: Zone Books, 2009).
2 Agamben, *The Signature of All Things*, 101.
3 Walter Benjamin, 'Surrealism', in *One-Way Street and Other Writings*, trans. Edmund Jephcott and Kingsley Shorter (London and New York: Verso, 1979), 229.
4 Karen Barad, *Meeting the Universe Halfway: Quantum Physics and the Entanglement of Matter and Meaning* (Durham and London: Duke University Press, 2007).
5 Giorgio Agamben, 'What Is the Contemporary?' is an essay published in Italian as 'Che cos'è il contemporaneo?' (2008), and in English as part of the collection *What Is an Apparatus? and Other Essays*, trans. David Kishik and Stefan Pedatella (Stanford, CA: Stanford University Press, 2009), 39–54.
6 Agamben, 'What Is the Contemporary?' 40.
7 Ibid., 50.
8 Giorgio Agamben, *Homo Sacer: Sovereign Power and Bare Life*, trans. Daniel Heller-Roazen (Stanford, CA: Stanford University Press, 1998), 44.
9 The *Homo Sacer* series is an ongoing project that began with the publication of Part I, *Homo Sacer: Sovereign Power and Bare Life* (1995), followed by a growing number of parts published out of chronological order. Part II comprises *State of Exception*, trans. Kevin Attell (Chicago: University of Chicago Press, 2003), *The Kingdom and the Glory: For a Theological Genealogy of Economy and Government*, trans. Lorenzo Chiesa and Matteo Mandarini (Stanford, CA: Stanford University Press, 2011), *The Sacrament of Language: An Archaeology of the Oath*, trans. Adam Kotsko (London, New York and Delhi: Polity, 2010), and *Opus Day: An Archaeology of Duty*, trans. Adam Kotsko (Stanford, CA: Stanford University Press, 2013). Part III is *Remnants of Auschwitz: The Witness and the Archive*, trans. Daniel Heller-Roazen (New York: Zone Books, 1999), and Part IV *The Highest Poverty: Monastic Rules and Forms-of-Life*, trans. Adam Kotsko (Stanford: Stanford University Press, 2013).
10 Leland de la Durantaye, 'Introduction', in *Giorgio Agamben: A Critical Introduction* (Stanford, CA: Stanford University Press, 2009), 1–25.

11 H. Gustafsson and A. Grønstad (eds), *Cinema and Agamben: Ethics, Biopolitics and the Moving Image* (New York, London, New Delhi and Sydney: Bloomsbury Academic, 2014), 2.
12 There are two further short texts on cinema by Agamben recently translated and published by Gustafsson and Grønstad in their edited collection *Agamben and Cinema*: 'For an Ethics of the Cinema' and 'Cinema and History: On Jean-Luc Godard'.
13 Christian McCrea, 'Giorgio Agamben', in *Film, Theory and Philosophy: The Key Thinkers*, ed. Felicity Colman (Durham: Acumen, 2009), 354.
14 Giorgio Agamben, 'Notes on Gesture', in *Infancy and History: Essays on the Destruction of Experience*, trans. Liz Heron (London and New York: Verso, 1993), 133–140.
15 Pasi Väliaho, *Mapping the Moving Image: Gesture, Thought and Image circa 1900* (Amsterdam: Amsterdam University Press, 2010), 31.
16 Deborah Levitt, 'Notes on Media and Biopolitics: "Notes on Gesture"', in *The Work of Giorgio Agamben: Law, Literature and Life*, eds Justin Clemens, Nicholas Heron and Alex Murray (Edinburgh: Edinburgh University Press, 2008), 193.
17 Giorgio Agamben 'Difference and Repetition: On Guy Debord's Films', in *Guy Debord and the Situationist International: Texts and Documents*, ed. Tom McDonough (Cambridge, MA and Cambridge, UK: an October Book for MIT Press, 2002), 313–320.
18 Benjamin Noys, 'Film-of-Life: Agamben's Profanation of the Image', in *Cinema and Agamben: Ethics, Biopolitics and the Moving Image*, eds H. Gustafsson and A. Grønstad (New York, London, New Delhi and Sydney: Bloomsbury Academic, 2014), 89–102, 92.
19 Giorgio Agamben, 'The Six Most Beautiful Minutes in the History of Cinema', *Profanations*, trans. Jeff Fort (New York: Zone Books), 93–94.
20 Garrett Stewart, 'Counterfactual, Potential, Virtual: Toward a Philosophical Cinematics', in *Cinema and Agamben: Ethics, Biopolitics and the Moving Image*, eds H. Gustafsson and A. Grønstad (New York, London, New Delhi and Sydney: Bloomsbury Academic, 2014), 261.
21 James S. Williams, 'Silence, Gesture, Revelation: The Ethics and Aesthetics of Montage in Godard and Agamben', in *Cinema and Agamben: Ethics, Biopolitics and the Moving Image*, eds H. Gustafsson and A. Grønstad (New York, London, New Delhi and Sydney: Bloomsbury Academic, 2014), 27–54, 29.
22 Ibid., 29.
23 Alex Murray, *Giorgio Agamben* (London and New York: Routledge, 2010), 90.
24 Trond Lundemo, 'Montage and the Dark Margin of the Archive', in *Cinema and Agamben: Ethics, Biopolitics and the Moving Image*, eds H. Gustafsson and A. Grønstad (New York, London, New Delhi and Sydney: Bloomsbury Academic, 2014), 191–206.

25 Henrik Gustafsson, 'Remnants of Palestine, or, Archaeology after Auschwitz' in *Cinema and Agamben: Ethics, Biopolitics and the Moving Image*, eds H. Gustafsson and A. Grønstad (New York, London, New Delhi and Sydney: Bloomsbury Academic, 2014), 207–230.

26 Carolyn Ownbey, 'The Abandonment of Modernity: Bare Life and the Camp in *Homo Sacer* and *Hotel Rwanda*', *disClosure: A Journal of Social Theory*, 22:1/5 (2013): 17–22, Special Edition 'Security'.

27 For example, Agamben's text 'Nymphs' appears in *Releasing the Image: From Literature to New Media*, eds Jacques Khalip and Robert Mitchell (Stanford, CA: Stanford University Press, 2011), 60–80.

28 Siegfried Zielinski, *The Deep Time of the Media: Toward an Archaeology of Hearing and Seeing by Technical Means*, trans. Gloria Custance (Amsterdam: Amsterdam University Press, 1999), 11.

29 Laura U. Marks, *Enfoldment and Infinity: An Islamic Genealogy of New Media Art* (Cambridge, MA and London: MIT Press, 2010), 180.

30 The most explicit description of the political urgency in this regard Agamben makes in the essay 'Time and History: Critique of the Instant and the Continuum' in *Infancy and History*. He writes, '… every culture is first and foremost a particular experience of time, and no new culture is possible without an alteration in this experience. The original task of a genuine revolution, therefore, is never merely to "change the world", but also – and above all – to "change time."' (91–105), 91. Agamben returns to this idea throughout his work, most poignantly in recent publications in his study of the relationship of messianic time in the Pauline text 'Letter to the Romans' and Benjamin's late work, 'Theses on the Philosophy of History', *The Time That Remains: A Commentary on the Letter to the Romans*, trans. Patricia Dailey (Stanford, CA: Stanford University Press, 2005).

31 William Watkins, *Agamben and Indifference: A Critical Overview* (London and New York: Rowman and Littlefield International, 2014), 4.

32 John Mullarkey, 'Animal Spirits: Philosomorphism and the Background Revolts of Cinema', *Angelaki: Journal of the Theoretical Humanities*, 18:1 (2013): 11–29: 18.

33 Giorgio Agamben, 'Fable and History', in *Infancy and History: Essays on the Destruction of Experience* (London: Verso, 1993), 128.

34 Matthew Calarco, *Zoographies: The Question of the Animal from Heidegger to Derrida* (New York: Columbia University Press, 2008), 101.

35 Jussi Parikka, *Insect Media: An Archaeology of Animals and Technology* (Minneapolis and London: University of Minnesota Press, 2010), xiii.

36 Akira Mizuta Lippit, *Electric Animal: Toward a Rhetoric of Wildlife* (Minneapolis and London: University of Minnesota Press, 2000), 189.

37 Anat Pick, *Creaturely Poetics: Animality and Vulnerability in Literature and Film* (New York: Colombia University Press, 2011), 116.

38 The last chapter of Graham Harman's *The Quadruple Object* (Winchester and Washington, DC: Zone Books, 2011) entitled 'Speculative Realism' recites the different positions of the philosophers named here, further elaborated in an edited collection, *The Speculative Turn: Continental Materialism and Realism*, eds Levi Bryant, Nick Smicek and Graham Harman (Melbourne: re.press, 2011).
39 Harman, *The Quadruple Object*, 6.
40 John Mullarkey, 'The Tragedy of the Object: Democracy of Vision and the Terrorism of Things in Bazin's Cinematic Realism', *Angelaki: Journal of the Theoretical Humanities*, 17:4 (December 2012): 39–59. See also Pick's rewriting of Bazinian realism in *Creaturely Poetics* and George Kouvaros's treatment in ' "We Do Not Die Twice": Realism and Cinema', in *The Sage Handbook of Film Studies*, eds James Donald and Michael Renov (London, New York and Delhi: Sage Publications, 2008), 376–390.
41 John Mullarkey, *Post-continental Philosophy: An Outline* (London and New York: Continuum, 2006), 7.
42 Manuel DeLanda, *A Thousand Years of Nonlinear History* (New York: Swerve Editions, 2000).
43 Giorgio Agamben, *Means without End: Notes on Politics*, trans. Vincenzo Binetti and Cesare Casarino (Minneapolis: University of Minnesota Press, 2000), 53.
44 Jodi Dean, 'Enclosing the Subject', *Journal of Political Theory* (Sage: December 1, 2014: DOI: 10.1177/0090591714560377), 1–31. Her critique of the emphatic production of individuality over and above other modalities underpins her analysis of the cultural horizon in a number of texts, for example *Democracy and Other Neoliberal Fantasies: Communicative Capitalism and Left Politics* (London and Durham: Duke University Press, 2009).
45 Eric Kluitenberg, *The Book of Imaginary Media. Excavating the Dream of the Ultimate Communications Medium* (Rotterdam: NAi Publishers, 2007).
46 Christian Janicot, *Anthologie du cinéma invisible: 100 scénarios pour 100 ans de cinema* (Paris: Jean-Michel Place, 1995).
47 Akira Mizuta Lippit, *Atomic Light (Optic Shadows)* (Minneapolis and London: University of Minnesota Press, 2005).

1

Girls and Other Incomplete Things: On Archaeological Method

Archaeology at the end of the world

Towards the end of an essay on non-knowledge, 'The Last Chapter in the History of the World', Giorgio Agamben offers an image of what this zone would look like were we able to see inside of it. It is not a view as such, but a partial and momentary sighting, 'one would only glimpse...an old and abandoned sled, only glimpse – though this is not clear – the petulant hinting of a little girl inviting us to play'.[1] This slight yet suggestive image, however, furnishes the method of archaeology with a key component. The idea that a zone of non-knowledge or potentiality is off to one side, tangential to the world in which we live and yet pressing in and shaping its contours, underpins the practice of a philosophical archaeology. That there is an invisible cast around what we inhabit as the known world is a concept variously elaborated across Agamben's work as potentiality, decreation, inoperativity and *in-fans*, from the earlier writings to the most recent. Yet the most potent figure that Agamben finds for non-knowledge is that of a small girl, a figure that operates recursively through both philosophy and film.

This petulant girl with the sled in the last chapter in the history of the world elides two images from the film *Citizen Kane* (Welles, 1941). The first is the famous sled that belongs to the boy at the beginning of the film and that is abandoned to the fire at the end, and the second is an image we never see but only hear about: a girl on a ferry sighted momentarily by Kane's business manager. As she passes by on a departing ferry, he recalls 'A white dress she had on. She was carrying a white parasol. I only saw her for one second,' yet '[s]he didn't see me at all'.[2] Carried in another direction to a different future, the young woman nonetheless remains a force in his life. The half-formed, liminal girl borders

Citizen Kane (1941)

on worlds but exercises distance and difference. She reappears as Dulcinea in Orson Welles's unfinished film, *Don Quixote*, who seems to know more than everyone around her. Wherever she is from, we do know the girl's language is that of gesture, not speech, and despite her peevishness she wishes to play, that activity which from Benjamin through to Agamben marks the suspension of the values of use and exchange. In this zone of non-knowledge, the laws of use and causality are arrested and the idea of completion is abandoned, for what proceeds here is a science of the potential and the partial.

This chapter practises and examines an archaeological approach to cinema through the prism of Agamben's thought. Unlike geological archaeology that seeks to reconstruct a version of the past from a fragment, philosophical archaeology works from small clues or signatures hidden in the open and from across history to make a phenomenon intelligible for the first time. These details are scattered across the past and we may at first only glimpse them as they appear in radically different contexts. The task of the archaeologist is to put these signatures into correspondence and, in doing so, to bring into being a paradigmatic case. The details that constitute the paradigm are exemplary in two senses: as an example, they provide a key to the other components of the set, and in their singularity they make sense apart from the group. It is worth noting that the paradigm never pre-exists the group but emerges through the relationship of each singular detail; the paradigm is, in other words, imminent in the detail of clues. The paradigmatic case that archaeology brings forth from cinema in the pages that follow concerns incomplete film, constituted through a set of objects that have in many respects the status of ruins. Treated as unprofitable waste in many contexts, the incomplete film is also the site of a potentiality retained in its state of possibility. The argument that proceeds finds its details in areas peripheral to the film text itself and builds towards an understanding of incompletion in various manifestations. That is to say, incompletion as a figure engages and suspends the laws of use, and the historiographic drive to establish an account of what has occurred. Before embarking on this exploration of incompletion, it may be strategic to set out at the beginning some key features of a philosophical archaeology that may act as particular points of entry.

First, a philosophical archaeology of cinema attends to seemingly insignificant details and is sensitive to the repetitions and reverberations between them. Precisely because they are peripheral, such clues reveal what has been marginalized or rendered more or less invisible through the process of establishing cinema *qua* cinema. Archaeology points to cinema's own non-knowledge, the potential that it hides from itself in a zone where half-thoughts, experiments and bits of machinery lie on a workbench. Included in this zone are the material forms of the apparatus that through exclusive attention to the image are rendered insignificant. Exemplary of the excluded features of cinema is the material substrate that supports its functioning yet is dematerialized in our version of cinema: the fabric of the screen, the electronic signal, the gelatin coating of celluloid, the rhythmic motor of the film projector. These materialities are features whose presence is not to be confused with structuralist interventions in cinema. They are rather the waste products of a system which are minimized and when this is not possible, psychically screened out, such as the glitch that disturbs the smooth surface of the image or the fly that infects the shot. Working from these details as signatures, signs that through resemblance carry a charge across historical periods, the archaeologist reveals the paradigm that underpins the functioning of cinema. If then we take the glitch to be the signature as it appears at critical moments in the century of cinema, the paradigm of the glitch requires us to consider what is at stake in its repression, or conversely, what becomes intelligible when it is taken into account.

The second feature of this approach is what we might think of as a revelatory decontextualization. In the practice of resonating the connections and correspondences between details (as it has been sketchily described above), the signature is lifted out of the context of its historical moment in order to appear as such. This attention to a detail bears the marks of an investment close to that of the collector or the bricoleur whose practice, Agamben suggests, 'extracts the object from its diachronic distance or its synchronic proximity and gathers it into the remote adjacence of history'.[3] Agamben makes this comment in a discussion of play, defined as a relationship between objects and human activity that suspends the use value and the temporality of an object. In one sense, the operation of a revelatory decontextualization perfectly describes cinematic montage as it is deployed against the grain of continuity; image sequences are lifted from one temporal–spatial context and set into relation with others to provide a new revelation, and this is perhaps why Agamben finds in Godard's project of cinematic recombination, *Histoire(s) du cinéma* (1988–98), the 'essential, constitutive link between history and cinema'.[4] Such a decreation of cinema rubs up against the imperfect question of whether the image is de-essentialized in this relation, that is, does the implied value and meaning of an image become mobile, or does archaeology reveal what has existed (but not been legible) all along.

To an extent, an archaeological method makes of montage a model for the practice of releasing images from the confines of their naturalized location (in the first instance the time and location in which they were recorded, and subsequently their naturalized position within the structure of a film) in order to reveal a relation that otherwise lies dormant. There is a link here to the practice that Laura Mulvey attributes to the pensive spectator of the digital video image who pauses to look ever closer, whose appetite for detail is whetted by the technology that allows one to pause, zoom into the image and scroll back and forth over sequences. There is also, and as Henrik Gustafsson and Asbjørn Grønstad observe, the influence of Aby Warburg's historian-as-necromancer bringing the phantasmatic image back to life from its seemingly fixed vocation.[5] There is in this chapter a particular phantom, the figure of a small girl who comes back to life in the archaeological tracing of her presence across texts and contexts. Released from her dead role in certain sequences of film (and philosophy), she returns as the limit-case of what we can know. Her presence here is instructive in two senses. First, as a child, she is an in-between figure who like the ghost is an 'unstable signifier', resistant perhaps to singular interpretation. Second, her form graces the scene of many events in this chapter as an opening onto the unthought or what resides as the underbelly of the intelligible in cinema or philosophy.

This leads neatly to the third aspect of cinematic archaeology which makes legible a potential cinema, one that has not taken place or completely fulfilled the entry criteria to count as cinema. One might take as an example of potential cinema the unfinished film, the incomplete project that remains a fragment either as an idea or a script or as reels of film that have not reached conclusion as a story, nor achieved the necessary closure to count as a commodity. The incomplete film presents other possibilities and iterations as pure fact, a feature that Sarah Keller identifies in Maya Deren's work as 'an aesthetic of open-endedness' that refuses to resolve the tension of oppositions into a neat synthesis.[6] Suspended in archives or consigned to the scrap heap (and one may read these as the same fate), unfinished works present not only the potential of cinema to have been otherwise, but its appointment with a future moment. This is an aspect of archaeology that Agamben draws from Benjamin's messianic thought, a familiar feature that both philosophers identify as an urgent task in the uncovering of relations between things that lie dormant in the ruin in order to arrest the forward march of progress. However, we may also take a less exigent view of this approach to the film fragment in which the form of the incomplete film may be appreciated as it offers itself to archaeological method. As a partial thing, it is always already positioned in relief against the naturalized background (and linear narration) of history and of cinema as an unrolling canon of successful completions in which it fails to register. Against this backdrop the incomplete film demonstrates the great reserve of a cinema that resides as the underbelly to the cinema that we know, a resource that is not only an untapped potential but a figurative presence that troubles the distinction between what has taken place and what has not.

There is a further dimension to an unactualized cinema that engages with potentiality in reverse, or what resides in the slip between im/potentiality. Agamben's valuing of potentiality as that which is not activated is not only the product of a philosophical engagement with Aristotle's meditation on what we understand by the term potential, but in its various iterations across Agamben's work it manifests as a political standpoint: the inhabiting of one's impotentiality as a mode of resistance to the current imperative to be productive, compliant and identifiable as subjects of a system (or in the case of cinema, the production of film goods for circulation). The exemplary and enigmatic figure of impotentiality who is a constant reference in this regard is the scrivener of

Wall Street in Herman Melville's story, Bartleby, who one day stops working because, he famously says, he prefers not to. His polite statement of a preference to not continue to copy the law may be read as a refusal to reproduce what is. Yet it is Bartleby's indeterminate formula that will not be confined to systems of will and resistance. For Agamben, Bartleby presents his capacity to not work, to actualize his incapacity as a state to be inhabited (rather than a refusal of an option).[7] Bartleby is a figure returned to in the final chapter of the book. Suffice it to say at this point that a further capacity of film archaeology is to value the dreams and fantasies of a cinema that never came to be over the one that we have. To choose not to produce cinema, a non-productivity that takes the course of impotentiality may be manifest in various ways, not only incomplete cinema but also in Pavle Levi's category of written films that actualized a capacity to not be films.[8] In this spirit, archaeology is also the imagining of a cinema that will not come into being, the writing of films that will never be made, the dreaming of works precisely as never to be actualized projects in the first instance.

Agamben's archaeological method is not, however, without controversy. The methodological approach of *Homo Sacer* (1998), in particular the third section of the book 'The Camp as Biopolitical Paradigm of the Modern', and of the book that followed, *Remnants of Auschwitz* (1999), has drawn significant critique for its deployment of the figure of *der Muselmann*, the close to death figure of the concentration camp and the camp itself, as paradigms. The critiques of Agamben's use of exemplary figures are, in Leland de la Durantaye's words, concerned with 'Agamben's aspiration to present paradigms as both real, concrete situations and representative instances'. Antonio Negri's difficulty with Agamben's use of the camp is precisely the exemplary nature of its treatment whereby the Holocaust becomes a model of other instances with similar properties, a form of analogy run wild that reduces the significance of the singular event, whilst Ernesto Laclau finds problematic the speed of Agamben's movement from a genealogy to a particular instance, which is then granted paradigmatic status. The identification of *der Muselmann* as the paradoxical figure of testimony who can never bear witness receives critique from Libby Saxton who, in reading Agamben's text with Claude Lanzmann's film of the Holocaust, *Shoah* (1985), warns of 'the dangers involved in attributing an exemplary or iconic status to any single kind of witness'. If *The Signature of All Things* engages with these questions, it does so by taking a distance from the role of the historian, positioning its reading as supplementary. He writes, towards the beginning of *The Signature of All Things*, that his aim is 'to render intelligible a series of phenomena whose relationship to one another has escaped, or might escape, the historian's gaze'. In this task, he draws allegiance with Michel Foucault, whose use of exemplary figures, such as the panopticon, is explicitly referenced by Agamben as a potent form of analysis that allows connections to be made across radically different periods and contexts.

These criticisms notwithstanding, the archaeological method pursued here engages with the obscure and the occluded, gathering to assembly the exemplary features of a paradigm that modulate our perceptions and understanding of cinema. It is a mode of critical reading, as we have noted, aligned with and indebted to both Walter Benjamin in his unfinished Arcades Project, the huge compendium of scraps and citations that are brought into relation, and the art historian Aby Warburg's similarly incomplete project, *Mnemosyne-Atlas*, begun in 1924 and remaining incomplete at the time of his death five years later. Comprising some forty wooden panels upon which over a thousand images from various sources were attached, Warburg's atlas featured the signatures that connect with intensity across time, that render legible in the present a transmission that until the moment of gathering had remained dormant. What follows in this chapter practises a version of, and reflects on, this method as it runs through cinema. Paying attention to the discarded and the partial as it manifests as unfinished film, the method is one of cross-referral, identifying figures, tropes and repetitions that will include a number of small girls, a suitcase, nymphs, a towering man, unwritten scripts, a dying actor, a ripped screen, a hidalgo,[9] a farmer and an Austin Mini Minor.

Incomplete film

Orson Welles is famous for proliferating incomplete film projects over the course of his rather vivid and eventful life. Welles, one might say, is the master not only of many monumental and canonized film works but also of unfinished and unreleased works, which tend to be regarded as failed or aborted efforts.[10] As the film scholar Jonathan Rosenbaum comments of this tendency in Welles's oeuvre and against the view of incompleteness as failure, 'Each one was unfinished in a different way and for somewhat different reasons.'[11] That Welles had many ideas and projects in various stages of development and production at the time of his death has been interpreted not as a source of celebration but rather as an indication of his slide into dereliction. Unfinished projects, in common lore, become the unsightly signifiers of creative impotence, fragments that testify to the 'ruin' of Welles's career as he failed to find focus, to comply with the demand for productivity, to live up to the success of his first film (*Citizen Kane*, 1941). Welles did not work in straight lines but zigzagged across surfaces. He worked across multiple projects simultaneously, creating his own networks of reference and resource not only within film but radio and theatre. Almost certainly the most obsessive of the unfinished films was *Don Quixote*, a project 'quite distinct'[12] from other unfinished works in that it evolved as different versions at different times, multiplying the possibilities of what this name could mean. A film that approached completion on several occasions, it was ritually set aside or suspended at the penultimate moment.[13] Rosenbaum considers this film a project unfinished by choice, a view that he supports by pointing to Welles's dissembling to those who worked with him, withholding critical information including a script and issuing contradictory instructions on how to edit the film. '*Don Quixote* is a dream which Orson Welles never finished, a dream from which he was never able to rouse himself,' said his lover Oja Kodar, shortly after Welles's death.[14]

Don Quixote was a project that Welles worked on for over thirty years intermittently between other projects returning to shoot with a cast that had become significantly older and in the case of the lead actor, dying. It was a phantom of sorts that became more phantasmatic as Welles shot parts of the film in different countries in different decades, resulting in the dispersal of some rushes across a number of continents whilst other parts of the film stock were destroyed. By the time Welles was working on the film in Italy, he had taken to carrying it around in a large black suitcase. The stages of Welles's production are, according to Rosenbaum, at least four,[15] beginning in 1955 as a project financed by television for a short programme featuring Sancho Panza and Don Quixote as characters in the modern world. Welles filmed screen tests in the Bois de Boulogne Park in Paris with Mischa Auer (an actor of Russian-American descent) as Don Quixote and Akim Tamiroff (of Russian-Armenian descent) as Sancho Panza. The television company declined to continue with the venture, and Welles decided to pursue and elaborate the project as a feature-length film with production located in Mexico City, beginning in June 1957. In this second version, he cast Francisco Reiguera as the knight and the twelve-year-old child star Patty McCormack as the young girl, Dulcinea, creating an additional dimension for the film by adding a framework; the girl meets a character (played by Welles) several times during the course of her visit to Mexico City and he tells her the story of Don Quixote. The girl then meets these characters herself during her stay. The third version was shot in Spain and Italy in 1959 with the two male actors and with a stand-in for Patty McCormack cast in Rome, although the rushes, according to Audrey Stainton[16] who worked on the production, show nothing of the stand-in other than a long shot of a girl on a balcony. The further stage of shooting took place two years later in 1961 when Welles made an essay film set in Spain. According to Rosenbaum, the second and third stages were the most intensive bursts of productivity, yet pickups and second-unit photography continued through the next decade, with a burst of activity to film Francisco Reiguera (Quixote) when he became critically ill, dying in 1969. Welles continued to work on various aspects of the production until his own death in 1985.

According to his biographers, there was not a chronological time of the film's production, but multiple overlapping times that jostle to be free of chronology. Welles worked on the various aspects of the film in his downtime. In Rome, a second-hand moviola was taken to a shed in the garden that Welles had converted into a cutting room to work on editing *Don Quixote* in the evenings.[17] During the day, he was acting in Huston's *Roots of Heaven* (1958). He openly referred to the film in his extended time in Italy as 'il mio bambino', a project with a fantastic gestation with Welles's expanding girth matching the metaphor.[18] Yet he was not going into labour with this project. The tantalizing trick was to keep the fine poise between potential and its realization, and in this sense, Welles resembles the character from Herman Melville's story. On many occasions Welles spoke of finishing the film *Don Quixote*, joking that it would be named 'When will you finish Don Quixote?';[19] yet we should be suspicious of this claim as we are also told by Audrey Stainton that he 'delighted in telling stories about himself that were notoriously, sometimes fantastically untrue'.[20] Did Welles hold on to the film as a living snow scene of a fantasy that he carried everywhere with him until his death, its potential never in doubt? Beyond his death, Welles continued to direct through misdirection, leaving the eccentric system of cataloguing slates that were impossible to fathom, in addition to his habit of saying to various people 'you are the one I can trust' to assemble the film.[21] Welles was working on four projects during the final week of his life. He died of a heart attack whilst typing the stage directions to a script that, reportedly, he intended to film later that day.[22]

A fragment of a ruin

One of the production team to work on the film from April 1969 until March 1970 was the Italian editor Mauro Bonanni. When Welles departed Italy in haste in 1970, he gave the print of the film to his daughter and left the negative in a film laboratory in Rome. Mauro Bonanni's wife worked there and four years later was witness to correspondence regarding the destruction of the negative. The fee for storing the film had not been paid and Welles could not be located. Bonanni eventually obtained permission from Welles to take the negative, which reportedly remains in his care.[23] In 2005, a fragment of the footage appeared on Italian television and now has a life on YouTube as a six-minute video. The images swim with blurred outlines, jump and flicker. A curtain of sparkle inserts itself at one point between clearer images.

The scene, which was shot without sound in accordance with the rest of the footage, features Don Quixote and his sidekick Sancho Panza attending a cinema. Sancho Panza enters the cinema after the film has started and the audience is seated. He is unaware of the protocols of cinema, of the silent viewing and rapt attention to the screen. From the aisle he whistles to Don Quixote to try and attract his attention, a whistle that is noted by a young girl in the audience who looks from Sancho Panza to Don Quixote and back again. He waves at his friend whilst receiving what in all likelihood are complaints and taunts to be quiet and sit down. He stumbles along a row of viewers before being made to sit next to a young girl, Dulcinea, who is now sucking a lollipop. She moves her things from the next seat so that he can be seated, and then, through a number of silent gestures, she inducts him into the ways of watching film. She tells him to be quiet; she points to his large hat and indicates that he should remove it; and she offers him a lollipop which he takes and begins to eat, but then she needs to show him how to take off the wrapper and suck the sweet. After this induction, Sancho Panza appears to become aware of the cinema in its fullness. He swivels in his seat to look at audience members seated behind him and then notices children on the balcony. Turning back again he sees as though for the first time the cinematic screen and image, at which point he rapidly becomes absorbed into the drama. In a parody of cinematic viewing, his expression moves from happy to sad and eventually weeping, and the young girl comfortingly strokes his arm and pats his back. This sequence is intercut with increasingly close shots of the face of Don Quixote in profile, stern by comparison, and transfixed by the action.

Francisco Reiguera as Don Quixote

The sequence of the film that they are watching comes to an end, the girl and Sancho Panza applaud, and a new sequence begins. We deduce from the faces of the audience that this sequence is different in nature. Sancho Panza looks concerned. He rises to his feet as though he will rush at the images and intervene, but the girl pulls him back down into his seat. At two minutes and thirty seconds into the extract, Don Quixote rises and climbs onto the stage, the point at which we see for the first time the cinematic images that the audience is watching: a battle between soldiers on horses, a woman in evening gown and a cross with a Christ figure nailed to its form. Are these a montage of sequences from films, were they scenes shot by Welles or selected by him? In this compressed and digitized version, figures are blurred, and movement inexact in a way that seems to intensify Don Quixote's own rigid movement as he strides in armour across the auditorium and stabs at the screen.[24] He ducks before galloping horses, slays attacking foe and stares at the towering figure of the woman. When the screen is destroyed, he turns to face the auditorium, exhausted and stunned. It is not clear whether he turns to face the small girl who stands in the aisle watching with disbelief and possibly anger, or the few remaining children (boys) on the balcony for whom he is a hero. As Quixote slays the screen, slashing at the representations of fair maidens until no more images exist, there are rents in the fabric, holes into which the images fall and disappear until 'nothing is left of the screen, and only the wooden structure supporting it remains visible'.[25] We could say that Quixote demolishes the idea of cinema in order to find out what is behind it, to look underneath official history and see what has been its support. But this ill-fated act only accidently leads to the destruction of the official elements of cinema; in truth, it is the misjudgement of sign and signifier, of mistaking the imagination for the real.

'The Six Most Beautiful Minutes in the History of Cinema'

Agamben writes about this particular fragment of film in a short essay entitled 'The Six Most Beautiful Minutes in the History of Cinema'. It contributes the final note to the ensemble *Profanations* (2005), a collection of essays that opens with a rumination on genius and closes with this final gesture of the destruction of a cinema screen and the experience of cinema. It is an act that Agamben reads as a gesture of misrecognition (Don Quixote's) that nonetheless retains a force of historical explication, the full meaning of which is only understood in relation to one of Agamben's earlier works, 'Infancy and History: An Essay on the Destruction of Experience', published in Italian in 1978.[26] The concern of this complex piece of writing is the separation of experience from knowledge. The essay opens with a citation from Benjamin's 'The Storyteller', in which he describes that when men came back from fighting in the First World War, they could not speak of their experience; an 'impoverishment of communicable experience' is the term that Agamben gives to this condition that he states became a widespread phenomenon. Through a series of vignettes, Agamben marks the historical features of a loss of capacity to communicate experience including notably the founding of modern science on the displacement of knowledge based on experience by an empirically validated source. Experience is discredited as a form of common and transmissible knowledge, resulting in a splitting of knowledge from experience. The characters from Cervantes's novel figure briefly in the essay as the ciphers of this schism:

> Don Quixote, the old subject of knowledge, has been befuddled by a spell and can only undergo experience without ever having it. By his side, Sancho Panza, the old subject of experience, can only have it, without ever undergoing it.[27]

In the fragment of film, Don Quixote utilizes his 'knowledge' of the chivalrous discourse, but this knowledge is now free floating, existing apart from experience. In front of the film, Don Quixote can only experience or undergo the effects of romantic lore, which in turn appeals to the small boys on the balcony as the purest of actions; experience rides him and the children are there to witness and celebrate this reversal. Agamben reads the scenario as a demonstration of the consequences of a historical division between experience and knowledge, where the imagination has lost its mediating power between the two terms and is now cut free. Detached from knowledge and experience, the argument runs, the imagination loses its grounding and the possibility of the fulfilment of a fantasy that had until this moment mediated the subject–object positions of love. 'But once imagination has been excluded from experience as unreal', he writes in 'Infancy and History', 'and its place has been taken by the *ego cogito* ... the status of desire changes radically: it becomes essentially insatiable'.[28] This diagnosis recurs at the end of the essay on cinema's six most beautiful minutes, when Agamben asks what we are to do with our imaginations. Whilst he does not provide an answer, the essay concludes with the observation that the price of such misrecognition is that 'Dulcinea – whom we have saved – cannot love us'. The neat analysis of the film fragment is precisely the identification of this historical shift as a dramatic situation. These are cinema's most beautiful minutes because of the synoptic force of the scene in which this complex and critical operation is acted out.

Yet there is more to be retrieved from this film fragment critically. It is the case, as indeed Agamben notes, that whilst Don Quixote through his stabbing kills the pleasure of the image world for the adult audience, he provides significant pleasure for the children in the audience, with the exception of Dulcinea. In their cheering, the children support an action that has blurred the world of the film and the world of watching, that has brought the activity on the screen into the realm of the everyday and the proximate. Taking this act at face value, as the chivalrous fight against an enemy, Don Quixote exposes the so-called childish investments that we all make in the cinematic image, which on some level we take to be a real fiction. That is, Don Quixote's actions lay bare both the psychic demands that the cinema makes on the viewer to disavow the image as fantasy ('I know that it is not real but. ...') and the disavowal of the material apparatus of cinema. When the screen is slashed and torn, the exposed structure supporting the projection screen is a shocking void, an absence of an image but also the revelation of cinema's materiality. In what we might describe as an extreme form of participation, Don Quixote brings into being cinema *by other means,* to draw on Pavle Levi's appellation, a cinema rooted in a practical engagement with things. In this light, Welles's film fragment presents a new version of cinema as praxis, precisely a *situation* in Guy Debord's terms, that is brought about through the rematerialization of the medium.

Attention to the material properties of cinema redirects the interpretation of this film sequence back towards an archaeological approach, and there is more to be said about the status of the scene as a fragment, or what we might think of as a film-ruin. In Benjamin's reading, a ruin is an incomplete object with philosophical benefits, potential 'allegories for thinking' as a form that allows the philosopher a way in through the handling of its rough edges.[29] Here, the archaeological ruin presents only a fragment of a larger whole that did not come to be rather than the collapse and decay of a once existing work. Nonetheless, there is the suggestiveness of the film that was never completed, inviting us to fill in and supplement the fragment with our own image sequences. But the most potent effect of this fragment is in a sense the opposite of our supplementary fantasies: it is the apprehension of the sequence as a detail out of context, an event out of time that is analogous to a still from a lost film. Precisely for the reason that it is incomplete, the piece of film stands apart from the time of its making just as it remains forever separate from the narratological prospect of a completed film called *Don Quixote*. The status of the sequence as fragment draws a circle around it, removing it from the flow of linear time and storylines where its meaning is fixed and frozen by its relation to the fictional and historical contexts. In contrast to a finished film, the sequence is thrown into relief as a series of gestures that casts a line towards us, demanding that we pay attention to these particular performances and these specific movements as bodies suspended from instrumental use.

There is one more detail to note about this brief essay. In asking 'What are we to do with our imaginations?', Agamben constructs what appears to be a question addressed to a wide audience, a rhetorical flourish that bridges the first paragraph describing the film sequence and the second paragraph that contains the interpretive key. And yet the pronouns that he adopts here betray a division. The 'we' and 'us' of the text that draw the reader into collusion with the writer are collective forms of address that, as we come to the final sentence of the essay, exclude the girl, Dulcinea. More accurately, the 'we' and 'us' of the essay are constituted only through their difference from the girl, or her difference from them. The essay closes with a line that pivots on the mention of her name: 'But when [our imaginations] reveal themselves to be empty and unfulfilled, when they show the nullity of which they are made, only then can we pay the price for their truth and understand that Dulcinea – whom we have saved – cannot love us.[30] The girl is a detail that remains external to the fallacy of the imagination, to the folly of pursuing one's own fantasy at all cost. Dulcinea will not join in, reciprocate and love 'us'. A figure that marks a different system of thought or mode of relating, Dulcinea may only signal her silent dissent. She is, I will argue, a critical component in Agamben's archaeological landscape.

Philosophical archaeology

The Signature of All Things: On Method (2009) is the most direct and full address of method in Agamben's work, although as Alex Murray notes, it presents as archaeology a re-articulation of a philological approach that has consistently characterized his method and in many places received direct treatment.[31] Explicit discussion of method occurs across his output, from the endnote 'Project for a Review' (*Infancy and History*, 1978), to the synoptic two-page 'Example' (*The Coming Community*, 1990) and the three essays published in English under the title *What Is an Apparatus?* (2009), to name but a few obvious choices. Method is further refracted through discussion of the work of others: Aby Warburg's practice as a 'nameless science' (*Potentialities*, 1999) for example, or the infamous exchange that takes place between Adorno and Benjamin, 'The Prince and the Frog: The Question of Method in Adorno and Benjamin' (*Infancy and History*, 1978). The term 'archaeology' rather than method begins to appear in the titles of Agamben's recent writings, his examination of the oath, *The Sacrament of Language: An Archaeology of the Oath* (2008), and Christian liturgy, *Opus Dei: An Archaeology of Duty* (2013). Whilst these are the explicit locations of method, procedure is bound up with each and every of his philosophical projects, from the notion of a creative criticism in *Stanzas* (1977), to the more recent theological engagements with Pauline doctrine and the messianic;[32] the eradication of a division between form and content is a repeatedly stated aim within Agamben's philosophical practice.

The book on method pays direct homage to Michel Foucault, citing Foucault in the prologue as 'a scholar from whom I have learned a great deal in recent years'.[33] It is well known that Foucault's examination of the history of thought in the social sciences, *The Order of Things: An Archaeology of the Human Sciences*

(1966), was the book that propelled the author into the limelight, selling out its initial two print runs.[34] Three years later *The Archaeology of Knowledge* (1969) followed on its heels, although both of these texts were prefigured by a number of projects in which history had figured prominently.[35] In the two books dedicated to an elaboration of method, Foucault develops a language of paradigms, apparatuses, epistemes and discursive formations that critically puts a distance between his work and historical investigation. Foucault of course was required to elaborate his method in response to the critiques that he received of playing loose and fast with history, of painting with broad sweeps of a brush and denying the detail of particular circumstance. His response came not only in the form of books but of essays, and most famously perhaps the essay 'Nietzsche, Genealogy, History', that drew for methodological inspiration on Nietzsche's critique of three modalities of history in *Untimely Meditations* (1876). In an essay that destroys the idea of origin and replaces it with moments of arising, Foucault swerves around the instrument of 'truth' as the object of enquiry and puts in its place the contingency of the evolution of knowledge. He writes that to practise genealogy is to practise a descent in which 'it is to discover that truth or being do not lie at the root of what we know and what we are, but the exteriority of accidents'.[36]

It has been widely noted in scholarship that Agamben's perspective on biopolitics and sovereignty diverges dramatically from Foucault's reading.[37] Foucault as we know postulates successive epistemic breaks running through history, in particular a rupture at the end of the eighteenth century that augured the arrival of modernity and the rise of institutional modes of management. In Foucault's account of sovereignty, power transitions from the centralized body of the head of state to be dispersed through the population as techniques of self-regulation ('care of the self'). In contrast, from Agamben's perspective 'biopolitics had emphatically not waited for modernity to set in', argues Anton Schütz, 'neither for the emergence of the modern practice of governance/ discipline, nor for the modern substitution of population for territory'.[38] In his account of sovereignty Agamben, influenced by the political legal thinker Carl Schmidt, retains the centralized power of sovereignty that demonstrates its potency through a suspension of the law creating a state of exception or legal lawlessness.[39] Sovereignty therefore remains a critical defining operative in the present that takes effect in the separation of life from bare life, or auspicious life from life in the camp. This division is not simply the construction of a binary (inclusion/exclusion) but the exception is 'that which is included in a set through its exclusion'.[40] In this sense, the exception is, as Justin Clemens argues, the twin of the example, which is placed on the outside of a group in the act of demonstrating its own inclusion. The example of course evokes its relation to the paradigm and to the issues that arise from thinking beyond the impasse of the general and the particular in philosophical methodology. If Agamben states his divergence from Foucault in terms of the biopolitical in *Homo Sacer*, in *The Signature of All Things*, he acknowledges his debt to Foucault.

With recourse to Foucault's use of paradigm, Agamben opens the first section of the book by identifying a number of features that demarcate the principles of method imminent to his own paradigmatic analyses. These are abstract principles, the first of these describing an analogical mode of proceeding that traces connections through resemblance. What this means becomes clearer when Agamben defines what this approach takes its distance from, which is a procedure of induction and deduction. The inductive is a form of knowledge production moving from the specific to the general, where each detail leads outwards to a wider application. Conversely, the deductive moves from the general to the particular, eliminating phenomena in the drive to move from the macro- to the micro-point of knowledge. Refusing binary oppositions and the falsity of moving from the specific to the general and vice versa, an analogical model proceeds by moving from singularity to singularity. The analogical model, that is, creates a series of relations through apparent likenesses. Furthermore, if the paradigm is produced through this analogical method, drawing relations between things, the paradigm is then immanent to things; significantly, it does not precede or predict them. Analogical procedure brings to the surface connections that configure paradigms, rather like Warburg's plates of images that are clustered according to a principle of gestural resemblance and drawn from various historical moments, or Joseph Cornell's boxes of seemingly unrelated objects, which we return to towards the end of this chapter.[41] The explicitly archaeological nature of this method, writes Agamben, is its position at the crossing of synchrony (meaning constituted relationally across discursive borders) and diachrony (the production of meaning over time).

The second part of the book moves into even closer proximity with Foucauldian thinking in the examination of signatures. It is instructive here to bear in mind the ambiguity of the translation of the term *signatura*, which does not exactly correspond with the English word 'signature'. The term commonly used for signing a name in Italian is *firma*, whilst *signatura* is closer to what Walter Benjamin calls an index, or to what William Watkins, in his discussion of this ambiguity, refers to as a mark. Agamben traces the concept through the work of scholars from medievalists Paracelsus and Böhm to Derrida and Foucault, and it is the latter's evocation of its form in the book on *The Order of Things* (1969) that has particular traction. Agamben writes, 'Foucault does not define the concept of signature, which for him resolves into resemblance,'[42] and yet it is clear that in this account the signature is the means by which resemblance is brought to attention. The signature, that is, operates as a kind of transmitter of links and correspondences. In practical terms, it both identifies a sign as a sign, and indicates how a sign might be interpreted. Its critical potency for Foucault resides in its position in the gap between semiology and hermeneutics, between which it traffics knowledge. In the period up until the end of the sixteenth century, Foucault argues, resemblance organized how knowledge was produced and made manifest, 'the earth echoing the sky, faces seeing themselves reflected in the stars, and plants holding within their stems the secrets that were of use to man'.[43] Whilst the signature partakes of resemblance, Foucault argues with reference to Paracelsus, there are no resemblances without signatures. Signatures act like hieroglyphs to mark the usefulness or efficacy of a thing, physical inscriptions that are there to be read.

In order to grasp the significance of the form of knowledge characterized by a system of resemblances, it is helpful to place this particular way of thinking within the larger context that Foucault provides in *The Order of Things*. The period predating the Enlightenment, he argues, is one in which resemblance, sympathy and analogy reign, describing knowledge established through the identification of kinship. The definition of kinship Foucault uses is precisely not the biological determination of identity through blood ties but the bonds produced through affinity, communion and rapport. Here is Foucault elaborating an approach to the history of an organism through the system of resemblance:

> ... to write the history of a plant or an animal was as much a matter of describing its elements or organs as of describing the resemblances that could be found in it, the virtues that it was thought to possess, the legends and stories with which it had been involved, its place in heraldry, the medicaments that were concocted from its substance, the foods it provided, what the ancients recorded of it, and what travellers might have said of it. The history of a living being was that being itself, within the whole semantic network that connected it to the world.[44]

But what follows as this system collapses is a triumph of representation, a period characterized by the classical episteme that establishes knowledge through practices of order and classification. Taxonomic principles dominate here and these are reliant upon, and in turn bring into being, a new power of observation. The transition identified by Foucault is similar to the shift Agamben was to describe in *Infancy and History* (1978) as the separation of knowledge from experience. In Agamben's account this is a transition that comes later than the Enlightenment, marking the rise of a scientific discourse in the nineteenth century through which experience is displaced by the knowledge produced with objects and instruments. Whilst for Agamben experience enters a decline, for Foucault the new episteme severs the web of relations through which a thing or event was known. The formerly thick weave of relations is replaced by a system of knowledge organization that restricts connections and confines thought as a series of hierarchically arranged divisions. Sign and signifier are no longer linked through physical or fabled means, leaving connections to be established as an order imposed rather than emerging in the immanent relations between things. Methodologically, it is the replacement of infinite resemblance with the search for finite difference. The establishment of difference according to Foucault yields the roots of an identitarian discourse in which the signatures of a person or a thing come to sign its essence or essential nature. In a final flourish, identity, he argues, becomes that which is represented in and as a sign, produced as an atomized unit of individualism or 'man'.[45] 'As the archaeology of our thought easily shows', he writes on the final page of the book, 'man is an invention of recent date', adding prophetically, 'And one perhaps nearing its end.'[46]

The science of signatures re-emerges, argues Agamben, under a different name, what is called the 'evidential'. Drawing on the work of historian Carlo Ginzburg, the evidential is the study of individual cases, instances and documents, the singular texts that retain in some small detail, a mark or stain. In this new context, signatures have become hidden things, or rather hidden in the open, to be sought out through the patient vigilance of detective work or the studious enquiry of the academic. Conan Doyle creates a method for Sherlock Holmes, overlapping with that of the art historian who seeks the clues of an artist's identity in the minor details of a painter's style, in the way in which seemingly unimportant details of finger nails or ear lobes are rendered across various canvases. Doyle's method, Agamben notes, attracted Freud's attention, who found a resonance with his own concern for critical traces left in residue matter, 'from the rubbish-heap, as it were, of our observations'.[47] The point that Agamben makes in this set of linked practices that pivot upon the evidential is that, following the demise of the concept (and efficacy) of the signature as resemblance after the Enlightenment, the signature surfaces in a context of excessive signification. Only in exceeding the semiotic dimension of the sign does the signature emerge as a trace of something more informative and efficacious. The signature puts into relation a series of details that direct the reader (or detective) to the subject or event. 'That is', Agamben sums up, 'the clue represents the exemplary case of a signature that puts an insignificant or nondescript object in effective relation to an event (in this case, a crime, in Freud's case, a traumatic event) or to subjects (the victim, the murderer, the author of a painting)'.[48] The signature that was once undisguised in a system of resemblances has become a discrete property, hiding in the gap between sign and meaning or semiotics and hermeneutics.

From these two versions of the signature first as resemblance and second as evidence hiding in the light, the significance of the term can be drawn out. The signature is first of all a connection across time and space, a relating of one thing to another through an unforeseen link or mark. However, more than this, the signature animates the sign or concept, and in doing so, sets the conditions for its use. Towards the end of *The Signature of All Things*, Agamben cites the assertion by Deleuze that philosophy entails two elements, the identification of a problem and the selection of concepts adequate to the task of exploring it. Agamben then says, 'It is necessary to add that concepts entail signatures, without which they remain inert and unproductive.'[49] The example that he offers at this point of the discussion, having travelled through the many iterations of the signature in philosophy, is of secularization, a signature that marks the concept of modernity. In philosophical discussion that sought to analyse secularization and modernity, the former was erroneously seen to operate structurally as the end of a period of religious belief and the subsequent compensatory investment in political systems. But, Agamben argues, the error here is to regard secularization as a concept, when it is in fact a signature that operates excessively, beyond its designation. It is a 'strategic operator', which in marking a political concept (such as modernity) refers back to a time of its theological foundation, of a potency that is subsequently redistributed to the emergent political regimes of modernity. Secularization invokes a history of its opposite, of a now-absent theology, animating the concept of modernization through its forgotten connections. In this sense, it is linked, but not reducible, to Derrida's trace carried forth in the supplement. The further point that Agamben makes in this analysis is this: the signature has primacy over the signified, or, the signature manages and so conditions the ways in which a concept is taken up. The extent to which the signature has ascended over and above 'meaning' is evident in Agamben's identification of this shift as critical to the twentieth century. He writes, 'it would not be wrong to state that the basis of one important part of twentieth-century thought presupposes something like the absolutizing of the signature, that is to say, a doctrine of the constitutive primacy of signatures over signification'.[50]

Typographic man

Don Quixote appears in Foucault's *The Order of Things*, situated as the pivot between the system of resemblances and the beginning of the new era of representation. Don Quixote, 'the negative of the Renaissance world',[51] exemplifies something of this shift in his practice of misinterpreting signs, finding resemblances where none exist with the effect of creating dramatic peaks from commonplace situations. Published in serial form as two books in 1605 and 1615, respectively, Cervantes' modern novel, as it has been called, marks its departure from the age of resemblance through parodic form. At the beginning of the seventeenth century, writes Foucault, '[s]imilitude is no longer the form of knowledge but rather the occasion of error'.[52] In a section of the book that displays Foucault's style at its most incisive, Don Quixote practises *homosemanticism*, he 'sees nothing but resemblances and signs of resemblance everywhere', because 'for him all signs resemble one another, and all resemblances have the value of signs' as man enters an age of madness in imagination.[53] Language breaks off its kinship with things. It is an epistemic shift attached to the practices of reading and writing, to the novel as a modern form of signs put into circulation, which is simultaneously the separation of the word from the world; the novel anchors the word sign so that its inked attachment is to the page rather than to a mobile set of objects and effects in the non-literary world. Quixote is himself a sign of typographic frenzy, no more than 'a long thin graphism' in Foucault's account, a definition of man got down to the few letters of a printer's block.

Cervantes' Don Quixote is nonetheless an animating force running a charge from Welles to Foucault to Agamben, and like a great shadow standing behind each of these men, Quixote threatens to parody their projects.[54] There are, we might say, serious risks attached to an engagement with him. For whilst Don Quixote features in Foucault's text as a hinge between two systems of knowledge, he seems to demonstrate the potentially bad practice of the archaeologist gone awry, the theorist who cannot determine a sign from a signature, whose clutch of signatures produces a paradigm that is a massive colourful projection onto a world with which it has no relation. The risk appears to be that if one stands next to Don Quixote, a family resemblance may become apparent. Not only Foucault with his appetite for resemblances is in danger here, but Agamben whose extraction of key figures from moments in history such as the starved and exhausted figure of *der Muselmann* in the concentration camps has drawn an accusation of the extraction of the sign (which is not a sign but a subject for his detractors) from its specific and singular context.[55] The figure with whom Quixote appears to risk a particular affinity is Welles who is also prone to the overproduction of texts that do not sit comfortably together as an ensemble but create angles and corners that he is forced to negotiate. Welles could not get *Don Quixote* down to one version over such a long period of time; his main actor becomes ill, his child actor grows up and Welles is left struggling with a set of signs that have peeled away from the world.

Audrey Stainton worked as Welles's secretary for a short period in 1958–9. She typed some of the versions of script, viewed some of the rushes on Welles's moviola and talked to those involved with the project. The notes on production that come from Stainton describe Welles's method as deeply secretive and eccentric. Welles started the project without a screenplay, a production manager or shooting schedule and whilst the self-funded nature of the project, as it became, conditioned a certain economy of practice, this by no means accounts for his method. The script would be written and rewritten by Welles himself the day or night before the shoot, and Stainton would have to type it no matter how late into the evening she worked. The scripts were never numbered nor ordered nor bound together, but Welles would insist that with each page typed, a carbon copy was made, and more meticulously, that a fresh carbon was used for the typing of each new page. 'Somewhere, hidden away', she writes, 'he kept an immaculate carbon copy of everything he wrote'. Shots and reels were not numbered as a result of his superstitious hatred of numbers, but were instead labelled with names such as 'sheep' or 'dreamers'. Through this process the mass of materials became an archive in which no one but Welles could find anything; no members of the production team worked continuously on the project over the full duration of the numerous shoots, and so Welles became the only figure with complete knowledge of what had been shot and how it had been labelled.

The last minute revisionist nature of the screenplay coupled with secrecy meant that actors had no lines to follow. According to Stainton, Patty McCormack 'never saw a script, only her own dialogue on loose pages that he kept rewriting and making her memorize all over again'. Similarly, any editing and post-production effects were done 'in house', meaning literally by Welles. Mauro Bonanni described how effects that could be achieved by technological means were hand-produced, with Bonanni and Welles hand-cutting white frames to insert alternately for slow motion effects, and removing alternate frames to speed up a sequence. In terms of sound, Welles shot much of the film mute and intended to revoice it in the editing stage. Here is Stainton's description of the unorthodox approach[56] that Welles took to creating the soundtrack, which is worth reproducing in full:

> Mauro Bonanni described the process to me as follows. First, before editing, Welles recorded the dialogue, sequence by sequence, wild, which means without screening the film and regardless of the actors' lip movements. In this way, he established the rhythm he wanted his editor to follow in cutting the film. The editor had to adapt the image to the voice, instead of vice versa. Only after this was done and Welles was satisfied with the rhythm of the sequence, would he study lip movements on the moviola and adapt his own speech accordingly, while recording an improvised guide track of his own on a small Philips tape-recorder.[57]

In this description, there is more than eccentricity at work. Welles demonstrates what film can be for him, which is not primarily a recording medium in which each element is 'captured' and fixed beginning with the visual. Rather, film has properties of malleability where rhythm can be teased from it, not only teased, but co-created in response to another element which in this case is Welles's wild track. The process that Bonanni describes to Stainton is an orchestration of elements that are adapted in response to one another; the wild track is produced from a written text, the film rushes are cut to its rhythms, the guide track is created to match the rough cut and the words of the text are changed (if necessary) to lip-synch with the actor's movements. The circularity of effects in post-production describes a world that has become an internal and hallucinatory set of signs.

As the years passed, Welles sifted and re-created versions in downtime between other projects. He wrote and revised the script according to what he was editing. In the footage that he worked with there were already multiple versions that threatened to reproduce again; the girl who played Dulcinea was no longer a girl and had to be played in all future shots by another girl who resembled a younger McCormack, but only at a distance. The film was 'set' in Spain, but through the camera the landscapes of Mexico, Italy and Malaga revealed the textures of various climates. It was the task in post-production of drawing such differences into a sympathetic relation that Welles laboured over. Voicing the characters of both Don Quixote and Sancho Panza, Welles had to play so many roles.[58] At the same time, his eldest daughter writes, 'he found fairly steady employment as a voice-over man, narrating documentaries and doing commercials on radio and television.'[59] Did Welles find himself in danger of becoming reduced to this disembodied voice, just as Quixote became a long thin graphism? 'I have to keep my name alive and my bills paid,' he tells his daughter, betraying an anxiety about whether life is located in a signature or in his body, which, like Patty McCormack and the image of the girl in the incomplete film, are becoming further and further apart.

The incomplete girl

In his fixation with Don Quixote, Welles, like others before and after, focuses on the sign and misses the signature. The clue that is out in the open and yet remains so obscure is the small girl. There are in the course of this story several girls. Indeed, Dulcinea by herself proliferates across genre, featuring as a textual love object in Cervantes' book, appearing in Welles's incomplete film as a 'contemporary' young girl in a scene in a hotel at the opening of the film, featuring notably in a 'found' sequence of Don Quixote at the cinema that in turn inspires the Dulcinea in Agamben's essay. McCormack is subject unwittingly, as all child stars are, to the parody of herself as she grows into an adult who no longer 'fits' her screen image. The child star McCormack is filmed silent in her scenes, but her voice features in the marginalia of film history, recounted by Audrey Stainton. McCormack tells Stainton that Welles was 'this terrifying man ... terrifying with everybody else, but astonishingly gentle with her', a man who gave the impression that he 'related better to children than to adults'.[60] Indeed, it is notable that Welles framed the whole film in terms of a dialogue between himself and the girl, constructing a scene on a terrace where he plays the character of a guest speaking to a child (played by McCormack). In this opening scenario, the adult man tells the girl the story of Don Quixote and Sancho Panza and after this, the girl begins to see the characters in her everyday life.

Welles appears to foreground the girl but then he loses her; he is not fast enough in his filmmaking and she outgrows him. 'Like King Lear, I have three daughters, but unlike Lear they have all been kind to me,' announces Welles to Dick Cavett on television during a ninety-minute interview. The eldest daughter writes this up in her autobiography as a startling memory of hearing herself described during the interview as 'frighteningly bright'. 'The phrase lodged in my mind,' she writes, 'Did my intelligence scare my father away? Would he feel closer to me if I were not as bright? I could speculate endlessly and arrive at no satisfactory answer.'[61] When in 1971 the film of *Don Quixote* has been cut (or one version of it), and Welles has left Rome without it, he sends his youngest daughter, Beatrice, who is sixteen at the time, to collect it. 'Mauro met her in the late summer of 1971, in Piazza del Popolo in Rome,' writes Stainton, 'where he helped her load Welles's big black suitcase containing the cut copy into the trunk of a silver-grey Austin Mini Minor'.[62] The oversized suitcase, the trunk of the small car, the competent figure of the girl driving into the centre of Rome to collect her father's baggage, or bagged potential. Is the daughter dutifully compliant or endlessly enraged? The girl-daughter says little.

These girls who conduct themselves with calm competence and patience seem to belong to a complementary world, an inviolable elsewhere. They are somewhere in the frame gesturing: the girl with the sled, the girl on the balcony, the child who tells Sancho Panza to sit down, the small figure driving the car away into the traffic and the girl watching her father on television. These are the signatures that are each their own singularity and simultaneously convene as a paradigm of the incomplete and the unspoken. They trace the contours of what is finished and said, but they are more than a remainder. For they ask us to go back and look again, to reconsider what was there, what it was that we saw and understood and conversely what we failed to see or listen to. They appear to be frozen in position, but when we look again, and when we consider them collectively, we notice that they are all gesturing in some way animating something of the past in the contemporary.

On the (im)possibility of (in)completion

In the book *Nymphs* (published in Italian in 2007 and in English translation in 2013), Agamben recalls the influences of Aby Warburg and Walter Benjamin on his conceptualization of gestural images, recalling their work when faced with the videos of artist Bill Viola.[63] Agamben identifies in the extremely slow nature of the images in Viola's series *The Passions*, which feature figures almost imperceptibly moving, the sense of a painting come to life. He writes, 'It was as if one entered the room of a museum and the old masters' canvases miraculously began to move,'[64] an effect that is at once commanding (the viewer needs to pay close attention to note the discrete changes in the image) and phantasmatic (the images appear to be both still and moving, dead and alive). The significance of Viola's video is, for Agamben, in the rendition of time that it obtains; movement and stillness are, for him, beside the point. What the video displays is the coming to life once again of the image. It is an effect that he links to the concept of the after-image, or *Nachleben* (meaning posthumous life or afterlife) in Warburg's account. The after-image is of course the physiological condition upon which cinema resides, the effect of an image that stays on the retina for a moment longer than its physical presence in front of the eye. This effect becomes in Agamben's reading, an analogy for the way in which images work historically: the image is produced at a moment in time and yet its effect lingers in memory where it continues to 'live' and to take different forms. The photographic and filmic image (there is nothing to choose between them here) is precisely not a record of an event mummified within the frame but a thing that continues to live phantasmatically with us.

This, according to Agamben, is what Warburg chased as he set about his compilation of images from antiquity in the Atlas selecting those that exhibited *pathosformel*, an emotionally charged visual trope. The images that interested Warburg were of nymphs in movement, captured in a gesture that defies the distinction between movement and stasis. Warburg's nymphs display a *dynamis* suspended yet nonetheless exhibiting a gesture of movement. The plates upon which a montage of images was assembled created what Warburg named 'dynamograms', assemblages full of energy generated by the paradox of their distance from each other in time and space and yet their shared transmission (as a paradigm) of an emotional charge. Contemplating the multiple images of a plate, Agamben argues, it is impossible to locate where the nymph resides, which is the original and which is the copy. The image of a nymph, of each nymph, is at once a glance back towards past images of the figure with an eye cast to the future, which is simultaneously 'an indiscernible blend of originariness and repetition, of form and matter'.[65] The nymph is, like the incomplete girl, an in-between figure belonging neither to childhood nor adulthood, neither humankind nor animal kind, a spirit that lacks a soul but who nonetheless eats and drinks as humans do. If the in-between the past and the future seems to describe a line, the nymph breaks with this linear version of time, demonstrating that the past is not fixed and complete but mutable, and this is where the relationship of Warburg's project to film becomes legible. For Warburg's fascination is with transmission rather than recording and this he shares with the incomplete girl; both are trying to tell us something about cinema.

Of the many desires that the term 'cinema' has conjured for audiences, critics and scholars, perhaps the most enduring has been in its capacity to record and document a moment in time. Whether this is within the realm of fiction or documentary is irrelevant; as Godard's majestic *Histoire(s) du cinéma* (1998) exemplified, film is suggestive of a capture of the twentieth century despite the fact that many of the films sampled in his story are fiction. Yet cinema in a sense shows us the waywardness of a desire to grasp and keep anything of the passing moment, and whilst the drive to do so is present in every new fantasy to render the experience of the recorded past as immersive (through surround sound and other techniques), cinema's ability to re-render a past moment in the present is a failure. What cinema delivers are fragments that may be assembled as partial things through its signature mode of montage. Cinema is composed of fragments not only in the sense of its multiple sequences that are strung together, but also in its framing of an image cut from a larger whole, and again in its positioning of the camera which can never be a totalizing point of view but only the multiplication of infinite points of view on an event. That is, in every act of recording, cinema demonstrates the opposite, the impossibility of documentation, revealing incompletion as its founding condition. The incomplete girl in her gesture towards a film that is never finalized nor total shows us not only the error of our desire to capture. Her gesture is telling us something concerning a renewed concept of time that the cinema alone may furnish us with: images of and from the past operate as a force in the present, connecting with and animating other images. The consequence of this is not only in the act of the past reaching into the present, but more importantly in the opening up of new meaning in the images of the past. Within new contexts and even more so as features of a paradigm, they come to speak differently. In so doing, the final stage of this process is the revelation of the past as mutable, always unfinished and incomplete, no matter how much time has passed nor how many accounts of an event are put into circulation.

We arrive at the point at which cinema may be defined as a force field of transmissions, and that to work archaeologically in the production of paradigms is to play to its strength. It is noteworthy in this respect that Agamben selects Godard and Debord as the prized operators of paradigmatic cinema; in both cases, paradigmatic gestures across cinematic history and across the sphere of the commodity, respectively, condition their practice. Yet whilst Agamben focuses on what he names two transcendentals of cinema as stoppage and repetition in his analysis of the work of Godard and Debord (which we come to in Chapter 3), he stops short of naming the full repertoire of cinematic tools that characterize its form as a force field of possibilities for animating the past. Cinema provides for an archaeological practice more thoroughly through four modalities that reconfigure possible relations with the image, or treat its form as incomplete fragment. These are schematically the variation of speed with which an image may be viewed; second, the facility of zooming in and zooming out of the image; third, the cutting together of images or image sequences from the same genre in new formations; and fourth, the extraction of an image or image sequence from its generic and temporal context. Each of these modalities treats the film image as a ruin, a fragment that when subject to various forms of scrutiny or placed in new relations opens itself up to reveal what was not until this moment evident. An archaeology of cinema reveals 'what was never written'.[66] To approach film as always already partial or incomplete leads us towards a further realization that the image sequences that exist begin to merge and ply with the film that was never made; ultimately, archaeology blurs the line that divides what has taken place from what has not.

Modern works of art are fragments from birth, writes Agamben in *Stanzas* (1977), by which token we can read film (artwork of the twentieth century par excellence) as always already a ruin.[67] It is important to maintain the understanding that all film is already a ruin, a fragment that is built around but never exhausted in its potentiality, open to reconfiguration merely in its re-projection.

The incomplete girl (ii)

When his daughter Beatrice collected the footage of *Don Quixote* from Mauro Bonanni in Rome, Orson Welles had fled Italy more than a year before in anger at publicity exposing his relationship with artist and actress Oja Kodar. Kodar was the lover and companion of Welles for the last twenty years of his life, an open secret whilst Welles remained married to Paola Mori. Kodar was to appear in Welles's final full-length film *F for Fake* (1974) as the object of desire as she walks down a street in Rome attracting the attention of many men in the locale who turn and stare. It is a 'fake' scene in which Welles has edited together sequences of images from different times and places to appear to be in response to one another. When Welles died in 1986, he left the incomplete films to Kodar in his will. Barely a year after his death, Kodar allowed the Cannes Film Festival to screen some of the footage, including that of *Don Quixote*. After some time, Kodar bequeathed the incomplete films to the Munich Film Museum with the stipulation that the footage must be screened at a non-commercial venue every two or three years. In 1994, Welles's eldest daughter Christopher met Oja Kodar for the first time after a screening of a version of *Don Quixote* edited by Jess Franco who had worked as assistant director on *Chimes at Midnight* (Welles, 1966) at the Museum of Modern Art, New York. The eldest daughter, now a woman in her forties, was excited to finally meet her father's lover. But Kodar was visibly upset by the film. Franco's edit had ruined the material.[68] And there was no sign of Patty McCormack in the film; the (incomplete) girl had been removed from the final picture, or this version of it.

What is the nature of this gestural yet silent girl and her iterations in film, biography and philosophy, or how might we conceive of her muteness if not as a historical silencing? With the publication of *The Unspeakable Girl: The Myth and Mystery of Kore* (2014), Agamben calls on another girl-figure, also mute, but this time she is at the centre rather than at the edges of his concerns as the mythological figure of Greek culture, Kore (a figure also known as Persephone). Agamben's interest in the tale of Kore is her fate, being suspended between states. Abducted by Hades and taken to the underworld, the violent grief of her mother Demeter (goddess of the harvest) threatened the earth with famine until her release was agreed. Persephone could leave the underworld for half of the year on the condition that she would be forever suspended between the states of the living and the dead, the world and the underworld, being a daughter and being a wife. In this essay, published with the suggestive images of artist Monica Ferrando, she exists on the threshold between opposing poles, between word and image, light and dark, keeping these in check. This is how the unspeakable girl appears, not as a silenced figure within history (although she does have affinity with the gestural stars of silent cinema that we turn to in the following chapter). She is, rather, that which cannot be spoken but can only be named. Kore inhabits 'the power and potentiality of a joyfully and intransigently *infantile* existence',[69] initiated into life itself rather than into language as the condition of humanity.

The trail of Agamben's thought here moves recursively, recalling the acquisition of language as the anthropological distinction separating man from animal. In this text, the unspeakable girl is initiated into life without entering language. The decisive meaning of the girl in her unspeakability is twofold: she remains unspoken and therefore undefined, or to connect her to the concerns of this chapter, incomplete, and second, she retains her potentiality to become.

There is a relation between the unspeakable girl and the incomplete girl. They are both exemplary of allied yet different concepts, and they form together the paradigm of the incomplete. These figures recall Michael Peck's painting of girl who stands with a book open as though thoroughly engrossed in the text. She stands on a path, as though she has been stopped in her tracks by the world of the book. Her face and head are not detailed but only given in outline; the space that would have been the features of her face is filled by the dreamy substance of clouds. The image in its sepia tones looks like a film still and by the style of the girl's clothes, this could be post-war America or Europe. But the image is in fact a painting that takes on the mantel of a film still, as though it is part of a larger sequence, inviting us to speculate on the nature of her incompletion. Certainly she does not appear to be lost, nor does she look as though she is in a hurry yet she invites speculation about what has come before this moment and what will follow.

The incomplete is a feature of history but one that is rarely celebrated, with the exception of the fragmented form of statues. The incomplete operates a negative productivity; it will not provide a category for prizes, nor will it conform to the demand of the commodity system that requires bounded and (legally) protectable closure. On the contrary, the incomplete marks decisively the entry points through which we may come to think history and thus time differently; in other words, it is an opening. Through unfinished works, the past remains fluid. How then might we understand the incomplete as a conceptual category? Interpreted through Agamben's prism there are two elements to its mode, the first belonging to Warburg's approach to history, and the second to Benjamin's. Following Warburg, culture is the site of gestures that lie dormant in images, their dynamic charge awaiting its ignition and time of transmission. Culture in this formulation is never finished in the sense of its meaning transmitted and exhausted, its moment of creation sealing its fate. In Warburg's *Atlas*, it is precisely as fragments that culture acquired from different epochs transmits itself potently, the act of transmission fused with the thing to be transmitted.[70] The image is always, in this sense, incomplete.

In Benjamin's writings, the incomplete appears here and there, never the title of an essay but appropriately at the edges of their borders. There is one essay in particular where the incomplete shines forth, an essay that Agamben writes about in 'Benjamin and the Demonic' (*Potentialities*): this is Benjamin's essay on Kafka (a text we return to in this book). Kafka's works are of course full of incomplete figures and characters and it is no surprise that Benjamin lights upon Kafka's short story on the subject of Sancho Panza, a piece of prose that he calls Kafka's 'most perfect creation'.[71] In this telling, Sancho Panza is a writer and Don Quixote is his protagonist who acts out Panza's demonic thoughts. This reading of Don Quixote as a puppet ventriloquized by the squire renders Sancho Panza a free man, a sedentary teller of tales rather than an adventurer. 'Sancho Panza, a sedate fool and clumsy assistant, sent his rider on ahead,' writes Benjamin.[72] In the figure of the sedate student and the assistant, Benjamin locates a critical manoeuvre: the deactivation of a system distinguishing what has taken place from what has not. This of course is the site of Benjamin's theory of history and redemption. What is redeemed of history is not that which has occurred, but the history that 'developed in the darkroom of the lived moment'.[73] Like rolls of undeveloped film, that which has not taken place exists in relation to that which has. The concept of the incomplete, therefore, engages and suspends the idea of history as that which has occurred, suspending its machinic division of what has been from what has not. This, for Benjamin, addresses what is at issue, which is the unsavability of a past that has taken place, a past that may only be repeated. The incomplete is an opening from this eternal return of the same (the fundamental rigidity of a past fixed and without possibility).

Agamben formulates it thus: 'What cannot be saved is what was, the past as such. But what is saved is what never was, something new'.[74] The incomplete draws us into a relation with this dialectic of what was and what was not, a dialectic that is fundamentally archaeological and ex-centric. At the door to this opening is the girl who straddles these worlds, who knows the stakes and who beckons to us. In a curious image to be added to the paradigm of the incomplete girl, a small upright figure rides an ass. Reminiscent of Sancho Panza travelling on the more lowly creature than his 'master' who rides a horse (Rocinante), the girl adds to Benjamin's vignette a figure whose meaning lies truly and yet enigmatically dormant and who interrupts the line of a critical male lineage. It is one of the few images by the photographer Eadweard Muybridge in which a child and a creature appear together. The relationship seems comfortable.

The reigns are slack, and one of the ass's ears is turned towards her as though she may be saying something to the creature as they journey forth. Muybridge, in his sequence of images, seems to allow for the possibility of a type of listening, of animating the potentiality of history through these two creaturely figures who show us what Agamben calls 'something new'.

Notes

1 Giorgio Agamben, 'The Last Chapter in the History of the World', in *Nudities*, trans. David Kishik and Stefan Pedatella (Stanford, CA: Stanford University Press, 2011 [2009]), 114.
2 Mr Bernstein, played by Everett Sloane, in the scene in which he discusses the meaning of Kane's last word, 'Rosebud', in *Citizen Kane* (Welles, 1941).
3 Giorgio Agamben, 'In Playland', in *Infancy and History*, trans. Liz Heron (London and New York: Verso, 1993), 72.
4 Giorgio Agamben, 'Cinema and History: On Jean-Luc Godard', in *Cinema and Agamben*, trans. John V. Garner and Colin Williamson, eds Henrik Gustafsson and Asbjørn Grønstad (New York, London, New Delhi and Sydney: Bloomsbury Academic, 2014), 24.
5 Gustafsson and Grønstad, *Cinema and Agamben*, 6.
6 Sarah Keller, *Maya Deren: Incomplete Control* (New York: Columbia University Press, 2014). See in particular the introduction 'Unfinished Business', 1–30.
7 For a fuller account of the figure of Bartleby in philosophy, see William Watkin's discussion 'The Two Bartlebies: Deleuze, Agamben and Immanence', in *Agamben and Indifference: A Critical Overview* (London and New York: Rowman and Littlefield International, 2012), 151–180.
8 See the chapter 'Written Films', in Pavle Levi, *Cinema by Other Means* (Oxford: Oxford University Press, 2012), 46–76.
9 A term for a member of the Spanish or Portuguese nobility.
10 A proponent of this view of Welles is David Thomson, in *Rosebud: The Story of Orson Welles* (New York: Alfred A. Knopf, 1996). For a counterview, see the review of Welles biographies by Jonathan Rosenbaum, 'The Battle over Orson Welles', in *Discovering Orson Welles* (Berkeley, Los Angeles, CA and London: University of California Press, 2007), 236–247. The controversial biographer Charles Higham provided a more psychological analysis of Welles in his account, *Orson Welles: The Rise and Fall of an American Genius* (London: St Martin's Press, 1985), which describes Welles suffering from a fear of completion, a view discredited by most other commentators and those who worked with Welles.

11 Jonathan Rosenbaum, 'When Will – How Can – We Finish Orson Welles's *Don Quixote?*', in *Discovering Orson Welles* (Berkeley, Los Angeles and London: University of California Press, 2007), 296–307, 297.
12 Ibid., 297.
13 During Rosenbaum's meeting with Welles in July 1972, Welles maintained that *Don Quixote* was almost finished with only sound work remaining in ibid., 298.
14 Oja Kodar cited in Chris Welles Feder, *In My Father's Shadow: A Daughter Remembers Orson Welles* (Edinburgh and London: Mainstream Publishing, 2009), 252–253.
15 According to Rosenbaum, other descriptions of the project add Malaga to the list of locations.
16 Audrey Stainton worked as Welles's secretary 'on and off' and 'more or less' throughout 1958 and 1959. 'Don Quixote: Orson Welles's Secret', *Sight and Sound* (Autumn, 1988).
17 It is perhaps a coincidence (a falling together) that the Italian filmmaker living nearby, Pier Paolo Pasolini, worked on several unfinished films including *Sao Paolo*, a script for a film of St Paul that he laboured over from 1968 to the end of his life in 1975. Welles had of course collaborated with Pasolini, playing himself as it were in the role of director in Pasolini's short film *Ricotta*, shot on the outskirts of Rome in 1962.
18 Orson Welles's contradictory relationship to Italy is the subject of the documentary *Rosabella: Orson Welles's Years in Italy*, directed by Gianfranco Giagni and Ciro Giorgini, Italy 1993 (sixty minutes).
19 Jonathan Rosenbaum, 'Notes on a Conversation with Welles', in *Discovering Orson Welles* (Berkeley, Los Angeles, CA and London: University of California Press, 2007), 50.
20 Stainton, 'Don Quixote: Orson Welles's Secret', 56.
21 Rosenbaum, 'Orson Welles's *Don Quixote*', 306.
22 Jonathan Rosenbaum, 'The Invisible Orson Welles' in *Discovering Orson Welles* (Berkeley, Los Angeles, CA and London: University of California Press, 2007), 73, 67–89.
23 Stainton '*Don Quixote*: Orson Welles's Secret', 56.
24 Jonathan Rosenbaum suggests that the scene is not a loose version of the knight tilting at windmills from Part 1, Chapter 8, but Quixote's attack on the puppet theatre in Part 2, Chapter 26.
25 Giorgio Agamben, 'The Six Most Beautiful Minutes in the History of Cinema' in *Potentialities: Collected Essays in Philosophy*, ed. and trans. Daniel Heller-Roazen (Stanford, CA: Stanford University Press, 1999), 93.
26 Giorgio Agamben, 'Infancy and History: An Essay on the Destruction of Experience', in *Infancy and History: Essays on the Destruction of Experience*, trans. Liz Heron (London and New York: Verso, 1993), 11–64.

27 Ibid., 24.
28 Ibid., 26.
29 Walter Benjamin, *The Origins of German Tragic Drama*, trans. John Osborn (London and New York: Verso, 2003), 178.
30 Agamben, 'The Six Most Beautiful Minutes in the History of Cinema', 94.
31 Alex Murray, *Giorgio Agamben* (London and New York: Routledge, 2010), 22.
32 For a discussion of Agamben's theological engagement and method, see Leland de la Durantaye's afterword 'On Method, the Messiah, Anarchy and Theocracy' in Giorgio Agamben, *The Church and the Kingdom*, trans. Leland de la Durantaye (London, New York and Calcutta: Seagull Books, 2012), 48-62.
33 Giorgio Agamben, *The Signature of All Things: On Method*, trans. Luca D'Isanto and Kevin Attell (New York: Zone Books, 2009), 7.
34 Alan Sheridan, *Michel Foucault: The Will to Truth* (London and New York: Routledge, 2003), 46.
35 Michel Foucault, *Histoire de la folie à l'âge classique: folie et déraison* (Paris: Plon, 1961), *Naissance de la clinique: une archéologie du regard médical* (Paris: PUF, 1963), and *Raymond Roussel* (Paris: Gallimard, 1963).
36 Michel Foucault, 'Nietzsche, Genealogy, History', in *Language, Counter-Memory, Practice: Selected Essays and Interviews*, trans. D. Bouchar and S. Simon (Ithaca, NY: Cornell University Press, 1977), 146.
37 For a succinct gloss on this difference, see Alison Ross's introduction to 'The Agamben Effect', Special Edition of the journal, *South Atlantic Quarterly* 107:1 (Winter 2008): 1-14.
38 Anton Schütz, 'The Fading Memory of *Homo Non Sacer*', in *The Work of Giorgio Agamben: Law, Literature, Life*, eds Justin Clemens, Nicholas Heron and Alex Murray (Edinburgh: Edinburgh University Press, 2008), 114-131, 119.
39 Giorgio Agamben, *State of Exception* (2005). See also Stephen Humphreys 'Legalizing Lawlessness: On Giorgio Agamben's *State of Exception*', *The European Journal of International Law* 17:3 (2006): 677-687.
40 Justin Clemens, 'The Role of the Shifter and the Problem of Reference' in *The Work of Giorgio Agamben: Law, Literature, Life*, eds Justin Clemens, Nicholas Heron and Alex Murray (Edinburgh: Edinburgh University Press, 2008), 53.
41 Agamben writes, 'Thus it is not so much the *bricoleur* as the collector who naturally appears as the figure closest to the player. For just as antique objects are collected, so are miniatures of objects. But in both cases the collector extracts the object from its diachronic distance or its synchronic proximity and gathers into the remote adjacence of history – into what, to paraphrase one of Benjamin's definitions, could be defined as 'une citation à l'ordre du jour', on the final day of history', in the essay 'In Playland', in *Infancy and History*, 72.

42 Agamben, *Signature of All Things*, 58.
43 Michel Foucault, *The Order of Things: An Archaeology of the Human Sciences* (London and New York: Routledge, 1989), 19.
44 Ibid., 140.
45 A point to note in Foucault's account is the changed ontology of the human subject in this shift of epistemic systems. The characteristic of a human being up until the late sixteenth century was figured in the same mode as the creature or object, as a thing revealed in its signature actions, the *being* of the human. In the era of representation, beings are separate from their signs and are instead represented by them. Signs we may misread or indeed may be adopted in order to deceive, cleaving a distinction between representation and truth.
46 Foucault, *The Order of Things*, 422.
47 Agamben, *The Signature of All Things*, 70.
48 Ibid.
49 Ibid., 76.
50 Ibid., 77.
51 Foucault, *The Order of Things*, 53.
52 Ibid., 56.
53 Ibid., 54.
54 One could add to this the film that Terry Gilliam attempted to make of the novel, which becomes a film of a failed effort in *Lost in La Mancha* (Keith Fulton and Louis Pepe, 2002).
55 In France, the most astute criticism of *Remnants of Auschwitz* came in the form of a book by Philippe Mesnard and Claudine Cahan, *Giorgio Agamben à l'épreuve d'Auschwitz* (Paris: Editions Kimé, 2001).
56 Stainton suggests that a more appropriate term for his method of post-synch would be pre-voice.
57 Stainton, '*Don Quixote*: Orson Welles's Secret', 56.
58 Ibid.
59 Feder, *In My Father's Shadow*, 231.
60 Stainton, 'Don Quixote: Orson Welles's Secret'.
61 Ibid., 232.
62 Stainton, 'Don Quixote: Orson Welles's Secret', 56.
63 The book also considers the work of amateur artist Henry Darger, whose paintings of small girls resisting the power of adults as Agamben describes them were discovered posthumously after his death in 1972.
64 Giorgio Agamben, *Nymphs*, trans. Amanda Minervini (London, New York and Calcutta: Seagull Books, 2013), *Ninfe*, 2007, 2.
65 Ibid., 15.

66 Ibid., 58. These phrases recur throughout Agamben's work, particularly in discussion of Walter Benjamin's account of history and the dialectical image.
67 Giorgio Agamben, *Stanzas: Word and Phantasm in Western Culture*, trans. R.L. Martinez (Minneapolis: University of Minnesota Press), 32.
68 This version of events derives from Chris Welles Feder's autobiography *In My Father's Shadow*, 250–268.
69 Giorgio Agamben, *The Unspeakable Girl: The Myth and Mystery of Kore*, trans. Leland de la Durantaye and Annie Julia Wyman (London, New York and Calcutta: Seagull Books), 38.
70 The relationship of culture as transmission and the aesthetic is the subject of Agamben's book *Man without Content*, trans. Georgia Albert (Stanford, CA: Stanford University Press, 2009).
71 Walter Benjamin, 'Franz Kafka', in *Illuminations*, ed. Hannah Arendt, trans. Harry Zorn (London: Fontana, 1973), 135.
72 Ibid.
73 Benjamin cited in Giorgio Agamben, 'Benjamin and the Demonic', *Potentialities: Collected Essays in Philosophy*, ed. and trans. Daniel Heller-Roazen (Stanford, CA: Stanford University Press, 1999), 138–159, 158.
74 Ibid., 158.

2

Gesture: Cinema Muto Mutato

Testing

In a piece of film lasting for seventeen seconds, two men clasp each other at the waist as they dance a waltz, whilst a third plays a violin. The violinist is standing next to a large conical horn. The men shuffle in rhythm with the bars of the song, *Les cloches de Corneville*, executing four complete turns.[1] The sequence has no diegetic context. The background is a black drape, for this is a test in which the recording equipment is at once the subject of the experiment and its witness. In this sense, the film is of its time, part and parcel of what Nietzsche had described as an 'experimental disposition' that had coloured the nineteenth century. The dancers are disposed to the project, and have given themselves over to the idea that something is being discovered through their movements and gestures. Yet there is an excess to this instrumentality that otherwise threatens to reduce dance to the means to an end. The posture and movements of the men disclose two bodies in synchronized step, not only performing a task or rehearsing a learnt routine, but in communication. They are, that is, an image of gesture, a mode of appearing in which the body exhibits its own mediality, where what is being revealed and the mode of revelation are indivisible.

This is Edison's Black Maria Studio in West Orange, New Jersey; it is winter 1894 or possibly spring 1895 and the test is a measure of how sound and image may be synchronized, one consolidating the presence of the other. More discretely, the scene is a demonstration of the body at the point of losing its hereto invisible ease (something is passing), and as it becomes subject to new methods of recorded imaging and capture (something is emerging). Does this new techne, or what is to become cinema, accelerate a crisis of gesture and bodily communication, or merely record its loss?

Test results: Inner life

Agamben's essay 'On Gesture' is in many ways the manifestation of a deeply archaeological approach to cinema. Through an imagined connection between the neurologist Gilles de la Tourette and the photographer Eadweard Muybridge at the latter part of the nineteenth century, a prehistory of cinema is conjured as a shared project of capturing the loss of a fluent locomotion in human gesture. Cinema emerges through, or even as a response to, a crisis in bodily movement. Bodies, Agamben argues, were in the process of losing their here-to invisible ease, transitioning towards a highly visible and self-conscious 'generalized disaster' for the realm of gesture, manifest in tics and spasms that atomized movement. The atomization of movement in turn atomized the subjects of a community whose dwelling had been located within the commons of a gestural language, and who were now isolated within the indecipherable language of a body unable to articulate itself. So opens the essay on gesture, which goes on to demonstrate cinema's turn-of-the-century appeal, located in its ability to summon both what was passing and what was emerging as a point of crisis, here taking the Greek root of the term as being between two states. It is an interpretation that undoes the positivist account of cinema's evolution as a journey from still images to film's fluent motion pictures. In contrast to this well-rehearsed story of origins, the oxidized footprints of de la Tourette's patients provide a semiotic account of corporal fluency gone awry, and Muybridge steps in (as it were) to frame and document the flailing human figure. The images of leaping, jumping, fencing men and women could be read as a manifest endeavour to triumph over a loss of bodily ease, with each frame a neurotic attempt to pin down the exact arc of gestural perfection, or indeed pathology. Cinema could almost be regarded as the accidental by-product of a drive to capture and redress the human figure's fall into incoherence.

If pre- and early cinema can be thought of as multifaceted attempts to orbit human gesture, it is probable that Agamben has in mind here Walter Benjamin's account of modern disaffection in his essay on Kafka. 'The invention of the film and phonograph came in an age of maximum alienation of men from one another,' writes Benjamin, 'of unpredictably intervening relationships which have become their only ones', he pens on the tenth anniversary of Kafka's death (1934). Cinema played back this alienation, according to Benjamin, almost as a form of detachment and objectification of the self. 'Experiments have proved', he continues, 'that a man does not recognize his own walk on the screen or his own voice on the phonograph'.² Taking Benjamin's account a point further, cinema is but one part of a mosaic of emerging institutions and effects that produce 'unpredictably intervening relationships', both between subjects and between the subject's notion of self and her body. Far from being simply an entertainment complex, cinema is aligned with a properly modern set of practices that, according to Foucault, capture, reproduce and administrate bodies, through the inculcation of the care of the self. Under the sign of the biopolitical, the modern subject is produced through a newly dispersed power moving through the populace as techniques of self-management cross-referred to statistically rendered classificatory norms. Whilst it is clear from the introduction to *Homer Sacer* (1995) that Agamben regards Foucault's examination of the biopolitical as unfinished work limited in its emphasis on the modern period, their thought is aligned, as Alison Ross remarks, in understanding the characteristics of modernity as 'an increasingly more radical tendency to take control of "life".'³ Modernity, according to Agamben, is but one particular rendition of a separation of life into bios (*polis* or common discourse of speech and action) and bare life (*zoe* or biological existence), where the latter may be utterly and fatally exposed to political instrumentality. This politicization of life under the sign of modernity, I will argue, acquires fuller detail and particularity when cinema is inserted into the dynamic scenario as a major link in the chain of administrative practices through which life is crafted, developed, preserved and managed.

This chapter follows Agamben's thinking on gesture as communicability in crisis at the end of the nineteenth century and pushes beyond this to explore not only how cinema manifests this crisis, but how this crisis made manifest the cinema that we have. In order to understand the disastrous consequences of the loss of gesture as the end of a common ground of an ethical–political relating, it is necessary to understand the crafting of an individuation over and against this gestural common. Key to this is what cinema became in its formative years, or more specifically the emergence of cinematic grammar as a vehicle privileging the enigma of human interiority, or 'inner life', over the shared and common power of communication. As Agamben writes, when life becomes indecipherable through a loss of gesture, the subject 'succumbs to interiority', and the realm of private thoughts, memories and affects becomes the critical locus of an essentialized yet obscure identity. Cinema, I will argue, is aligned with those institutions and disciplines that evolve a mode of investigative practice focused on the deciphering of the subject as enigma. Akin to physiology, cinema's attention to the external features of the subject is but the decipherment of an 'internal' world, identifying truth effects *within* the subject, rather than through a matrix of common exchange. As the techniques and practices of cinema evolve, its language shifts from the observational mode of fixed-position camera recording to a more mobile syntax of camera positions that align the spectator with characters. As early as 1911, the technique of shot reverse shot offered faces of characters for scrutiny, privileging emotional tension as the engine fuelled by the challenge of decipherment. Fostering an interrogative mode at once subtler than that of forensic criminology, psychiatry and physiognomy, cinema made the internal processes of a character the key that unlocks and makes intelligible the (diegetic) world.[4]

In the second part of the nineteenth century, unruly gesticulating bodies were on their way to becoming fully encoded within various registers, subjected to all manner of trials, performances and experiments in front of experts and audiences in medical theatres, laboratories, on couches, in photographic studios and latterly in cinema. The excitement pertaining to bodies was generated through these multiple processes of examination that instituted the body as the site of a mysterious truth, a verity that remained veiled to the subject himself or herself. Cinema's very potent appeal was manifest in its disclosure of a subjective interiority to a lay rather than a specialized audience, a popularization of investigative processes that brought about an affective discharge with its revelation. The curve of this chapter brings cinema into an alignment with the multiple biopolitical investitures of the time within an archaeological paradigm, a constellation of discourses. In the following pages, cinema enters a zone of undecidability, a realm where fictional entertainment is not in opposition to factual knowledge but where such distinctions are dissolved. Entering this zone, the definition of cinema becomes loosened and in the course of the chapter we will find that the apparatus famed for its ability to record is always also a machine for transmission.

Running man

In the eleven volumes of photographs by Eadweard Muybridge held at the Kingston Museum, London, entitled 'Animal Locomotion: An Electro-photographic Investigation of Consecutive Phases of Animal Movements', the editions draw attention to a distinction between bodies clothed (or 'draped' as Muybridge preferred) and those that are naked. There are other distinctions to be made, between the bodies of men and bodies of women, adults and children, human beings and animals, and between bodies that are 'able' and 'disabled'. This survey of locomotion, developed at and financially supported by the University of Pennsylvania in 1884, presented a consolidation of Muybridge's working methods developed over a number of decades, famously deploying fast shutter speed with multiple lens cameras activated electromagnetically.[5]

General view of Muybridge's experimental track circa 1881. (Eadweard Muybridge)

The most frequently reproduced images show a subject in movement photographed from the side (with the subject in profile) against a graphic patterned background, but cameras were also installed at the front and rear of the walkway to provide a 180° perspective. The resulting plates offer a version of the photographed subject in excess of human vision, not only in terms of the famous revelation of the body in movement at frozen intervals but the body as a three-dimensional object in space. The images of 'man running', depicting the body from the front, behind and the side, seem to move around the subject as though time itself is slowed and suspended.

The critical commentary on Muybridge's work is a dense palimpsest of links to anthropology, anthropometry, physiology, medicine and travel. The photographic grids of differently marked bodies are in Elspeth Brown's terms, on a continuum of evolutionary race science necessary to an age of colonial expansion.[6] Marta Braun has argued with a different emphasis that Muybridge's sequences of women were erotic stories.[7] Braun identifies gaps and absences in the grids of images that testify to a form of post-production, a crafting of non-chronological images into micro-dramatic narratives that Muybridge is able to control. Muybridge shoots the sequences in a certain order that bears out the theory that a narrative drive is at work as Muybridge's favoured model, twenty-year-old Blanche Epler in 1885, is required to lie down, rise, pray, pour water, descend stairs and leave. The sequences provide, Rebecca Solnit argues, a narrative more sophisticated and layered than a train arriving at a station or workers leaving a factory; the text here has patterns, arrangements and gaps. In a continuation of this thought, Solnit speculates that psychically Muybridge is rehearsing a form of distanced intimacy, an intense drama that resides on the other side of a glass partition.[8] Certainly, the female figures recall the art historian Aby Warburg's nymphs, who 'seem to be moving in a dreamy, self-absorbed time in which the most basic gesture is stretched out into a series of images'.[9] In the studio built specifically for Muybridge on the north-east corner of the campus, the women carry baskets on their heads, use watering cans, dispense water from a jug to a bowl, sweep the floor, fan themselves, pour water over each other, shake linen, wash their faces and get into bed.[10] The men leapfrog over other men, ascend and descend stairs, swing pickaxes, carry dumbbells, throw and catch balls, carry baskets on shoulders, walk planks, row imaginary boats, wield cricket bats and bowl cricket balls.

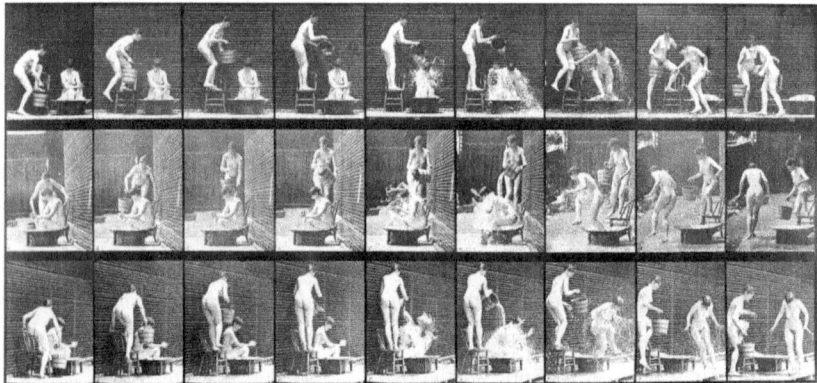

Woman pouring water over another nude woman in bath (Eadweard Muybridge)

In the subsequent books in which figures are clothed, the tasks are more pronounced and the social stratification of subjects is brought into relief as clothing, posture and activities begin to cohere as chains of signifiers. Women in long blousy dresses play tennis, a woman in a bustle dress sits demurely on a chair, a woman in a dress that sweeps the floor carries a child under a parasol, a woman fans herself whilst descending steps, a woman under a parasol waves a handkerchief. A shoeless girl carries a bucket and kneels, rakes hay, carries a bucket and an urn, bundles hay into her hands and, in another sequence, carries hay on her head. A shoeless girl, in the most obviously pleasurable activity of all, throws herself forwards onto a pile of hay. And then there are the couples, one pair dancing, another pair walking towards each other and two women kissing. Clothed or naked, the body, rather than the speaking subject of the body, has some truth to reveal to the observer.

Two women kissing (Eadweard Muybridge)

Agamben, as we have noted, writes about Muybridge in 'Notes on Gesture'. The essay travels from the bourgeoisie's loss of gesture in the late nineteenth century through to the 'pure gesturality' of human beings in the realm of the ethical and political. At the centre is the cinema, an apparatus that at once captures the waning display of gesture and more importantly continues to function as the locus of a pure gestural mode, allowing Agamben to assert that '[t]he element of cinema is gesture and not the image'.[11] In addition to the naked and clothed bodies in the locomotion study, another division (which is also a binary pairing) takes place in the opening section between the happy and suffering bodies. Muybridge's exercising figures are 'the happy and visible twins of the unknown and suffering creatures'[12] in the work of the French neuropsychiatrist Gilles de la Tourette, an expert on epilepsy, hysteria and hypnotism. Agamben opens the essay with Tourette's publication from 1886 of a clinical study of the human gait, *Études cliniques et physiologiques sur la marche*.[13] In this study, Tourette had analysed the common human gesture of walking through a particular method of imprint, and with the precision and detail of a gaze that Agamben finds prophetic of what 'cinematography would later become'.[14] Tourette's method was to attach a roll of white paper to the floor and draw a line down the centre whilst his subjects, their feet smeared with iron sesquioxide powder, were required to walk the line to the best of their abilities. The resulting footprints provided a trace of movement that could be calibrated and compared according to length of step, cadence, direction, symmetry and so forth. These are the marks of an invisible series of people whose only inscription recorded testifies to their malady, besides which the naked and clothed figures of Muybridge's series are permitted to fully 'appear'.

A year before the study of the human gait was published, Gilles de la Tourette had published the results of related research into a nervous condition that gave rise to a lack of motor coordination, *Étude sur une affection nerveuse caractérisée par l'incoordination motrice accompagnée d'écholalie et de coprolalie*. The work supplied a description of a range of uncoordinated involuntary motor and vocal tics, spasms and tremors that, for Agamben at least, 'cannot be defined in any way other than as a generalized catastrophe of the sphere of gestures'.[15] It is as though the subjects of these movements are subjected to something that reads like an electrical current. He writes of these patients, 'If they are able to start a movement, this is interrupted and broken up by shocks lacking any coordination and by tremors that give the impression that the whole musculature is engaged in a dance (*chorea*) that is completely independent of any ambulatory end.'[16] Figuratively, it appears as though the shockwaves of modernity run through these bodies, a mimetic encounter with the increasingly automated world. Both Muybridge and de la Tourette produce a notion of evidence as a forensic trace. Furthermore, their dissection of movement into units is suggestive for those concerned with the efficiencies of factory labour and economy. The physiologist and chronophotographer Étienne-Jules Marey (also referenced in Agamben's essay), unlike Muybridge, believed that 'his analyses could cut down on fatigue and increase productivity in almost all areas of social life'.[17] In addition to the other polarities in operation in the essay, efficiency and waste, energy and fatigue make their appearance.

The essay 'Notes on Gesture' is structured like a report with a series of points that read almost as intertitles in an early film underscoring and interleafing the action.[18] The opening title states that by the end of the nineteenth century the (Western) bourgeoisie had lost its gestures, followed by the second point that the cinema attempts to both recover and record the loss. The third point is that which redeems cinema in the assertion that the element of cinema is gesture and not the image, a hinge in the argument that turns towards potential salvation. The fourth and lengthiest point is this: 'Because cinema has its center in the gesture and not in the image, it belongs essentially to the realm of ethics and politics (and not simply to that of aesthetics).'[19] The final title closes the circle by bringing politics back to gesture: 'Politics is the sphere of pure means, that is, of the absolute and complete gesturality of human beings.'[20] The essay closes on this statement with no elaboration beneath the subheading, as though this silent film may run on and we viewers imagine the consequent scene. The simplicity of the headings, however, belies the complexity of thought compressed into this gnomic piece of writing that leads from the identification of pathology in motor coordination in the late nineteenth century, to cinema, ethics and politics, declining aesthetics along the way. How is it possible to unpack this assertion that cinema is summoned from the field of the image and aesthetics to take its place as a gestural medium belonging with ethics and politics?

The image is not in itself a priority in Agamben's work but, as Benjamin Noys writes, it appears as a 'minor' concern in the sense given to the term by Deleuze and Guattari, as a continuous flight to release the image from the function of representation and classification.[21] 'Although the image is nowhere a *sustained* point of reference for Agamben's work,' writes Noys, 'his momentary reflections and fragmentary comments on the image attests to the necessity continually to *displace* its centrality.'[22] Where the image does appear, it is often associated with the spectral system of capital, a moniker for the captivation of human desire (and gesture) in a system that returns this as a reified and ultimately unattainable condition. Across his work, pornography and advertising are attributed the ambiguous role of 'hired mourners' that escort the commodity image to the grave.[23] Here Agamben draws on his friend, Guy Debord's analysis of the society of the spectacle, a condition that refers us not to the image itself but the way in which the image comes to constitute the relations between human beings, and indeed between humans and things. Under the sign of the spectacle, the image mediates relations, getting between and separating a seductive and ultimately unattainable image of 'life' apparently present in the image from the living being. Yet this account is inflected by a Benjaminian sense of salvation in which the image is not irredeemable, rather it is situated within a force field that Agamben elsewhere calls a zone of undecidability, the site at which two elements coincide. Here, the image may be deployed by capital to deaden its dynamic capacity (its call to act), or conversely it may maintain its own potentiality, its capacity to release a dynamic energy within the image that has been frozen but not destroyed. Out of these two elements, the deadening effect of capital is described by Deborah Levitt as gesture expropriated by the spectacle, which silences its communicative capacity; 'we could read the spectacle as an in-between of object (image) and invested desire (eye) that suspends the two from a state of dialogue'.[24] On the other hand, if the system of reification has fixed the gestural potential of the image, that is, made static the energy of gestural display, the image retains the possibility of revivification when the image is reappropriated. This is the argument made by Jessica Whyte that through the notion of profanation, the image (or other commodity form) may be taken from the space of a 'sacred' separation and inserted back into common use.

Cinema as image and as gesture would seem to be situated ambivalently at the crossroads of capital and salvation, respectively, a position that arises from its footing in photography and the frozen gesture. The emergence of cinema *qua* cinema is subtly treated by Agamben in that the distinction between photography and cinema is not notable. Indeed, Garrett Stewart goes as far as to claim that Agamben 'defers all questions of medium-specificity to the phenomenological "plane of immanence" (the touchstone Deleuzian formulation), where motion is visible as such'.[25] If photographers such as Muybridge appear in Agamben's writings (and Muybridge assumes a particularly prescient position), it is not as a predecessor to the cinema as entertainment complex, but as a progenitor of the study of bodies and their capacities, creating a different non-chronological alliance of photography and cinema that is concerned with what it is a body can do. It is of course an arising of a biopolitical investiture in the body as the site of investigation and the seeking of 'truth', but we come to this in fullness later.

A prismatic figure, Muybridge turns his camera towards the body, many bodies, and charts their capacity to jump, throw, step and run. He is not interested in portraiture (the common use for photography up until this moment), in who these people are or presume to be, but in the abstract and virtual capacity of bodies to act. He creates images that at once attest to movement as linear modality and capture something more, its potency. He breaks the fluid motion of running into a series of staccato steps. In a contortion of Laura Mulvey's formulation that cinema presents stillness (or death) at twenty-four times a second (and thus centralizing the effects of recording), Muybridge brings into being the still image as movement captured as *engram*, privileging transmission.

Engram: Encryptions and transmissions

The significance of the division between a cinema of gesture and a cinema of the image that Agamben cleaves has a further legacy through his attachment to Warburg.[26] In 'Notes on Gesture', Warburg is evoked in the second section of the essay as a researcher whose practice and investigations into the image uncovered gesture as 'a crystal of historical memory'. 'Because of the fact that this research was conducted through the medium of images,' writes Agamben, 'it was believed that the image was also its object',[27] a belief that Agamben sets about dispelling. Warburg, through his method of collecting and tracing connections between thousands of images from antiquity to the twentieth century had, according to Agamben's corrective, achieved a transformation of the image into 'a decisively historical and dynamic element'.[28] Each image is less an autonomous reality, writes Agamben, than a film still; that is, each image is part of a larger set or paradigm that it both establishes and is established by.[29] A film still, like a photograph, is characterized both by a mode of belonging (to other similar images) and by a relationship to movement. Yet caution is needed here as movement for Agamben and for Warburg is not motion traced across a sequence but the mobility captured by the image in its 'still' form. One could say that Warburg might have valued Muybridge's images not for their sequential motion but for the iconographic capture of movement within one and each frame.

The method of intuitive gathering that Warburg employed and his peculiar analysis of detail produce an iconography concerned not with an era but the anomalies that reveal continuity that is 'out of time', or 'historical' in

Benjamin's sense. At the centre of Warburg's practice was a concept of culture as transmission, a concept influenced by anthropology at the turn of the twentieth century, in particular the evolutionary biologist Richard Semon, who Agamben identifies as a critical influence on Warburg's thought. He tells us that in 1908, Warburg had bought Semon's book *Mneme* (named after the Greek goddess of memory) and it is in this text that Semon proposes a theory of memory binding culture and biological function. Rather startlingly, memory is defined not as a property of consciousness, but as a quality distinguishing living matter from that which is dead. In this text, Semon proposed that every external stimulus producing an effect on the body leaves a trace, or imprint, which he named an *engram*, and in a thread that leads back to the medical investiture of Tourette, he argued that this potential memory affect was located within the nervous system; included in his list of inscriptions are involuntary spasms and discharges in response to stimuli. Capturing this energy, the *engram* is a type of residue, a trace of memory encoded and open to future transmission across time, retaining a potential for reactivation within the appropriate conditions. Whilst one can see the evolutionary strains of Semon's work as biological transmission, Warburg took from this the concept that a potentiality existed within culture to conserve energy in a gesture, whose dynamic force could be discharged at a later date. In a radical appropriation of the theory, Warburg traces the thousands of gestures in the images and symbols of ancient art as encrypted *engrams* that at once stand alone as transmissions and correspond in relation.

In Agamben's version this gestural charge caught within the image becomes akin to 'electricity condensed in a Leydan jar',[30] and in another of Agamben's texts written shortly after his period of research at the Warburg Institute, *Stanzas: Word and Phantasm in Western Culture* (1977), we find an earlier version of this emphasis when he writes that 'every culture is essentially a process of transmission and of *Nachleben*'.[31] Agamben retains the German term which does not correspond directly with a single term in English but which approximates to survival, or a continuation of life in this world.[32] Gesture is a cultural form of something continuing in this world not as a supernatural force but as a transmission that cuts across and reconfigures chronological time. Related to Benjamin's concept of the dialectic at a standstill, the gesture is a force in two senses. It is a current that engages thought with disregard for temporal origin, that is, images may connect and fire with images from other periods. Second, the dynamis encrypted in the image betrays the potency of contingency in that its release is associated with unpredictable situations and unlikely encounters. In this sense, gestural qualities are those poses that conserve an energy or dynamis silently or perhaps invisibly until a contingency provides their moment of discharge (or what Benjamin might have named the kairological time of the event). In addition to the animating force of the gesture, however, there is something potentially explosive or misfiring in the concept of the *engram* as transmission that is encoded in Agamben's brief essay on gesture.

In his account of Muybridge who animates the essay as a figure 'it is impossible not to think about' in relation to Gilles de la Tourette,[33] Agamben attributes a set of images to the photographer that do not exist. In what he calls 'running man with shotgun', the philosopher splices together the separate photographic sequences of 'man running' with 'man with a rifle', a misfiring that cannot but recall Muybridge's own unorthodox transmission. In 1874, Muybridge famously travelled some seventy-five miles to track down Major Harry Larkyns, the lover of his wife and probable father of the child Muybridge had considered his, and shot him.[34] Larkyns, shot at close range, died that night. 'Running man with shotgun' perfectly captures the journey, the intent of the act and the heat of the event. It was in fact the French photographer Etienne Jules Marey (mentioned in passing by Agamben in the gesture essay) who recorded sequences of a man running with a gun (1891–2), captured by Marey's hybrid machine, the gun camera or the chronophotographic gun.[35] Agamben creates for us a vignette in which the gestures that came to characterize Muybridge's life, shooting photographs and shooting a man, are superimposed, distilling a life to these dynamic features. Curiously there is also a shooting incident in the life of de la Tourette that occurred some years after his studies of the human gait and of nervous disorders. In 1893, de la Tourette was shot by a former patient, Rose Kamper, who claimed that she was hypnotized by de la Tourette against her will. Rose Kamper appeared one day at his treatment rooms and stopped the flow of his conversation in the most startling of ways, but not for good. De la Tourette survived the relatively superficial head wound but according to his biographer, his reputation was permanently damaged in the suggestion of an abuse of power. In summary, in the late nineteenth century, movement and stillness, motion and its arrest, suspended states and broken sentences are rife in acts of transmission that do not necessarily obey the law of intention. Whilst the pre-cinematic physiological sequences of photography exhibit a body ostensibly brought under analytical control and made legible, there is always a dimension that escapes this capture.

In the decades in which cinema came to be recognized as cinema, there was a certain obsession with traces and transmissions that was to become buried in the years that followed. Perhaps Muybridge was closer to Warburg's intent in his ambition to develop a method that captured *dynamis*, preserved its form and transmitted it via a photographic recording. In contrast to the standard accounts that seek an origin for cinema, Warburg's conceptualization disrupts the polarization of recording and transmission; the fixed taxidermic nature of photographic images and a liveness communicated in transmission are situated together at a site where their contours become indistinguishable. The metaphor of electricity that runs through Agamben's account of gesture is suggestive of a capacity to both store and transmit at a later date, the image of the Leyden jar describing the captured potency of the images Warburg assembles. The electrical current is also present, we may recall, in his description of the gestural figurations of Tourette's patients whose movement is 'interrupted and broken up by shocks'. What is apparent in these various activities of imaging at this moment is that cinema is not, properly speaking, necessary to this system of capture, preservation and transmission. Photography as a medium by itself was effective in its ability to adapt itself to these demands. For if the photographic image contains gesture, or to put it in reverse, if gesture is a dynamic form within the still image, what would be the imperative to literalize movement as cinema did? The notion of Muybridge as a necessary forerunner of cinema lays a path of almost inevitable consequence, that photography is the stuttering early manifestation of what was to become realized in the work of the Lumières, Méliès and others. And yet the volumes of images of moving bodies, animals and humans are rewritten here as a capacity to store gestural motion in stillness, a captured motion that is made to move in a literal sense through the circling discs of the zoopraxiscope that Muybridge also created as only one method of display amongst others.

This alternative modelling of a number of prismatic developments (cultural, medical and technical) posits gesture and transmission rather than media ontology and recording, at the centre of a conceptualization of cinema. There is, in addition, a further aspect to the essay on gesture that has received sparse critical treatment but which I will argue reconceives the task of early cinema in biopolitical terms. Agamben's essay on gesture features a line in which a considerable shift in communication and communicability takes place, a shift that is signalled by the obsession with bodily gesture, but leads to a number of transformations in the manifestation of being, creating an identity located in a space internal to the subject. The two sentences that come before this line are these: 'For human beings who have lost every sense of naturalness, each single gesture becomes a destiny. And the more gestures lose their powers, the more life becomes indecipherable.'[36] These lines, and the one that follows, appear in all versions of the essay and concern, once again, the bourgeoisie: 'In this phase the bourgeoisie, which just a few decades earlier was still firmly in possession of its symbols, succumbs to interiority and gives itself up to psychology.'[37]

Cinema gives itself up to psychology

One might say the same of cinema during the first decade of the twentieth century, as its modality transferred from one of gestural, externally oriented *cinema muto*, to a cinema of psychological drama located 'within' the character. It is not the case that cinema simply reflected a social phenomenon but that cinema came into being as a properly institutionalized form through discourses of internalization that were born a century earlier.[38] If, for Foucault, identity had been produced and stabilized through the long nineteenth century with the institutionalization of 'identity effects' through medicine, education, juridico-legal discourses and labour practices, such processes gave form to an emergent cinema as it too became regulated and standardized. The shift that cinema underwent in its twist from aberrant music-hall ephemera and eclecticism to psychological drama delivered it to the services of an individualizing culture, parallel to what Roberto Esposito has designated the move from a paradigm of *communitas* to one of immunization (*immunitas*).[39] But this is to leap ahead.

There are many gags in the archives of early cinema pertaining to bodies, which are routinely subjected to accidental or intentional harm, imaged by cinema, according to Lisa Trahair, as 'preposterous figurations',[40] defying the laws of the physical universe: crushed, flattened, dropped, broken, run over, the body almost always seems to get it, only to be magically rejuvenated in the course of a short film. There is however an early film that reverses this story, the famous short, *The Big Swallow* (James Williamson, 1901: 68 seconds). A man, wearing a bowler hat and carrying a cane, stands direct to camera and appears irritated and argumentative in response to the camera's presence. He moves towards the lens in a mode that is both tentative and threatening, continuing a highly gestural rant. Moving into extreme proximity, his mouth covers the lens and he appears (for the viewer) to have swallowed the camera. At this point (shot two), the screen becomes as black as the inside of a mouth would be without illumination. The shot then becomes illuminated to reveal an imagined space, dimly lit, inside of the man's mouth showing the cinematographer and the camera as they meet their fate and are swallowed. The third shot withdraws from the mouth, passing back over the teeth, returning to the exterior of the body to show the first man chewing and swallowing, ending the event with a satisfied smile.

The Big Swallow (James Williamson, 1901)

There is something more to be said of this act in terms of ingestion that requires us to question what it is that was swallowed with the emergence of cinema. This film, in open display, performs cinema's movement into the interiority of the body, an *engram* that demonstrates in just over a minute the potency of cinema to dramatize an interest in the internal space of the body. In 1901, in James Williamson's innovative comic short, the horizon of a biopolitical condition is there to be seen, disguised as a gag. In Akira Lippit's reading of this film, he draws a similar connection to dramatized internal space with reference to Freud's dream of his analysis with the patient Irma. Freud dreams of Irma's mouth, its resistance to his desire to reach her subconscious and the spectre of formlessness that it presented. The camera's move into the man's mouth in *The Big Swallow* suggestively echoes 'Freud's X-ray entry into Irma's mouth', he writes, continuing: 'It marks the passage of the subject into the illusory body of the other, but also the loss of oneself elsewhere, in an other, deep inside an other'.[41] For Lippit, cinema teeters on the edge of an anatomical excursus into the inside of another and the dissolution of the self. The psychotherapist may get swallowed whole too. Yet there is something of the mechanical registration of this excursion into the interior space of the body that stabilizes and distances the threat. Writing of Jean Martin Charcot's infamous use of photography in his study (or invention) of hysteria, Georges Didi-Huberman notes, 'photographic endoscopy, finally able to unveil the most secret anatomy – as it is'.[42] Photography of hysterical 'pathology' invites a performance of the 'inside' that translates as the interior made visible and legible.

The first decade of cinema (1893–1904) offers, according to Jonathan Auerbach, a prime opportunity to think questions of the body and its importance for this emerging technology with its probing attempts at coherence and intelligibility. 'How do we read a film made at the turn of the twentieth century,' he asks, 'that has no clearly demarcated characters or actors, settings or plot?' continuing, 'What is a body without a comprehensible story to give it some context?'[43] If one of the first popular British films of the early nineteenth century dramatizes these questions, it also provides the answer in a figural way and during the following decade the grammar of cinema evolves to consolidate the internal 'world' of characters as the site and anchor of intelligibility. There are various fronts that this quest to secure interiority as truth moves forward on cinematically, including medical science films on the one hand and popular entertainment on the other, their efforts jointly efficacious in driving attention towards the join of physiognomy and psychology. Through early film experiments and figural instances it is possible to circle back to the statement and find greater force in its assertion that '[i]n this phase the bourgeoisie, which just a few decades earlier was still firmly in possession of its symbols, succumbs to interiority and gives itself up to psychology'.[44] Succumbing to interiority, however, is no facile trick; the subject is made to articulate the inner world to the best of her or his ability and the couch is ready and waiting to facilitate the process. The speaking cure, well underway before *cinema muto* breaks out into babbling song and speech with the talkies in 1927 (*The Jazz Singer*, Alan Crossland), appears intent on removing the gag, releasing the secrets of this interiority to flutter out like so many butterflies. Foucault names this psychologization a 'clinical codification of the inducement to speak',[45] part of a set of procedures that are not a repression of talk about sexuality, but on the contrary, are the site of an excitable proliferation of discourses.

Cinema's turn inwards has to be seen as part of a broader re-articulation of the relations of interiority to exteriority, a phenomenon that rises like a swell across the social sciences. Francis Galton, cousin to Charles Darwin, had shown the way with his taxonomy of fingerprints as a body's signature. Galton famously added photographic portraiture to the practice of physiognomy, finding that the physical form and the external surface of the body were indices of a hidden internal condition. Galton's statistical focus generated the exception and the rule, a similar logic that Foucault was to identify retrospectively in 'exceptional' perversions that come to produce the general rule of heterosexuality. He writes, 'since sexuality was a medical and medicalizable object, one had to try and detect it – as a lesion, a dysfunction, or a symptom – in the depths of the organism, or on the surface of the skin, or among all the signs of behavior'.[46] The outside speaks of the inside, or the inside ruptures the surface tension of the exterior, creating a methodological problem. Practices and approaches are shared, appropriated and contagious. De la Tourette's study of a nervous condition manifest in the disruption of composure was in all likelihood etymologically linked to an earlier piece of research on a typology of posture cited by Foucault as one of the most determining works in the conceptualization of sexuality in the nineteenth century (and beyond): Carl Westphal's article, 'Contrary sexual sensations' (1870).[47] To this study Foucault ascribes the moment in which homosexuality was defined as an identity, characterized 'less by a type of sexual relations than by a certain quality of sexual sensibility, a certain way of inverting the masculine and feminine in oneself'.[48]

Westphal's article reported on two cases, a 35-year-old woman (Miss N), who dressed as a man and desired women, and a man (Ha), who dressed in women's clothing and spoke 'in an effeminate tone with a lisping voice'. The diagnosis of Miss N's 'morbid pathology' is supported by her own confessional statements and her sister's testimony, whilst for Ha, the signifiers or symptoms of his incapacity are inherent to his disposition and comportment, described as 'a hundred tiny unconscious nuances'. The site of truth is a mobile feast, and it is fortunate that Ha's pathology is visible for all to see, as the doctor finds him otherwise a mendacious and deceitful person. His performative role play, for example, led to his obtaining by deceitful means an exemplary collection of feminine toiletry. Ha's style is not confined to the feminine although this is his preferred mode. He is also a performer of subjects of various social classes including the aristocracy. Westphal writes, Ha 'rather skilfully played [the] role of an unhappy and therefore highly strung illegitimate son of a baron'[49] for some time (ha! as Ha might have shouted and Westphal duly noted down). Westphal transcribes the external evidence into a report, which in turn becomes a diagnostic tool, marking a categorical shift in the understanding of sexuality. The report provides a departure from the comprehension of a sexual practice (cross-dressing), to the designation of a sexual sensibility (inverted gender), whereby the location of identity is fixed *within* rather than created as a contingency *between* subjects. This shift from imaging sexuality as a fluid state of being in actions, to sexuality as a fixed internal nature, transposes ambiguity 'onto a kind of interior androgyny, a hermaphrodism of the soul',[50] describing a movement from the external world to the space of a metaphorical and literal interiority.

The manifestation of a film grammar takes its form in correspondence with the pairings of speech and silence, gesture and image, bodies and their meaning as they exist across numerous fields. How film in this era might be said to 'succumb to interiority' concerns the establishment of a set of production techniques that stabilize around the period 1910–13. The construction of space and time through the break-up of the tableau image, the placement of the camera within the scene itself and in multiple locations within the scene, and an emerging attention to the matching of the sightlines of actors collectively bring into being a grammar that establishes point-of-view shots, aligning the viewer with the camera. This was, to a certain extent, achieved in *The Big Swallow*, as the viewer is taken into the mouth of the irate man along with the camera, traversing the flat space of the tableau. In addition, there are early examples of reverse angle camera placements, indeed a film made by Williamson in the year before *The Big Swallow* contains a reverse angle set-up. The film, *Attack on a China Mission* (1900, 1 minute 24 seconds), showed an approach to the mission from two different angles. However, it is not until 1911, according to Barry Salt, that the reverse angle shot becomes more directly aligned with the viewer's perspective.[51] In this year, Arthur Macklay's 'The Loafer', used reverse angle shots to stage a scene between a farmer and a character called simply 'a stranger' who approaches the farmer for money. The reverse angle shots play the tension of the conflict by creating opposing views. The 180° stage rule that began to be imposed through this technique was as many film historians have described the division of screen space into two half circles in which the camera could be positioned anywhere within one portion, but was prohibited from transgressing this boundary line.

These developments successfully fragmented the tableau scene of the earliest films, where the fixed camera at the front of what was effectively a stage had created a field of vision viewed from a single, static point. In varying the camera's placement, the tableau was fractured, splintering into a number of images that the viewer was able to place psychologically within the overall scene. The relocation of the camera from the front of the stage into the space of the action brought the possibility of greater proximity to the faces of actors, focusing attention on the emotional register of the face. The faces of the actors could be given over to a type of surveillance, but this suggestion of omnipotence was overridden by the new style of editing that alternated close-ups: the shot reverse shot. The increasing alignment of the viewer with characters (over other features of the set such as objects or animals) intensified the need for emotional legibility; the face became the screen within a screen through which 'character' could be read. With the move from long shots to medium shots to close-ups, the bodies of actors became sliced into segments (knee to head, waist to head, face and neck), with the close-up on the face the critical point of an intensification of emotional tenor of these early films. Moving away from a cinema of capers (a cast of bungling characters acting on a stage being observed by the viewer as a simultaneous event), the new grammar demanded that the viewer assemble the various shots psychologically as parts of a whole picture, bearing in mind the order of their sequence. The further effect of reverse angle shots then is temporal and rhythmic, producing a chronology and tempo through expressions that move from the face of one actor to the face of another.

In the lexicon of early cinema language, there is however a shot that retains the deepest degree of ambiguity in terms of its intelligibility: the close-up. It resides ambivalently in the codification of the body, oscillating between description and immersion, a celebration of surface and an aggressive desire to know the other. Jean Epstein magnificently rides the cusp in his writing on cinema's magnifying qualities. 'Even more beautiful than a laugh is the face preparing for it,' he writes, 'I love the mouth which is about to speak and holds back, the gesture which hesitates between right and left, the recoil before the leap, and the moment before landing, the becoming, the hesitation, the taut spring, the prelude.'[52] Epstein's obeisance in front of the close-up permits a submission to its graphic nature, its texture and its variable form. Yet the essay also testifies to an intensive desire to be inside of the screen other, evident when he writes of a situation in which a character is going to meet another. 'I want to go along with him not behind or in front of him or by his side, but in him,' he states, pressing the thought further: 'I would like to look through his eyes and see his hand reach out from under me as if it were my own; interruptions of opaque film would imitate the blinking of our eyelids,' as though film could not only facilitate the desire but combine the two bodies.[53] Cinema presents an invitation, to Epstein at least, to go inside of another and it is this interior space that remains forever an enigma.[54]

The cinema moves from its earliest manifestation, the recording of external actions between characters, towards a cinema located in the ability to read the grammar of a character's interior life. The interior world of the character is constructed as the enigmatic site of a barely accessible truth. The grammar of cinema in this early period comes into line with the proliferating range of discourses concerned with reading the traces of the subject on the exterior of the body, traces that reveal the inner workings of the subject in whatever codified form. The call to truth demands a cast of specialists in the form of criminologists, psychologists and we might add, film directors, those able to read the inscription of internal perturbations from surface effects. It produces subjects whose (problematic or enigmatic) legibility creates a sense of excitement in interpretive possibility, revealing the creative flair of those trained to observe within the intense confinements of clinics, prisons and studios (and here it is worth noting that the class distinctions operating across and through these institutions locate a bourgeois subject at the opposing end of the prison, which at this moment is an emerging 'cinema', deracinated from its roots in the music hall). There is no surprise that the vocabulary is colourful with expressions drawn from a heady mix of science and mysticism, for what is empirically sought is the empirically evasive non-matter of identity, truth and emotion.

Seeing inside: Cinematic X-ray machines

What is in the ether, rather literally, is of concern here, and the phenomena of electricity and magnetism step in as vectors of potent yet invisible forces. Electricity is everywhere and what is more, sending other things everywhere else: the telegraph, the telephone, the speaking clock all contribute to a mystical world in which things that cannot be seen to act nonetheless have empirical effects. The collective investment in electricity held an affective dimension, according to Wolfgang Schivelbusch, in the belief that it restored the state of fatigue; electricity, energy and life, he writes, were synonymous.[55] Carolyn Morvan recounts a story of the early days of telegraphic transfer, where people in the United States visited telegraph offices to 'see it go through', as though the message could be seen to pass through the atmosphere.[56] Miss N speaks of an irresistible magnetism that 'gripped her', pulling her suddenly towards a certain woman. Westphal notes the metaphor, yet no amount of controlled observation or incitements to speech seems to make manifest explicitly that which is sought in the spirit of clarification and classification.

The desire to 'see' inside or beneath or through is, according to Tom Gunning, prevalent in literature of the late nineteenth century where the flâneur oscillates with the detective, the former an oneiric floating observer, whilst the latter prevails through a moral framework of intense scrutiny.[57] The detective, like the psychologist and the criminologist, needs to read the surface of things to organize a picture of what lies beneath. It is no coincidence that a discovery of this nature occurs in 1895, as Lisa Cartwright notes, 'The histories of the X-ray and the cinema coincide in concrete and matter of-fact ways.'[58] When Wilhelm Röntgen, a German physicist, was experimenting with the path of electrical rays passing from an induction coil through a partially evacuated glass tube, he noticed an uncanny effect. The tube was covered in black paper enclosing the light rays, and the room was blacked out, yet the rays appeared on an illuminated screen at one end of the room. The 'screen' was a small piece of card covered in fluorescent materials (barium platinocyanide). In further experiments he discovered that objects of diverse thicknesses interposed in the path of the rays showed varying degrees of transparency. The experiment that clinched it involved a body, not his but that of his wife Anna Bertha, whose hand Röntgen placed over a glass photographic plate. The resulting image famously showed the bone structure of her hand and the detail of her wedding ring, offering a perception of the body beneath the skin and apart from the flesh. The 'new rays' as they were called were produced by the impact of cathode rays on a material object, but their newness defied naming; Röntgen called them X-rays, drawing on the principle from mathematics that 'X' represents an unknown quantity. The paper that he wrote reporting the research, 'On a New Kind of Rays',[59] was published in December 1895, the same month that the Lumière brothers were publically screening their invention at the Salon Indien du Grand Café in Paris, and ten short films including *Sortie des Usines Lumière à Lyon*.

The fantasy and reality of seeing beneath a surface is, according to Steven Connor, an inherent feature of modernism, for the modern experience (according to Connor) is of being permeated.[60] Figuratively, these two positions as it were, of 'permeation' and of 'seeing through', mark the respective polar lines that converge in the subjectification of bodies to the many practices of observation and taxonomy throughout the nineteenth century. X-rays were, according to Connor, during the first ten years of their recognized existence considered akin to the photographic apparatus, requiring an alchemical process (development) in which a transformation occurs to deliver a revelation (the image). What the X-ray brings to the foreground is seeing, the act of vision caught in its own mediality: 'X-ray vision was linked with photography's power to arrest and anatomize vision, to get on the inside of seeing itself,' writes Connor, 'making the invisible, the act of seeing itself, visible'. Another inside opens up, the 'inside of vision', that through which an action can be exhibited in its own mediality. Seeing, far from being a naturalized operation of sight as knowledge, becomes detached from the body just at the moment that the body becomes see-through to itself. But X-rays articulated a body not exactly see-through; more accurately the term described the various dimensions and properties of the body as a composite of diverse and mutating matter. 'The term *artefact* perhaps best describes the X-ray image,' writes Akira Lippit, 'which is at once buried and revealed, invoking its archaeological nature as spectacle'. He continues, 'The X-ray image determines a kind of living remnant, a phantom subject.'[61] Despite how solid the bones of the X-ray appeared to Anna Bertha, her exclamation that she had seen her own death produces an opposite assurance, that the body (all bodies) are subject to inertia and decay. In fact, it is this 'intermingling and reversibility of the positive and the negative', writes Connor, 'the radiating and the fixed, the interior and the exterior, the force and the form', that is 'the essential feature of magical thinking regarding the making visible of the invisible'.[62]

The interior of the body becomes the site of an investiture of truth and identity, but one to which access is obscure, requiring magic, or inventiveness at least. The cinema, the X-ray, the many taxonomic tests, practices and observations are all driven by the same quest to unravel the enigmatic subject, which is simultaneously a process that inscribes as much as it discovers the enigma as an internal form. The language describing this investiture of the interior of the body as a locus of truth begins to be influenced by its own descriptions, evolving this as metaphor; there are the acts of 'seeing through' someone, or 'getting under the skin' of another. The paradox that places the subject at the centre of a biopolitical discourse as axes of meaning is this: that the subject herself or himself may never be the agent of discovery of her or his own 'truth'. Writing on the interplay of psychic, physical and metaphysical discourses in the inventory of unseen forces (of which the X-ray is an instrument of taxonomy), Marina Warner writes that '[t]he capacity to see through solid matter did not have the effect of disenchanting empiricism and turning such vision mundane', on the contrary, 'doctors now seemed endowed with supernatural powers'.[63] Psychoanalysis must be added to this list, with Freud as the arch-prince of the turn away from the flesh of the body to the treatment of a mediated inside, its method dependent upon verbal articulation, famously the recounting of dreams and the slippery double meanings fossilized within language. In the occupational transfer from physician to the founder of psychoanalysis, Freud reconfigured the fleshy inside of the body as an imagined space and in this psychoanalysis is thoroughly attuned to cinema's project. Akira Lippit writes, 'Three *phenomenologies of the inside* haunt 1895: psychoanalysis, the X-ray, and cinema seek to expose, respectively, the depths of the psyche, body and movements of life.' Arguing that each of these modalities appropriated the other's techniques and rhetorical strategies, Lippit asserts that collectively, they 'transformed the structure of visual perception, shifting the terms of vision from phenomenal to phantasmatic registers, from a perceived visuality to an imagined one'.[64]

Biopolitics versus the donkey that craps gold coins

We might pause here to consider what is at issue in aligning cinema with the register of institutions and practices that came to administrate life in the modern era in the manner of Foucault's analysis, devolving such regulation to the subject herself or himself. And if this alignment brings cinema within Foucault's orbit, what of the distance that Agamben takes from this reading of biopolitics when he asserts, for example, that the 'Foucauldian thesis will then have to be corrected or, at least, completed?'[65] Is cinema only complicit in the production of an interior truth through the evolving grammar of the apparatus and scripts, or are there other modes in which it operates as a determination of the biopolitical? Furthermore, and from a different angle, if this line of enquiry leads towards cinema's complicity with new forms of dispersed institutional power, what becomes of the potential of gesture that cinema also provides for, the Warburgian genie in the image that may emerge at any moment to animate and ignite revelatory connections across time in the manner of a transmission?

In order to address these concerns it is necessary to turn in greater depth to Agamben's critique of the model of disciplinary power proposed by Foucault, of when 'natural life begins to be included in the mechanisms and calculations of State power, and politics turns into *biopolitics*'.[66] Whilst Agamben pays homage to Foucault in many of his essays, in *Homer Sacer*, the central premise of the book works against Foucault's account of biopolitics as a distinctly modern phenomenon. To recall, Foucault's politico-theoretical move had been to question the explanatory force of a theory of juridical power, a power imposed on the populace under the threat of death, and to posit instead a model of dispersed power operating through micro-forms of administration and regulation (such as his studies of the arrangements of sleeping quarters in schools, the design of hospitals and prisons). He writes: 'Power would no longer be dealing simply with legal subjects over whom the ultimate dominion was death, but with living beings, and the mastery it would be able to exercise over them would have to be applied at the level of life itself; it was the taking charge of life, more than the threat of death, that gave power its access even to the body.'[67] This shift in the location and operation of power Foucault anchored in the domain of the modern world, specifically the late eighteenth and early nineteenth centuries, related to a number of complex events, including the French revolution and the deposition of the monarch. As Eric Santner comments, this event in particular 'mark[s] the period of transition from kings to "people" as the bearer of the principle of sovereignty', and it is this shift in the modality of power that Foucault's work describes.[68] The departure that Agamben takes from this account of the biopolitical is critical of two related aspects. The first point of contestation concerns Foucault's delimitation of the biopolitical to the modern period. Agamben argues, in contrast, that the biopolitical determination of life goes back at least as far as antiquity. Identifying as a foundational moment the separation of *bios* from *zoe*, in Greek antiquity, he finds in Roman politics the figure of *homo sacer*, the sacred man who is excluded from the social domain and killed, but who can never be sacrificed. Schematically, the sacred man is the paradoxical figure who is placed outside of the law and whose rights are suspended in order to guarantee the sovereign status of the one who suspends the law. This figure is the limit case of the political system, designating a place of privation external to its enclosure upon which it is dependent; therefore, this ancient ban effects an inclusive exclusion critical to the functioning of the polis. Thus, for Agamben, Foucault's reading not only contracts the biopolitical to a historically narrow range, it also misses the foundational presence of an included exclusion (the *homo sacer*) upon which modern politics rests.

Cinema's relation to this excluded term is difficult to trace except perhaps as a cinematic representation of the excluded, for example in films of genocide or camps. Even here, as Libby Saxton argues in relation to films of the Holocaust, Agamben would be critical of the film's status as a recording instrument, as a means of witnessing the 'unspeakable'. Cinema's relation to the institution of biopolitics, as I have argued throughout this chapter, can be traced through the evolution of an apparatus and grammar that atomizes the subject within an internal psychic and affective state. Cinema's relation to the biopolitical at the turn of the twentieth century is visible then mainly in its designation of a certain form of subjectivity, a subjectification of the viewer that is instituted in multiple, historically variable ways. But do we need to take sides with either Foucault or Agamben on this issue, or can the relationship of sovereignty and biopolitics and the transfer of power be thought differently? Roberto Esposito argues against Foucault's proposition that one system of power gives rise chronologically to the other, yet without aligning his position neatly with that of Agamben, Esposito provides a way of thinking exclusion in more local and specific instances; power does not take an exclusive form but on the contrary, one system of power opens up inside of the other at unpredictable historical junctures.[69] In the event of the Holocaust, he argues, in which sovereign power returns inside of a system of dispersed governance, the two systems of power are revealed to be non-exclusive. From here, Esposito moves towards his own formulation of the operation of biopolitical power that is worked through a single, historically variable paradigm: that of immunization. In tracing this term back to its etymological root, *immunitas* appears as the negative form of *communitas*. In these terms Esposito finds a model of political inclusion and exclusion that brings together the ethos of Foucault's delegated power in the care of the self with the potency of sovereign exclusion. It is through this model of biopolitical power that we can bring cinema once again into view.

Esposito's model or paradigm draws its strength from a bodily metaphor; the political life of the subject is conditioned by notions of corporeal exposure. The concept of immunity in a sense dissolves social bonds, facilitating a withdrawal of the individual from collective forms of life and the living community where a risk contagion is present. The mode of immunization is one of self-protection, the maintenance of borders that prevents sociality, relationality, cross-referentiality and appropriation. He writes: 'If *communitas* is that relation, which in binding its members to an obligation of reciprocal donation, jeopardizes individual identity, *immunitas* is the condition of dispensation from such an obligation and therefore the defence against the expropriating features of *communitas* ....'[70] The project of immunization defends against risk and threat across different materials and conceptual thresholds, protecting the community through its fortification against 'foreign' matter. But in so doing, the individual as the base level of immunization is preserved over and against another and all others within the community. Therefore, the scene of *communitas* dissolves as the community begins to operate something akin to an autoimmune disease whereby what is preserved at the level of the individual unit or cell is counterproductive to the larger collective. Immunization becomes 'the fold that in some way separates community from itself'.[71] If Esposito's model appears to speak only to a political determination of life, I will argue that we can follow a link to cinema through Jonathan Crary's description of what we might call the immunizing effects of a narrowed field of attention, within which the cinema is a critical component in its nascent form.

If an axiom of modernity is that seeing becomes torn from itself and is no longer a naturalized bodily activity by the late nineteenth century, a critical and anxiety-inducing feature of this is the matter of attention. The late nineteenth century is written about by Crary as a period in which a subjectification of vision took place through a mosaic of practices, technologies and pedagogic techniques. Cinema was amongst them, inducting the viewer (or observer as he prefers), in ways of paying attention. The paying of attention is a complex feat, demanding the subject's disengagement from a broader social context with competing modes of visual and aural stimuli. Examining the period from 1880 to 1905, Crary argues that the suspension of other dimensions of, and stimuli within, the environment effectively isolates the subject, whose world becomes eventually a 'patchwork of such disconnected states'.[72] Cinema is situated, like other 'new' attractions, as a means of commodifying and quantifying a culture of transmissible images and sounds. In Crary's view, 'Edison saw the marketplace in terms of how images, sounds, energy, or information could be reshaped into measurable and distributable commodities and how a social field of individual subjects could be arranged into increasingly separate and specialized units of consumption.'[73] The effect of such dispositifs in the fervid environment of the time was to isolate subjects from one another, creating a social sphere of individuals over communities, subjects rather than peoples, individual viewers rather than audiences. Cinema, we might say, was productive of a polis predicated on immunity. The architecture of the auditorium famously brought together a collective, and yet the arrangement of fixed seating directed attention towards a screen rather than towards one another securing a cultural experience conditioned by anonymity and producing atomization. The ways in which cinema came to be crafted as a particular experience during the decade of the 1920s is well documented by historians as a reduction of sensory effects and possibilities for collective interaction. Cinema, that is, intensified the experience of the subject's singularity and the image that spoke directly to her or him as gesture. Immunity, however, is not cinema's only or dominating modality. At this point, it is useful to recall the other side of cinema as gesture rather than image, to return to Warburg's version of an image that communicates only its own ability to communicate, to install what in Esposito's terms would be *communitas* in the power of gesture to transmit only its own power of transmission. Gesture becomes the term for a residue common ground, the potential for a common dwelling in the image that displays its own communicability, and in this account gesture is akin to magic, to 'the genie in the bottle at one's side' and 'the donkey that craps gold coins'.[74]

Gesture as potentiality

The play of interiority and exteriority as alluded to in the essay on gesture can be traced back through Max Kommerell in one particular version of Agamben's essay. 'On Gesture' has more than one manifestation, existing as variations on the theme in three languages published during the 1990s.[75] It is in the essay, 'Kommerell, or on Gesture', published in the collection *Potentialities* (1999), where Agamben offers the fullest account of the emergence of the concept as it appeared in the work of the writer Jean Paul and in Max Kommerell's study of the writer. Kommerell, a German critic and a contemporary of Walter Benjamin, finds in Jean Paul's writing three types of gesture: gesture and the soul, gesture and nature, and pure gesture. These three forms serialize a relationship to gesture that moves from a disappointment in the failure of gesture to mediate inner and outer worlds, to the projection of interiority onto nature, to finally a rendering of gesture as the operation of language itself. Kommerell finds in Jean Paul a mourning of the inability of the soul to find its expression through language, regarding language as a distortion of interiority, and as such unable to connect to the exterior world of nature. Yet a different interpretation is possible, according to Paul Fleming, who reads Jean Paul's relation to language as one of suspicion that language can provide a definitive statement or express an affect adequately. The pure gesture that Kommerell identifies in Jean Paul's writing exists as the origin of the other two, existing somewhere 'above' or over the other gestural types. Pure gesture bears no relation to a reality beyond itself, but is manifest in 'fragments from another world, an over-world', writes Fleming. 'The pure gesture is not a sign at all,' he continues, 'It belongs to no semiotic order per se, for it [is] only "the pure possibility of speaking itself". The pure gesture is not language saying *something*, but rather the very possibility of saying.'[76] Agamben is not concerned with Kommerell's differentiation of gesture into this tripartite arrangement, nor of Kommerell's diagnosis, through gesture, of a crisis of art and therefore of society. Agamben is drawn to Jean Paul's exercise of language as the pure possibility of speaking, and following from this, the pure potentiality that is not speaking.

This brings us to a critical point in an understanding of gesture in Agamben's work, which is that gesture is rooted in language *and* in the bodily form that becomes cinema. Gesture is the capacity for language, connected to the question of, 'Is there a human voice?', and furthermore, 'And if it exists, is this voice language?'[77] Where, in the tradition of western metaphysics, language is often thought apart from the body as an effect of consciousness, and the question of the body follows literally as an 'after-thought' (as animal flesh), in the concept of gesture the two reside together, or more accurately they are inextricable. Both language and the body have the capacity not only for communication (to convey something to another), but of *communicability*, to register the being in a medium itself. 'Those who have not reached, as in a dream, this woody substance of language,' he writes in *The Idea of Prose*, 'which the ancients called *silva* (wildwood), are prisoners of representation, even when they keep silent'.[78] To reverse the proposition, to regard language as a tool for expression or a description of a world beyond itself, treats the material form of language as a natural and neutral matter, leaving us prey to the pictorial representation as truth effect. To be in language as a medium, however, is to be in touch with the material form that is shared, the common ground of our experience. For Agamben, there is no other common form than this being in a medium that is communicability, which he also names the potential to support.

The gestural body of cinema is not distinguished from spoken language, but part of the same system of communicability. Language issues from the mouth, which is the body, which has the potential to speak and act, or not to do so.[79] To remain silent, or still, is not to be mute but to reside in the medium in a different mode, a being in pure potentiality. The more we speak, writes Agamben, the more the unsaid stacks up around us; every speech act forecloses other possibilities for speaking in that moment, possibilities that do not evaporate and disappear, but stay around like phantasms. In this sense, language 'en-frames' for us our relation to potentiality. Cinema, as a corollary, en-frames the body's communicability, a concept that as Benjamin Noys points out, Agamben borrows from Heidegger: 'cinema is the apparatus of the *Ge-Stell* (En-framing) of the gesture'.[80] Like the woody substance of language, the gestural body of cinema displays the material form of being. Cinematic gesture in its pure form is neither the actor's expression of an inner life nor the action that leads to an end (the closure of narrative), but the display of being in the medium of the body with its limits and possibilities. This may be why, for Benjamin, 'man' does not recognize his own walk or voice when he watches cinema precisely because the cinema denaturalizes the body's everyday gestural form.

In the essay on Kommerell, it is the gag that conjoins language and corporeal form. In language, we have nothing to say other than 'what is said in language',[81] and gesture only demonstrates this being at a loss for what to say. It is a gag, he says, in the literal meaning of the term, the significance of which is double. To gag a person infers the stopping of the mouth with a cloth to block speech, and at the same time, the gag is the joke that the performer steps in with to improvise for this impossibility of speaking. The gag dissolves the tension but has nothing to say. Agamben writes: 'there is a gesture that felicitously establishes itself in this emptiness of language', a gesture that demonstrates the emptiness without compensating, 'without filling it', which 'makes it into humankind's most proper dwelling'.[82] The gag as the limit case of language brings to mind the centrality of the body as vehicle for comedy in early cinema, a gestural body that establishes itself in this emptiness of language. In early film, the body is open to others and to its own possibility. The comic effect is often the body dancing with its limits, as it teeters along a window ledge at a height, or at the last minute moves sideways to avoid a collision with traffic. The comic body is also open to interruption. Its course through the world is subject to deferral, distraction and rerouting, as Chaplin or Keaton navigate situations through which they discover more about the body's capacity as it brushes up against obtuse objects and invisible forces. The overt gestures of the actor, we might say, perform a body displaying its own existential mediality. When Agamben cites early cinema in the gesture essay, it is not the literal silence of film that he draws attention to, but the potentiality that exists in the capacity for the body to signal itself whether in the presence of language or not. 'The pure gesture is language that is content with itself,' Fleming writes of Jean Paul's work, 'with its affective possibilities, freed from the burden of reference'.[83] It is also the case for cinema, in Agamben's reading, that the pure gesture is the body freed from the burden of reference, and that is perhaps why he places the crisis in gesture 100 years later than Jean Paul and Kommerell, as the apparatus of cinema is assembled.

Gesture en-frames the body in its communicability over and against the biopolitical drive to locate, examine and fix its meaning. Cinema can go either way, and it does, funnelling into the confines of melodrama and the desire for truth and meaning, whilst simultaneously flowing into corporeal comedy, science films, education, amateur footage amongst the many contingent modalities. Gesture in cinema is potentially the body liberated from the biopolitical demand for meaning and exactitude, for bodies to be calculated, calibrated and known. The body in cinematic moments of flight, conversely, allows gesture to inhere in its form in a manner that refuses exact interpretation. In so doing, gesture as a mode works against the apparatus of identity effects, of being reduced to a set of descriptors that details a human profile. In the face of a demand for an account of the self, gesture points only to the failure of such a system, for the gesture does not speak the subject, but is the demonstration of its contingency. Gesture is the empty space of identity, a space that cannot be inhabited as a permanent or fully knowable phenomenon. In an essay on authorship and gesture, Agamben ends the text in this way:

> A subjectivity is produced where the living being, encountering language and putting itself into play in language without reserve, exhibits in a gesture the impossibility of its being reduced to this gesture. All the rest is psychology, and nowhere in psychology do we encounter anything like an ethical subject, a form of life.[84]

If Agamben opposes psychology (or the turn to interiority) to an ethical form of life, the link between the ethical and the openness of the body is elucidated in a short essay, 'Without classes', in *The Coming Community*.[85] The essay opens with the denouncement of the triumph of a single planetary bourgeoisie, the inheritors of the earlier turn of the century bourgeoisie who lost gesture and lost all pathos. This class, within which all social classes and differences are now dissolved, is the triumph of a nihilistic individualism that tragically precludes any recourse to the common being, to community. If this humanity, instead of searching for a 'proper identity' in individuality, sought 'a singularity without identity, a common and absolutely exposed singularity', he writes, continuing, 'if humans could, that is, not be-thus? in this or that biography, but be only *the* thus, their singular exteriority and their face, then they would for the first time enter into a community without presuppositions and without subjects, into a communication without the incommunicable'.[86] The potential of early cinema was the possible site of community, of singular exteriorities, faces and contingencies, being only this, or in Agamben's phrasing, 'the thus'.[87]

Transmitting cinema

In the tales, elaborations and digressions of this discussion of gesture, there are other details, details other than the body and language and interiority and exteriority that are visible in the corner of the various passing frames. These details are in the form of activities that keep appearing and dissolving, the acts of running, kissing, balancing, shooting and dancing. These are the enlivened bodies and enlivening activities that resist the deadening effects of photography, that won't be stilled by the camera lens and committed to history as an eternal pose. Muybridge, like Chaplin, balances on the window ledge of cinema, unsure of whether he is inside or out, whether in his studio he captures the absolute *dynamis* of a body, or commits it to premature rigor mortis. A glare of the flash emits from Muybridge's camera and the scene is lit by an electrical current that transmits its energy to the room. The image that emerges oscillates wildly between a recording and a transmission. Sent into the future, the photograph and the film are transmissions, and it is this term that comes in late in the day. It comes some 100 years after the fact, and only now does its incipient presence challenge the primary account of cinema as record.

The diversionary route then is characterized precisely not by an itinerary but an impulse; and the impulse that emerges in this account is to transmit, to send an image on a journey without control of the carrier, the transmitter or the destination. Transmission is praxis and as such compels the image to partake of its own system, whether that be the writing of the image in code or chemical form, through projection devices or light-emitting diode displays. The transmission of the cinematic image has a corollary to the body in gesture; there is nothing to report but the medium itself. What is sent (through the practice of making or distributing) is an address to the other, an openness to communication across time and space. Distinct from the recording of the dynamics between characters' internal worlds, the transmitted film is open, outwards, faced about. It is an electrical charge that skips chronological time and makes its connections unpredictably. This is a Warburgian cinema: the image operates across time, not chronological but archaeological time. It is memory defined not as that which articulates consciousness, but memory as that which distinguishes the living from the dead. The image conceived as a live form of memory is sent across time, secure in its profanatory impulse to bring back into common use that which has been removed from everyday life.

Kafka, according to Benjamin, took gesture to be something that cannot be known in advance, but from which the author attempts to find the meaning 'in ever-changing contexts and experimental groupings'[88] and it is this approach that I wish to borrow for the end of this discussion. There is a presence that runs through the discussions of gesture and the body, which skirts the edges of commentary and image sequences, but never quite steps into the centre. But it is a stepping movement. This familiar and yet slight presence is the activity of dance, appearing in these scenarios in 'ever-changing contexts and experimental groupings'. For dance is a peculiar kind of support and communication; often conducted with another, it is a manifestation of the body, its praxis and potentiality. It makes a prominent appearance in photography and cinema in the late nineteenth century, and a particularly peculiar appearance in one particular scenario recorded between September 1894 and April 1895.

We are once again in Edison's Black Maria laboratory (so called for its likeness to the sinister police vehicles of the day) in West Orange, New Jersey, where Edison's assistant, William Dickson and his colleagues worked on the development of moving image technologies. It was an experimental grouping and the studio had been constructed and designed for their purposes, namely the exclusion of light and the production of a black space in which figures may be conjured, as though by magic perhaps. Philippe-Alain Michaud describes it in this way:

> Before a syncretic style combining different types of representation (mimetic, symbolic, diagrammatic) came to the fore in cinema in 1895, films were based on a system of relationships that proceeded from the figures alone, independently of the place in which they were filmed, as if the latter were purely and simply annulled. The description of the space remained schematic, the field of vision was not clearly delineated, and the black cloth hung at the back of the set manifested not the creation of place but its absence.[89]

For the months between September and April, the group laboured to realize Edison's plan for a kinetophone. The idea for this invention was the synchronization of sound and image, following the development of the kinetoscope viewing device and the kinetograph motion picture camera a few years before. Edison had many ideas that were patented and thus claimed whilst the business of working out the practice followed.[90] In the dance of technological invention, Edison, we might say, was the leading partner. The idea of the kinetophone was the connection of sound and image recordings, yet it was rather different from a contemporary concept of synchronized sound.[91] Sound was recorded onto a wax cylinder, whilst the camera filmed the visual element and the two recordings would later be synchronized. This concept was materialized in 'The Dickson Experimental Sound Film'. The film is a test and at the beginning an off-screen voice announces 'Are the rest of you ready? Go ahead!'

The Dickson experimental sound film (1894)

The dance appears to be at once improvised for the moment of recording and loosely based on a waltz. It is the capture of a bachelor moment in the enclosure of the workshop; the men who make are caught at play and have an edge of embarrassment laced with seriousness as they shuffle around together. Is the embarrassment a feature of the slippage between gender and sexual relations as they swirl around the small enclosure? Two men dance, a third plays an instrument (Dickson), whilst a fourth (Edison) slips almost imperceptibly into the scene behind the conical horn just as the sequence comes to an end. Who knows how many times this scene had been enacted before this moment of registration? Who knew if this time it would work and the dance and the violin were rhythm communications duly inscribed by their separate apparatuses? Who could know whether the scene would be resisted by the apparatus, or indeed sent into the future? And why is it dance that features at this scene of experiment and not a recitation or conversation? Dance, unlike the recitation reliant on verbal language, emphasizes the body as the privileged mode of articulation, and it marks the transmission of the body across space; dance, it could be said, describes the body as gesture. The men perform in time to the movement of the violin bow, their bodies instruments and instrumental to what is being formed. These are bodies at the intersection of labour and leisure, bodies that offer themselves as technologies materializing and transmitting a musical rhythm into pictorial form.

Some seven years earlier, on Monday 27th February 1888, Eadweard Muybridge had paid a visit to Edison's laboratory in Orange, New Jersey.[92] Muybridge was conducting one of his many tours to demonstrate and publicize his zoopraxiscope, the circular discs that rotated a series of images to appear to the viewer as moving pictures. According to Muybridge, the conversation between the two men involved discussion of a scheme that would 'reproduce the gestures and the facial expression of [a person].... in the act of making a speech', with Muybridge proposing that Edison should provide the phonograph to this end whilst Muybridge would provide the visuals.[93] Edison denied that this conversation ever took place, but he did in the autumn of that year employ William Dickson to begin work on a project to combine moving images with sound. Perhaps Edison recalled some of Muybridge's images when he set up his experiment, for there had been dancers on the zoopraxiscope plates, and other dancers, if we recall, in the locomotion series: women dancing in long white fluttering gowns, a man and a mannequin woman clothed, respectively, in suit and dress appear to waltz, whilst two naked women perform a dance together.[94] The ballet-dancing woman who is named 'fancy' by someone who provides captions along the way looks absorbed in her gown and its flowing form. The man and mannequin-like woman look as though they may be rehearsing for a life of heterosexually modelled relations as he sweeps her off her feet. The two naked women, their feet firmly on the ground, look down as though in concentrated effort to move together in the 'right' way. Perhaps they are negotiating who should lead, or coyly avoiding each other's eyes. Or possibly they are paying attention to the fleshy contours of the other's body.

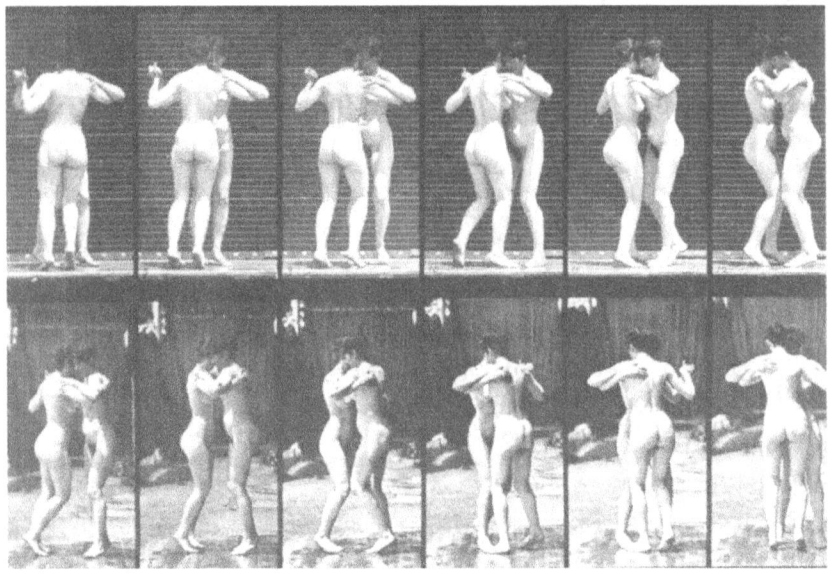

Two women dancing (Eadweard Muybridge)

In these images, a tension is transmitted as a live question of where the performance ends and the non-performed begins? What intimacy is produced and captured when Muybridge photographs two naked women dancing together? It would seem an intimacy against all odds as the women, surrounded by a battery of cameras, within the confines of a photographic studio located on the campus of a university, perform in front of the large bear-like bearded figure of Eadweard Muybridge.

These dances are gestures whose meaning could not be known in advance and only guessed retrospectively as the transmission connects us to its electrical charge. What has been sent to us readers of gesture and how might we attune our receptors? The chuntering cinematic projector is part of the *techne* of transmission as the other side of the capturing-recording device, the camera. We watch these scenes of figures running from here to there, fall from this height onto a bale of hay, engage in a kiss that mends the circuit break or more accurately installs a new connective channel. We receive the transmission, and years later it may as an engram infect us with its *dynamis*. In these scenes of pre-cinema or what we might name cinema's arising, identity is located in what a body *does* rather than what *it is*. The terms of ontology shift so that these oppositions are braided but not dissolved. The body on display in Muybridge's studies, and in early cinema, is the site of a struggle between polarities. The body, on the one part, is the location of an emerging and diffuse biopolitical power that seeks knowledge and management of bodies, which subjects it to an identitarian politics, establishing ontology as a categorical definition. Yet the body is also the site of a mobile communicability, a gestural play that is open to transformation through an encounter with the contingencies of each and every situation. The project, for both cinema and for Agamben's gestural politics, is to refuse the resolute demarcation between these definitions, and to create a zone where the border between dance, gesture and communication is indistinct.

Dance puts the body on display, and in early cinema it foregrounds the body as gestural, marking out its mediality rather than its utility. 'If dance is gesture,' writes Agamben, 'it is so, rather, because it is nothing more than the endurance and the exhibition of the media character of corporal movements'.[95] The boundary between the gestural body and the body losing its gestures is not clear. It is here instructive to recall Agamben's description in the earlier part of the essay of de la Tourette's patients:

> Patients can neither start nor complete the simplest of gestures. If they are able to start a movement, this is interrupted and broken up by shocks lacking any coordination and by tremors that give the impression that the whole musculature is engaged in a dance (*chorea*) that is completely independent of any ambulatory end.[96]

Again, a page later, he describes Nietzsche's *Thus Spoke Zarathustra* as 'the ballet of humankind that has lost its gestures'.[97] As a mode, dance in the late nineteenth and early twentieth centuries provides a precarious opportunity to materialize the body as a failing object of communication, or conversely, as the making visible of the means of an ethical communicability. Nietzsche, it is well known, had a deep fondness for dance and perhaps this is what Agamben has in mind when he writes the line about ballet. Thought in its most free and lively manifestation could aspire to be like dance, in Nietzsche's view. 'I would not know what the spirit of a philosopher might wish more to be than a good dancer,' he writes.[98] Nietzsche writes of thinking as good dancing and Agamben of chorea as a misplaced ballet of loss. What kind of dancing is this in the early scene captured by film, which is simultaneously an emergence of various objects, energies and thoughts as a thing, a practice or an object that was given the name of cinema? It is dance as improvisation, and endless rehearsal and repetition, seeking to engage its own kairological moment. It calls to us across the century. A voice from off-screen commands through the question 'Are the rest of you ready?,' a voice that is scratched by the crack in the wax cylinder that announces the medium of recording, the click, click, crack of a sound glitch transmitted over the course of a century. 'Are the rest of you ready?,' it asks, a voice always and forever only a voice to an unseen body. Each of the actors in the situation prepares again to grasp this moment, to make the time of the dance, *this* dance, the time of the now. The lights are brought up, the air is static and the camera is ready. 'Go ahead!' it calls.

Notes

1 *Les Cloches de Corneville*, the English language version *The Chimes of Normandy*, was a popular operetta by Robert Planquette (1877).
2 Walter Benjamin 'Franz Kafka', in *Illuminations* (108–135). Benjamin uses this diagnostic scenario to situate Kafka's practice, thus 'the situation of the subject in such experiments is Kafka's situation; this is what directs him to learning, where he may encounter fragments of his own existence, fragments that are still within the context of the role. He might catch hold of the lost *gestus* the way Peter Schlemihl caught hold of the shadow he had sold. He might understand himself, but an enormous effort would be required!' (*Illuminations*, ed. Hannah Arendt, trans. Harry Zorn, Fontana, 1973), 133.
3 Alison Ross 'Introduction', *South Atlantic Quarterly*, Special issue *The Agamben Effect* 107:2 (Winter 2008): 1–15, 2.
4 We may consider expressive monologues of melodrama in cinema as types of confession.
5 Muybridge's models, or experimentees, were drawn from the university staff and student cohort; animals were selected from the nearby Philadelphia Zoo (opened in 1874); and the Philadelphia Almshouse (next to the University of Pennsylvania campus) provided models with various disabilities.
6 Elspeth H. Brown, 'Racialising the Virile Body: Eadweard Muybridge's Locomotion Studies 1883–1887', *Gender and History* 17:3 (November 2005): 627–656: 631.
7 Marta Braun, 'Muybridge's Scientific Fictions', *Studies in Visual Communication*, 10:3 (1984): 2–21. For a longer discussion of Muybridge's works in the context of the late nineteenth century including the campaign against 'lewd' images of nudity

by the Citizen's Representative Committee of Philadelphia, see Martha Braun's *Eadweard Muybridge (Critical Lives)* (2010). Remarkably, Braun notes, Muybridge escaped the wrath of the committee whose target was 'art', a category from which photographs were exempt (Braun, 2010), 218.
8 Rebecca Solnit, *River of Shadows: Eadweard Muybridge and the Technological Wild West* (New York: Penguin Books, 2003), 226.
9 Ibid., 223.
10 Muybridge was also given space in the Biological Hall (University of Pennsylvania University Archives and Records Center). http://www.archives.upenn.edu/histy/features/muybridge/muybridge.html (accessed 15 March 2013).
11 Giorgio Agamben, *Means without End: Notes on Politics*, trans. Vincenzo Binetti and Cesare Casarino (Minneapolis: University of Minnesota Press, Minneapolis, 2000), 54.
12 Ibid., 50.
13 The full title of this text is *Études cliniques et physiologiques sur la marche: la marche dans les maladies du système nerveux: étudiée par la méthode des empreintes*.
14 Agamben, *Means without End*, 49.
15 Ibid., 50.
16 Ibid.
17 Deborah Levitt, 'Notes on Media and Biopolitics: "Notes on Gesture"', in *The Work of Giorgio Agamben: Law, Literature and Life*, eds Justin Clemens, Nicholas Heron and Alex Murray (Edinburgh: Edinburgh University Press, 2008), 198.
18 Deborah Levitt rather nicely describes the mode of these intertitles as 'telegraphic'. See Levitt, 'Notes on Media and Biopolitics', 194.
19 Agamben, *Means without End*, 55.
20 Ibid., 59.
21 Gilles Deleuze and Félix Guattari, *Kafka: Toward a Minor Literature*, trans. Dana Polan (Minneapolis and London: University of Minnesota Press, 1975).
22 Benjamin Noys, "Film-of-Life: Agamben's Profanation of the Image", in *Cinema and Agamben: Ethics, Biopolitics and the Moving Image*, eds H. Gustafsson and A. Grønstad (New York, London, New Delhi and Sydney: Bloomsbury Academic, 2014), 89.
23 See 'Dim Stockings' for this connection of cinema to advertising and commodification, in which the hired mourners appear in the final sentence, in *The Coming Community*, 49.
24 Levitt, 'Notes on Media and Biopolitics', 166.
25 Stewart, 'Counterfactual, Potential, Virtual': Toward a Philosophical Cinematic", in *Cinema and Agamben: Ethics, Biopolitics and the Moving Image*, eds H. Gustafsson and A. Grønstad (New York, London, New Delhi and Sydney: Bloomsbury Academic, 2014), 161.

26 Leland de la Durantaye, *Giorgio Agamben: A Critical Introduction* (Stanford, CA: Stanford University Press, 2009), xviii.
27 Agamben, 'Notes on Gesture', 53.
28 Ibid.
29 See Agamben's extensive treatment of the term paradigm in *The Signature of All Things*.
30 Giorgio Agamben, 'Warburg and the Nameless Science', *Potentialities* 89–103 (1999): 94.
31 Giorgio Agamben, *Stanzas: Word and Phantasm in Western Culture*, trans. R.L. Martninez (Minneapolis: University of Minnesota Press, 1993), 112.
32 Leland de la Durantaye points out that Agamben does not translate this German term into English although in the English edition the translator does, offering the term 'afterlife' in brackets. Durantaye draws attention to the misleading effects of this interpretation; 'afterlife' directs attention to the end of a life and the possibility of another, whereas Agamben's meaning is closer to survival, a continuation of life in this world.
33 Agamben, 'Notes on Gesture', 49–50.
34 Robert Bartlett Haas, *Muybridge: Man in Motion* (Berkeley, CA and London: University of California Press, 1976).
35 Etienne-Jules Marey and George Demeny *Homme Soldat* (1891–2), and *Hommes, Course Avec Fusil et Sac* (1892).
36 Agamben, 'Notes on Gesture', 52.
37 Ibid.
38 For a fuller account of this phenomenon and the fascination of gesture as movement, see Pasi Valiaho, *Mapping the Moving Image: Gesture, Thought and Cinema Circa 1900* (Amsterdam: Amsterdam University Press, 2010).
39 Roberto Esposito, *Bios: Biopolitics and Philosophy*, trans. Timothy Campbell (Minneapolis: University of Minnesota Press, 2008).
40 Lisa Trahair, 'Preposterous Figurality', in *The Comedy of Philosophy: Sense and Nonsense in Early Cinematic Slapstick* (Albany: State University of New York Press, 2007), 191–212.
41 Akira Mizuta Lippit, *Atomic Light (Shadow Optics)* (Minneapolis and London: University of Minnesota Press, 2005), 73.
42 Georges Didi-Huberman, *Invention of Hysteria: Charcot and the Photographic Iconography of the Salpêtrière*, trans. Alisa Hardtz (Cambridge, MA and London, England: MIT Press, 2007 [1982]), 34.
43 Jonathan Auerbach, *Body Shots: Early Cinema's Incarnations* (Berkeley, CA and London: University of California Press, 2007), 2.
44 Agamben, 'Notes on Gesture', 53.

45 Michel Foucault, *The History of Sexuality, Volume 1*, trans. R. Hurley (London: Penguin, 1981), 65.
46 Ibid., 44.
47 Carl Westphal, 'Contrary Sexual Feeling', *Archiv für Psychiatrie und Nervenkrankeiten*, 2 (1870): 104–116.
48 Foucault, *The History of Sexuality*, 43.
49 Westphal, 'Contrary Sexual Feeling', 73–108: 75.
50 Foucault, *The History of Sexuality*, 43.
51 Barry Salt, *Film Style and Technology: History and Analysis* (New York: Starword Books, 1982).
52 Jean Epstein, 'Magnification and Other Writings', trans. Stuart Liebman, *October* 3 (Spring 1977): 9–25: 9 .
53 Ibid., 10–11.
54 This enigma is of course the attraction for Béla Balázs in his study of human physiognomy in the cinematic close-up. Béla Balázs, *Theory of the Film: Character and Growth of a New Art*, trans. Edith Bone (New York: Arno Press, 1972).
55 Wolfgang Schivelbusch, *Disenchanted Night: The Industrialization of Light in the Nineteenth Century*, trans. Angela Davis (Berkeley, CA and London: University of California Press, 1988), 71.
56 Carolyn Morvan, *When Old Technologies Were New* (New York and Oxford: Oxford University Press, 1988), 111.
57 Tom Gunning, 'From the Kaleidoscope to the X-Ray: Urban Spectatorship, Poe, Benjamin, and *Traffic in Souls* (1913)', *Wide Angle* 19:4 (1997): 25–61.
58 Lisa Cartwright, *Screening the Body: Tracing Medicine's Visual Culture* (Minneapolis and London: University of Minnesota Press, 1995), 109.
59 Wilhelm Röntgen, 'A New Kind of Rays', trans. Arthur Stanton, *Nature*, 53 (1896): 274–776
60 Steven Connor, 'Pregnable of Eye: X-Rays, Vision and Magic'. http://www.stevenconnor.com/xray/ (accessed 14 May 2013). This is an expanded version of a text given as a talk for the annual conference of the British Society for Literature and Science, Keele University, March 29, 2008.
61 Lippit, *Atomic Light (Shadow Optics)*, 53.
62 Steven Connor, 'Pregnable of Eye: X-Rays, Vision and Magic', a presentation delivered in 2008, accessed 12 March 2013: http://www.stevenconnor.com/xray/
63 Marina Warner, *Phantasmagoria: Spirit Visions, Metaphors, and Media into the Twenty-First Century* (Oxford: Oxford University Press, 2006), 256.
64 Lippit, *Atomic Light (Shadow Optics)*, 58.
65 Giorgio Agamben, *Homo Sacer: Sovereign Power and Bare Life*, translated by Daniel Heller-Roazen (Stanford, CA: Stanford University Press, 1998), 9.

66 Ibid., 3.
67 Ibid., 142–143.
68 Eric L. Santner, *The Royal Remains: The People's Two Bodies and the Endgames of Sovereignty* (Chicago, IL and London: University of Chicago Press, 2011), 89. In Santner's reading of this moment, the transition of power from the King to the people is a troubled one, producing an excess, an extraneous matter of flesh that had always haunted the figure of the King and his 'two bodies'. The fleshy matter of bodies remains a problem when the populace collectively inherits this problem.
69 Esposito, *Bios: Biopolitics and Philosophy*.
70 Ibid., 50.
71 Ibid., 52.
72 Jonathan Crary, *Suspensions of Perception: Attention, Spectacle, and Modern Culture* (Cambridge, MA: MIT Press, 2001), introduction.
73 Ibid., 31.
74 Giorgio Agamben, 'Magic and Happiness', in *Profanations*, trans. Jeff Fort (New York: Zone Books, 2007), 19.
75 The essay on gesture appears in *Means without End* (1996) and *Postmoderne und Politik* (1992), and a shorter version is added to the English translation of *Infancy and History* in 1993.
76 Paul Fleming, 'The Crisis of Art: Max Kommerell and Jean Paul's Gestures', *MLN*, 115:3 (April 2000): 519–543, 534.
77 Citation from Agamben's introduction to the 1993 English edition of *Infancy and History*, 3.
78 Giorgio Agamben, *The Idea of Prose*, trans. Michael Sullivan and Sam Whitsitt (Albany: SUNY Press, 1995), 37.
79 This recalls Nietzsche's warning in *Thus Spoke Zarathustra* 'the body and its great reason: that does not say "I" but does "I"'. *Thus Spoke Zarathustra: A Book for Everyone and No One* trans. and introduced by R.J. Hollingdale (London: Penguin Books, 2003), 146.
80 Noys, 'Film-of-Life: Agamben's Profanation of the Image', 90.
81 Giorgio Agamben, 'Kommerell, or on Gesture', in *Potentialities: Collected Essays in Philosophy*, ed. and trans. Daniel Heller-Roazen (Stanford, CA: Stanford University Press, 1999), 77–88, 78.
82 Ibid., 78–79.
83 Fleming, 'The Crisis of Art: Max Kommerell and Jean Paul's Gestures', 535.
84 Agamben 'The Author as Gesture', *Profanations*, 72.
85 Giorgio Agamben, 'Without Classes', in *The Coming Community* trans. by Michael Hardt (Minneapolis and London: University of Minnesota Press, 1993), 62–64.
86 Ibid., 64.
87 Ibid.

88 Benjamin from the essay 'Franz Kafka', cited in Agamben's essay 'Kommerell, or on Gesture', 80.
89 Philippe-Alain Michaud, *Aby Warburg and the Image in Motion*, trans. Sophie Hawkes (New York: Zone Books, 2007), 51.
90 Charles Musser argues that Edison's method of working was not exploitative but collaborative: 'Significantly, Edison and his colleagues employed collaborative methods during the process of developing their modern motion picture system. Rather than argue whether it was Thomas A. Edison or William Kennedy Laurie Dickson who really invented the kinetograph and kinetoscope, we need to see them as working together. Moreover, this team, which formulated general principles and established priorities for research, overlapped with another team dealing with the actual hands-on mucking about that typified the Edison lab'. Charles Musser (1996) 'Pre-classical American Cinema: Its Changing Modes of Film Production', in *Silent Film*, ed. Richard Abel (London: Athlone, 1996), 86–87.
91 The film and sound recording were archived separately, with the wax cylinder having been damaged and split into two parts. The parts were assembled together in 1998 at the Rogers and Hammerstein Archive of Recorded Sound, Lincoln Centre, New York, with the editor Walter Murch responsible for finding the correct frame speed to match sound and image. In Murch's view, the film was shot at forty frames per second.
92 Rebecca Solnit offers a full account of this meeting in *River of Shadows*, 228–231.
93 Ibid., 228.
94 The plates are, respectively, 'Dancing (Fancy)', 1887. Vintage collotype. Plate 192 from 'Animal Locomotion'. Image measures 7 × 16 inches on 19 × 24 inch sheet. 'Couple Dancing' Plate 197, and Plate 196, captioned 'Two women dancing a waltz'.
95 Agamben, 'Notes on Gesture', 57.
96 Ibid., 50.
97 Ibid., 52.
98 Friedrich Nietzsche, *The Gay Science*, ed. Bernard Williams, trans. Josefine Nauckhoff (Cambridge: Cambridge University Press, 2001), section 381, 246. Here, towards the end of the book, Nietzsche is speaking of the nourishment required by those undertaking the type of joyful scholarship that has been presented: 'There is no formula for how much a spirit needs for its nourishment; but if it has a taste for independence, for quick coming and going, for wandering, perhaps for adventures of which only the swiftest are capable, it would rather live free with little food than unfree and stuffed. It is not fat but the greatest possible suppleness and strength that a good dancer wants from his nourishment – and I wouldn't know what the spirit of a philosopher might more want to be than a good dancer. For the dance is his ideal, also his art, and finally also his only piety, his "service to god"'.

3

Dim Stockings and Pornography: Community, Spectacle and the Example

What is disappearing?

In *The Three Disappearances of Soad Hosny* (2011) by Lebanese filmmaker Rania Stephens, gesture floats to the surface of a sea of images. In this film, which may also be described as an essay, a cinematic compendium or a repurposed film, the iconic Egyptian actress Soad Hosny performs in short sequences of images assembled from eighty-two of the eighty-six films spanning her thirty-year career. Structured in three acts, the film opens with short bursts of action as Hosny drives a car recklessly, runs the final metres of a race and dances manically. The second part finds a more measured tempo as she sits motionless on a stool whilst an artist paints her portrait, relaxes on a sandy beach and reclines on a luxuriously large bed, whilst the third act is a concatenation of trauma. Dreams of falling and running are intercut with sleeplessness and death. Her actions performed are the common bodily phrasings of a shared culture and yet in this film there is neither causality nor conclusion, only the gestures and tropes of an actress who repeats the same actions in different films, a repetition of movements that with each performance registers a slight difference. Isolating one gesture at a time, Stephan gathers together a movement as it appears across the corpus of her films: a glance in a rear-view mirror, a certain way of entering a room. If this film seems to exhibit the common bodily phrasings that coincide with the rules and expectations of genre, that operate within familiar paradigms of action clusters, there are also those gestures that inhere as traces of her singularity. Despite her iconic status in Egyptian culture, the film emphasizes through repeated play the moments when Hosny seems to break the spell of the fictional cast and asks the question, 'Am I Egyptian?'

The structure of Stephan's film as it moves between fixed and clichéd versions of Soad Hosny and moments of utter fluidity seems to speak to the dilemma of belonging and community that concerns Agamben in the wake of the fall of communism in the late 1980s. The question of what kind of being together is possible after this and other destructive events of the twentieth-century Agamben examines in *The Coming Community* (1990), a book that opens with a description of a new form of singularity without identity upon which community could be built, the curiously named 'whatever being'. The turn of phrase denotes a political figure for whom being is not unimportant; 'whatever' refers to a capacity to make use of the self in a given context, with whatever resources, alignments and attachments are to hand. It describes a mode of being without recourse to the defining terms of substantive identities (being Muslim, British and athlete). Whatever being marks the possibility of a community that operates without any demands or conditions of belonging. This is the subject of the many brief essays that constitute *The Coming Community*, the title of which in the Italian is *La comunità che viene*. Translated as 'the coming community', the emphasis is placed on a future-oriented event, an event to come. Yet in Italian the title bears a different inference, literally the community that comes, giving emphasis to the event of community as transient and ephemeral, a gathering that assembles momentarily and again disperses. The event of community is not a temporally fixed becoming, but on the contrary, a transient being together without conditions for belonging.

What, we may ask, is the place of cinema in this enquiry. This chapter examines the ground between Agamben's thinking-through of the possibility of community on the one part, and on the other his engagement with the potentialities of cinema. In tracing the many appearances of cinema across his essays, it is apparent that cinema is a particular kind of ethico-political gesture machine that is nonetheless part of the apparatus of capital. In alignment with mid-century political theorists of the image, Agamben's cinema is receptive to the laws of commodification and alienation that have come to dominate twentieth-century socio-political life as it has been defined largely through a culture of images. In this respect, cinema is critical to, and at times complicit with, the unfolding of an image-based culture that exhibits the separation of our desires from our selves and plays them back in commodified form. Yet cinema is also an apparatus that functions through what Agamben describes as two transcendental terms provided by montage: to arrest the image (stoppage) and to replay it (repetition), and here resides cinema's ability to deactivate the smooth flow of commodity images. Cut, removed, repositioned and replayed, the naturalized sequences of ideal bodies and lifestyles become jagged-edged, unruly, uncomfortable to watch. In a further interpretation of cinema's potential to break with the commodity's spell, Agamben identifies in the genre of pornographic film the repeated gesture of a woman who looks to camera and cuts through the enchantment of the scene. In this choice of genre, Agamben is perhaps adhering to Walter Benjamin's invocation of a philosophy that locates truth in the most banal and quotidian details of life.

But it is also in this discussion of a returned look that Agamben's appeal to cinema becomes a reductive account by arguing that the breaking of the diegetic spell within the scene of pornography is a radical manoeuvre. This particular look is, I will argue, a gesture entirely at home in mainstream pornographic film that presents its viewers with the proposition of a window onto a real event, a hyperreality underwritten by the knowing look to camera. There are two further points to follow from this, the first of which is that Agamben's account is perhaps indebted to Benjamin's exhortations on the animating property of pornographic language, yet he fails to attend to the difference between obscene language and pornographic image sequences. The second point is that in reading for a profanatory gesture in the performance of the porn star, Agamben misses the potentiality that inheres in the material form of the image, or what I will call the example of imperfection. In contrast to the perfect surface of the commodity image as it is put into circulation, the cinematic image comes to bear the marks of its exhibition, or to put it a different way around, it loses the sheen of its status as fixed record and moves into a zone where recording and transmission become indiscernible. In the final part of the chapter we return to Rania Stephan's film as the site of the exhibition of cinema's materiality as it surfaces in celluloid, video tape and digital video discs. In the glitches, sparkle and crackle that pattern the images of Hosny, the commodity is subjected to the registration of its history, to contingency, finitude and decay.

Community to come

The function of the image in post-war late capitalist culture brings to mind Guy Debord's writings and his many strategic practices during a lifetime committed to exposing the alienation endemic, as he saw it, to this period, and Agamben explicitly draws on the work of his friend in several essays written in the 1990s. The text 'Marginal Notes on *Commentaries on the Society of the Spectacle*' appeared in 1990 in the collection *Means without End: Notes on Politics*, a book dedicated to the memory of Debord. A section of this same text was published in the same year under the chapter title 'Shekinah', in the book *The Coming Community* (1990). A further essay, 'Difference and Repetition: On Guy Debord's Films', first delivered as a lecture in 1995, was published and translated into English seven years later in an edited collection of essays by and about Debord and the Situationist International. This last essay appears in memoriam as on 30 November 1994, Debord had taken his own life. Debord's polemical analysis of a late capitalist condition in *The Society of the Spectacle* (1967) famously identifies a society whose relations are thoroughly mediatized and whose capacity for communication has been separated from humans, captured and displayed as a totalizing image world. The prescience of such a critique for what was to follow in the decades after the book's publication is notable: 'Debord's books constitute the clearest and most severe analysis of the miseries and slavery of a society that by now has extended its dominion over the whole planet – that is to say, the society of the spectacle in which we live.'[1] The system of images, of which cinema is a part, structures and mediates the relationships of individuals to their own desires and annuls their singularity, their potency and their capacity to act. Furthermore, the spectacle has come to mediate relations between the individual and the community, and the one and the many, which in the context of globalization is also a structuring of the particular and the universal.

There are other events that play a part in the philosophical landscape of the time. Agamben's essays on the spectacle, and specifically the volume *The Coming Community*, were written in the wake of the spectacular collapse of the communist East that began in 1989 with the fall of the Berlin Wall and continued with the demise of Eastern European communist states throughout the following year. *The Coming Community* has to be seen, as Leland de la Durantaye argues, as a response to these events as well as a continuation of a philosophical conversation concerning the concept of community.[2] In 1993, two books provided a spur to such debate, both turning on conceptions of community derived from the late Georges Bataille. These were Jean-Luc Nancy's text, 'The Inoperative Community'[3] (published first as an essay and extended into a book three years later), and Maurice Blanchot's *The Unavowable Community*,[4] with Alphonso Lingis's *The Community of Those Who Have Nothing in Common* (1994)[5] following in their path. The question of an im/possible community derives from Bataille's notion of a negative formulation constituted through the concept of the unavowable, or the inoperative. For such a formation, or group, there may be no grounds for inclusion or exclusion on his terms. Events of the Second World War had demonstrated the corruption of the idea of community as a group unified by a shared history, throwing into relief the potentially exclusionary and persecutory nature of communal ideology. Blanchot's rendition of a community without rules or conditions for belonging avoids such a possible application, yet it lacks a description of a form that community may take. Nancy's examination of the concept takes a different approach in the tracing of a nostalgia for an original belonging that accompanies every instance of community, not only in the recent past but through far earlier instantiations, a belonging founded on land, language, ancestry or blood. Conceptualizing a version of community as commonality of any kind carries risks.

The exigencies of the project present themselves during the last decade of the twentieth century with the crisis in a communist definition of community and its provision of an alternative to capitalism. 'If the idea of community, and a corresponding idea of communism, is to survive its present crisis,' writes de la Durantaye, 'for both Blanchot and Nancy it is only on the condition that it discover new means for discussing what communities have in common'.[6] Agamben's response to this crisis of the term is, according to de la Durantaye, 'totally unique'. In *The Coming Community*, the problem of commonality, or the relation of the part to the whole, is parsed through the concept of the example. The example is a singular entity that nonetheless has a relation to others. 'It is one singularity amongst others, which, however, stands for each of them and serves for all,'[7] Agamben writes in the short exegesis of the example that features towards the beginning of *The Coming Community*. The example would seem to belong to a group, an exemplary part of a whole, but it is precisely its exemplary quality as example that determines its separation from the group, its standing apart in this moment of display. The example comes about through an act of naming which is also a setting to one side, or from the Greek *paradeigma*, shown alongside. Produced through the act of exemplification, examples (as he states in *The Signature of All Things*) have no intrinsic identity and no common property. They are the means through which the coming community may be conceived and *The Coming Community* is indeed an inventory of examples of such a community formed in each act of exemplification. 'Tricksters or fakes, assistants or 'toons, they are the exemplars of the coming community,'[8] he writes, and the text takes this wide-ranging approach to its subject in a series of ruminations on topics that include halos, the Swiss writer Robert Walser, the character Bartleby the scrivener, the event of Tiananmen and the advertisement from French cinema for the brand of 'Dim' stockings. It is perhaps the latter, above all, that displays the unlikely provenance of Agamben's choice of examples.

Barely discernable: Dim Stockings

'Dim Stockings'[9] is a meditation that recalls cinema of the 1970s, and a particular advertisement screened in Paris movie theatres in which smooth-legged smiling women danced together to display the sheerness of these inexpensive stockings. This advertisement, that 'wafted over the audience a promise of happiness unequivocally related to the human body',[10] also registered a 'strange disjunction' between the individual dancers. This vaguely discernable fault line had been created by a 'facile trick' in the editing together of images that were filmed separately, presented on screen as though they were of one moment in space and time. The image of a 'community' of dancers was in fact a composite of bodies patched together to create the illusion of a group dynamically engaged together in movement. In its dissembling through open display, the advertisement perfectly performs the role of the image within a culture of spectacle. The commodity of stockings appears to create a shared point of contact between these women, and the images openly exhibit this apparent commonality through the dance that is at display. This sequence of images presents to the women their own desires but at a remove: the pleasure of dancing is channelled through the commodity of a brand of stockings; furthermore, the 'community' of dancers is brought together by the commodity that rather literally mediates the relations between the women. The brand of Dim Stockings, in a final act of mediation, interfaces the relationship of the viewer to the image sequence. There is, however, a more positive aspect to this advertisement, and advertising more generally, which we come to in due course.

The fetishistic nature of the commodity, its partial and mesmerizing potency, is an aspect of Marx's work that Debord claws back following its marginalization by an Althusserian reading emphasizing the state apparatus. In the concept of fetishism, Marx models the fetishistic extraction of the thing from its context and its further abstraction as a sign, and here we draw closer to understanding the function of the image within the system of commodification. The visual potency of the fetish is key to this formulation, and in an essay entitled 'Marx; or, The Universal Exposition', in *Stanzas* (1977), Agamben turns to the Great Exhibition of 1851 in London to give emphasis to the visual potency of capital manifest in its exhibitionary form. The products of the Great Exhibition, arranged for display in the glass building designed by Paxton, were not to be viewed as separate units but uniformly as an enchanted scene. It is a magically auratic scene that, speculatively at least, may have furnished the imagination of Marx. 'Marx was in London in 1851 when the first Universal Exhibition, in Hyde Park, was inaugurated with great fanfare,' he writes, 'and it is probable that his memory of that occasion contributed to his reflections on the character of the commodity-fetish'.[11] It is a moment and a scene that Agamben returns to, years later, in the essay on 'Marginal Notes on *Commentaries on the Society of the Spectacle*', to make a similar point. That is, the shift from use value to exchange value in Marxist thought was fundamentally bound to a visual sense, an image of things as detached promises of an endlessly deferred desire. And it is this transition, from use to exchange to spectacle, that Debord so thoroughly inventorized in his essays, books and films about a culture given over to the spectacle, to the mediation of all social relations through a visual realm.

The spectacle, according to Debord's many formulations of its manifestation, captured human desire only to reveal it in the land of the commodity in an alienated form. Desire, if we recall, was captured, distanced and replayed as a commodified image. The spectacle eroded not only the relationship of the labourer to the materials and forms of productivity, but the common substance of communicability that unified people as community, a being in common. The image therefore takes a particular place in the history of community, a place from which an abstraction of relations can be achieved, and towards which the image can contribute to (if not determine) the ultimate failure and impossibility of community under the sign of the spectacle. As Agamben is at pains to underline, Debord situates the spectacle not in the realm of the image itself, but in the realm of relations, in the space of communication and the possibility of communicability itself. However, the image is not simply a lost cause. It is rather an intersection at which the commodity faces community, and communication confronts exchange, a site where we may find once again the paradigmatic feature of gesture. In Agamben's words:

> The gesture is neither use value nor exchange value, neither biographic experience nor impersonal event: it is the other side of the commodity that lets the 'crystals of this common social substance' sink into the situation.[12]

Gesture is the paradigm that both eludes definition (it is neither nor) and sits between terms. It is tied to neither use nor exchange because it is never a simply purposeful act nor a decadent indulgence. Gesture is the other side to the spectacular commodity in its mode of appearing, its being given to be seen. It is praxis, a corporeal manifestation of communication that is neither an expressive act of personality, nor performance at a remove, rather it is a location where community may be situated, or in the terms borrowed from Marx, the ground that is receptive to the crystals of a common social substance.[13]

What relevance does Debord's analysis have for a politics that comes after it? Whilst Agamben's essay opens his 'marginal notes' with the assertion that Debord's books provide the clearest and most severe examination of a system that has permeated the globe, the conclusion to the essay suggests that in the midst of such misery, a coming community takes form. The subsection entitled 'Tiananmen', returns to the events of China, 1989, as a situation in which a demonstration produced an exemplary instance of a community without name, a commonality with no identifiable features of belonging. He writes that the threat presented by this community was precisely its unwillingness to present an identity 'what the state cannot tolerate in any way is that singularities form a community without claiming an identity, that human beings co-belong without a representable condition of belonging (being Italian, working-class, Catholic, terrorist, etc.).'[14] The demonstrators had no specific demands, but only generic ones such as democracy. What this exemplary instance fulfils in Agamben's terms is the possibility of the spectacle falling foul of its own methods. For whilst social bonds are diminished and dissolved under its power, and the populace reduced to singular individuals whose relations are without conditions of belonging, such a situation produces unanchored beings, or *whatever* singularities as Agamben names them. In an argument that resonates with Hardt and Negri's analysis of capital as empire, whatever singularities have the capacity to elude capture, to slip the net of social control because they have no located community and no lasting social bonds, and therefore have no means of recognition for the state.[15]

Written only a year after the Tiananmen protest, the analysis of this event closes the essay on the society of the spectacle with a note of possibility, despite the deaths of the occasion. Yet the image that circulated internationally of a man standing in front of a tank on Chang'an Avenue refusing to move, a gesture of peaceful defiance, Agamben does not directly comment on. The fact that it is an image that 'captures' the event is surely of some importance to this argument. The image as news discourse performs its task of mediating the event, but in the course of its distribution, the potentiality of the image is rendered dead.

The gestural dynamic of the image as a force of opposition becomes, through endless dissemination and repetitive exposure, a banal icon reproducing a generic concept of 'protest' and 'the fight for democracy' and is readily appropriated by state powers elsewhere to service their own agendas. Agamben's analysis swerves away from the spectacle and the question of the meaning of images in this final section, moving problematically to the unmediated event itself. The curve of the argument ultimately refracts the analysis of spectacle into multiple sites and all possible relations. In the spirit of a general mediating function of the spectacle, his essay locates the social spectacle everywhere and yet in no particular medium, and at times free of media altogether. In order to understand the designation of cinema in the system of spectacle, it is necessary then to refine this term, the spectacle, which is used loosely and at times simultaneously to mean an epoch, a political system, a relationship and a mediated culture.

The spectacle and the mass ornament

Is the spectacle of cinema synonymous with the general spectacularity that Debord identifies as the condition of the society of the spectacle? Judging from the cover of the American edition of the book issued in 1967, featuring a cinema audience made uniform by the wearing three-dimensional glasses, there is a particular relation between the general condition of the spectacle and the cultural institution of cinema. And yet as Thomas Levin cautions, it is a mistake to completely elide the spectacle with the image, for in Debord's writings it is clear that the spectacle is the mediation of a social relation between people, with the cinema as but one manifestation of this 'getting in-between'. A degree of confusion concerning the nature of the spectacle is however, as Levin notes, produced by a slippage in Debord's use of the term, at times invoking the sphere of representation as *the* privileged site of spectacle, whilst at others, insisting on the spectacle's separate manifestation in relations between things. Levin writes, 'The conflation in turn stems from Debord's rhetorical employment of the notion of spectacles qua images or representation to concretize his reading of "spectacle" as *the* allegory of late capital.'[16]

To avoid a wholesale running together of the alienation and passivity of the spectacular condition with the particular apparatus of cinema, we might ask what kind of cinema Debord has in mind at this moment in time? Levin suggests that the cinema that Debord takes aim at is in fact a historically specific set of practices named classical cinema, a model of cinema produced predominantly in America in the first half of the twentieth century. The coherence of such a cinema is derived from its narrative, commercial and industrial features. Citing a statement from Debord that goes some way towards qualifying the cinema of his critique by way of an alternative, Levin argues that for Debord, there were many possible cinemas rather than the singular version that was prevalent: 'It is society and not technology that has made cinema what it is. The cinema could have been historical examination, theory, essay, memories,'[17] argues Debord in a text published in 1978. It is also the case that the cinema was, for the Situationists, a major cultural institution. In 1958, the first reference to cinema appears in Situationist literature, announcing 'Cinema is the central art of our society.' Debord was of course to adopt cinema as a main channel of critique, precisely because such critique must locate itself 'in the taking-place of what it wants to overthrow',[18] with all of its attendant risks.

Jonathan Crary identifies a further difficulty to the term 'spectacle' as Debord wields it in its lack of a historical dimension. Crary writes, 'A striking feature of Debord's book was the absence of any kind of historical genealogy of the spectacle, and that absence may have contributed to the sense of the spectacle as having appeared full-blown out of the blue.'[19] In the original publication of 1967, Debord fails to reveal what he perceives to be its inaugural occasion, but some years later, with the publication of his *Comments on the Society of the Spectacle* in 1988, he inserts what Crary takes to be a clue. Debord dates the spectacle as barely forty years old at the time of his original analysis of the term published in 1967. He provides, however, no further indication of why this may be so, which leaves Crary to speculate on the reasons for this quite precise date of the late 1920s, or even 1927 itself. Probing possibilities, Crary considers a number of dissimilar events as occurrences that may be implicated in the advent of the spectacle, specifically three interlocking technological, social and cultural developments that redefine regimes of visual power and attention. In 1927, the technological perfection of television was achieved by Vladimir Zworykin, who created the seeds of a culture in which images travelled free of a permanent physical support and were transmitted with speed and ubiquity across space. The prospect of broadcast commanded a response involving a military, corporate and state division of the apparatus and its reach, defining the territory of the spectacle at this early stage. Another development in the same year was the arrival of sound in film, a transformation that brought with it the vertical integration of film production, circulation and exhibition, and secured the dissemination of the diffused spectacle. Significantly, this event of the sound film signified the end of cinema muto and the cinema of explicit gesture.[20] The third critical change of the period is the rise of fascism and shortly after, Stalinism, ushering in a culture of the concentrated political spectacle. An interesting adjunct to this is the crafting of television as a collective form. Both Hitler and Goebbels, according to Crary, regarded television as a medium to be engaged with collectively, designating public television halls that would accommodate up to 400 people.

In Crary's sketch of a genealogy, the spectacle is integral to a number of restrictions, in particular the locking down of film to a soundtrack and to specific national languages that in turn secured the domination of the producer over the exhibitor of film (and of Hollywood over indigenous film cultures), and the related consolidation of geopolitical power through the management of televisual transmission. If these restrictions secure the spectacle through efforts of administration, the aesthetic dimension of the spectacle is secured through the visualization of fascism, an image of power at once ubiquitous and seductive, fetishized images of leadership extracted from daily life and put on general display. One only has to recall Leni Riefenstahl's propaganda films to appreciate the potential of the moving image to effect an abstraction of power, to transform the mass into an elegant body, a collective or machinic assembly of moving parts. A concomitant effect of such spectacular abstraction is its designation of a perpetual present, a time that denies history and historical knowledge in favour of novelty. The 'new and different' features of the world of the spectacle were of course only the cover image of a potentially disturbing juxtaposition of things; the array of shining commodities of the department store removed from any meaningful context were the reverse image of an anthropological surrealism prevalent during the period here designated by Crary as the consolidation of the spectacle.

If Crary's speculations are correct and the instance of the spectacle's emergence derives from the late 1920s and the peak of modernism, it is a moment in which cinema is a privileged vehicle for critics of the time who are noting features of abstraction. In their writings on cinema, the spectacle emerges through framing devices, close-ups that fetishize things, as an abstraction of bodies and with a preoccupation with surface detail. This attention to spectacle in the writings of both Walter Benjamin and Siegfried Kracauer, Agamben references in 'Dim Stockings', where he claims that their fascination with surface novelty is deceptive. Seemingly enchanted by a depthless abstraction, the novel surface figure is rendered through their rumination on the insightful detail. Whilst Benjamin's eye was attracted to the discarded and abandoned detail of everyday life rendered invisible by its lack of utility, Kracauer's gaze slides across the shimmering surface that posited the secret unconscious of a society in full view. These 'unheeded impulses' that texture the surface of things, 'by virtue of their unconscious nature, provide unmediated access to the fundamental substance of the state of things', Kracauer writes at the opening of the essay 'The Mass Ornament'.[21] The famous girls whose dancing legs conform to exercise regimes in turn produce geometric patterns in the gathering of bodies into an abstracted mass. They are 'no longer girls', he cautions, 'but indissoluble girl clusters whose movements are demonstrations of mathematics'.[22] The description of abstraction applies not only to their bodies as object parts and their movements as geometric patterns, but also to their hovering above any idea of community; community is marked as the property of the people (*Volk*), whereas the girl clusters are of the mass. The mass ornament, the term famously coined by Kracauer to describe these displays, is borne by and arises from the mass, and is significantly an '*end in itself*'.[23]

When Agamben recalls this analysis of the body under the sign of spectacle, it is, however, not without positive qualities. The body as an abstract designation is freed from what he calls the 'stigma of ineffability',[24] of which there are two modes: the mysterious body of biological life, and the enigmatic individual body subject to interpretive scrutiny as biography. The emancipation of the body from these confinements of thought, which are also its theological foundations, releases the body into a *whatever* body, a singularity that is free from the claims of being knowable and from the claims of identity (being British and being Muslim). The whatever body is a body that displays its belonging as such, a manifest condition. The promise of happiness that wafts over the audience of Parisian cinemagoers as they are confronted with dancing girls, those wearers of the inexpensive brand Dim Stockings, may be traced back to a similar prospect identified by Kracauer in the 1920s when faced with the spectacle. In alliance with Kracauer, Agamben writes of a particular appeal of the commodified body, an appeal rooted in the emancipation of the body image from its 'destiny' in biology and biography. Detached from its materiality, the body is no longer audited, monitored and explained by these dual procedures of naturalization. Not only the dancing girls, but those figures in advertising, on fashion runways, and in pornography all exhibit a body freed from its material constraints. That is, they display the *body as image*, for Kracauer, abstracted as surface pattern. Yet, '[w]hat was technologized was not the body, but its image',[25] which leaves the lived body as remainder, or remaindered. For Agamben the spectacular immaterial body as image hides the frail human form in its precarity, and here a radical cleaving separates the mask (Agamben's term) from the thing itself. As the body images, ever more abstract and perfect, peel away from the material form of lived bodies, the human body, he implies, may be discarded, de-categorized and abandoned to the camps.

The convergence of regimes of visual power that characterizes for Crary the arising of the spectacle works through (in Agamben's reading) to effect a radical separation of body from its image, of life from its potential, but also of people from their governance. The separation most exemplary of the domination of the commodity over all aspects of life is pornographic film, singular in its illumination of the body as an instrument of endless pleasure and generic in its conforming to the laws of exchange value. In pornography Agamben identifies, as we have noted before, a potential to break the spell of the commodity and this lies in the actor's look to camera that splinters the screen of viewing. If the body is hopelessly subject to commodification, the look retains the potential for salvation of some sort but not through promissory connection. On the contrary, it is a mark of indifference towards the imagined viewer. This look, which is seen to radically disarm the abstract power of the image world, Agamben makes central to an argument that I will argue is flawed in many respects.

Pornography

Pornography, as with many other examples in Agamben's work, is a subject that is potent in its ability to transgress categories and ultimately to erase the distinctions between them. Pornography belongs conventionally to the sphere of the profane, yet the line that divides the profane from the sacred is in the course of its treatment (in Agamben's readings) confounded. Not simply an example of the permeation of the commodity into all aspects of life, pornography moves from this site of commodified abjection to become exemplary in the jamming of the system of commodity exchange. Pornography, that is, contains the means of its own undoing. In the most recent account of pornography, Agamben names a particular figure in association with such a profanatory power, the actress and star Chloë des Lysses, the one whose signature look to camera exhibits a striking form of indifference. To whom Chloë des Lysses is indifferent is a question that opens the relationship of her look to the spectacular system of which she is part. But before giving due consideration to this reading of de Lysses, there is the task of tracing a not uncomplicated, shifting approach to pornography in Agamben's work. Over a period of fifteen years, the subject of pornography makes an appearance in at least six essays published between 1985 and 2005, and in each it figures as a means to break the spell of commodity forms. In this apparently marginal genre, furthermore, Agamben locates in a highly schematic mode the formulations of an idea of community.

One of the first mentions of pornography appears midway through the book *The Idea of Prose* (1985), a text comprised of short segments listed under chapter titles as philosophically charged as 'The Idea of Thought', as politically motivated as 'The Idea of Power' and as affective as 'The Idea of Shame'. The book is a meditation on the necessity for indirect, patient forms of thought, and this indirection it engages in its own formal structure. The chapter that concerns us is entitled 'The Idea of Communism', which opens with the statement that in pornography, there exists a utopian image of a classless society. The utopian element of pornography, writes Agamben, is produced by a double movement. In the first instance is a 'gross caricature' of class traits manifest in the actors' wearing of uniforms that identify roles and hierarchies. The second movement describes an alteration of hierarchical formations and their intelligibility through sexual practices that transgress and mix categories and classifications. This literal and analogical undoing of meaning is then open to reinscription, or what Agamben terms a transfiguration, a word that comports an element of theological weight to a mode of appearing. Most notably, transfiguration is a term used in the New Testament to describe the appearance of Jesus to his disciples as Son of God when he prepares them for his fate and suffering to come.[26] It is a term then slightly at odds with the Bakhtinian-like subversion of everyday categories through the excesses of bodily pleasure that has been invoked in the description of a pornographic scenario. In eschatological mood, he writes:

> The starched caps and aprons of maids, the worker's overalls, the butler's white gloves and striped waistcoat, and more recently, even the smocks and half-masks of nurses, all celebrate their apotheosis at the moment in which, set like strange amulets on inextricably tangled naked bodies, they seem to trumpet forth that last day on which they are to appear as the emblems of a community we can still barely glimpse.[27]

The last day is subject to treatment in another chapter entitled 'The Idea of the Last Judgment', but hear its effect is jarring in the forced comedy of pairing pornography with eschatology, the profane with the sacred. Whilst this is certainly characteristic of Agamben's stylistic treatment of these binary terms, the forging of these particular characters with the sacred moment of transfiguration appears to risk their ridicule. Furthermore, when we look more closely at Agamben's list of stock figures from across the classes, the markers of class derive from a rather narrowband of lower-middle- and working-class professions. The scene of pornography is not classless, but rather could be characterized as a vision of the lower classes typically eroticized by those 'above'. This reading resonates with Stallybrass and White's model of the eroticization of domestic labour in the nineteenth century, lodged in the spatial dimensions of the home, above and below stairs, facilitating the squire's pursuit of the lowly maid, the master's fantasy of the sex life of his butler and cook.[28] It is also reminiscent of the scenarios constructed in Muybridge's studio; when participants were photographed with props including clothing, the power relations between subjects in terms of their class position are evident, whereas the photographs of naked figures take the appearance of classical subjects. In striving for a form of neutrality on Muybridge's account, and the deactivation of class differences in Agamben's,[29] there remains the trace of hierarchy that might be described through Heidegger's *sous rature*, a term crossed out and yet legible.

In Leland de la Durantaye's reading, pornography in Agamben's work functions as a paradigm in which 'property, propriety and possession would be transformed'.[30] Yet there is something of the order of the beatitude in Agamben's treatment of the subject, where his language lists dangerously close to caricature in its claim for a community realized through the scenario of pornography. The emphasis of his reading, however, undergoes a sea change in work published in the period immediately following the collapse of communism in Eastern Europe. When pornography makes an appearance at the end of 'Dim Stockings' in *The Coming Community* (1990), the tone is contrastingly melancholic. He remarks, 'never has the body, above all the female body [been so] massively manipulated as today... by the techniques of advertising and commodity production'.[31] In the triumphant rise of a capitalist world order, bodies have become thoroughly investigated, revealed and exposed, becoming image detached from their material counterpart. The task for a now precariously poised humanity, he writes, is to bring the image and the material form of bodies together in a space where such separation is no longer possible. The final line, often cited, is an advocation of pornography to aid this task. He writes, 'Advertising and pornography, which escort the commodity to the grave like hired mourners, are the unknowing midwives of this new body of humanity,' the extreme limit of a spectacular exposure, they are also that which is unprofanable.[32]

In the treatment of pornography in Agamben's memorial lecture for Guy Debord, and again in *Means without End*, attention has turned to a specific feature of the genre, a signature that operates across image sequences: the actor's returned look to camera. In this essay, Agamben draws our attention to an early instance of this in the film *Summer with Monika* (Bergman, 1953), where the main character (played by Harriet Andersson), casually smoking a cigarette, exhales and turns her face to the right, looking directly into the camera. Bergman's description of this look as the moment in which a 'direct, shameless'[33] contact is established with the viewer is cited approvingly,[34] and Agamben finds a link from this shamelessness to pornography and advertising, where the same device has been put to work. His interpretation of this signature is that the demonstration by the woman that 'she is more interested in the viewer than her partner'[35] breaks the fourth wall of fiction, exposing the image as image. Similarly, in an essay entitled 'The Face' (1998), which concerns still photographs rather than film, the look to camera is also an acknowledgement that a scenario has been fabricated for the pleasure of the viewer; the viewer is caught unawares, it would seem, by the actors who look back. This gesture conveys the actors paradoxically as 'more real precisely to the extent to which they exhibit this falsification.'[36] The rather subtle argument that is being made in this essay is primarily for a political interpretation of the face as a locus for community. In the conventions of our time, we look to the face, argues Agamben, for evidence of truth or lies, openness or concealment. And yet this search for truth presupposes that humans are in control of expression and appearance. In fact, the face is not a register of a subject's intentionality because the subject has no essence and thus nothing to hide; it is only appearance itself, and if the face attempts to dissimulate anything, it is this being nothing other than a face, an appearance. It is curious then that Agamben would want to orient the face in the genre of pornography towards a mode of manufactured disinterest, a mode that enticingly invites the viewer to read intention into the expression: is the returned look of the porn star feigned boredom or hostile disaffection? Is it a dismissal of the director and the whole apparatus of pornography or the rehearsal of a mode 'in character'?

The final orientation of pornography arrives in the book *Profanations* (2005), in an essay on parody, and again in the title essay 'In Praise of Profanation'.

Harriet Andersson in *Summer with Monika* (**Bergman, 1953**)

The essay on parody (which returns in Chapter 4 of this book) brings together pornography and love poetry, the former a parody of the latter. Where love poetry announces the desirability and yet the unattainability of its object, pornography offers an intangible fantasy and yet 'in the same gesture' brings it closer 'in a mode that is unbearable to look at'.[37] In this reading, Pasolini's *Salò* (1975) is a parody of Elsa Morante's *History: A Novel* (1974). In the essay on profanation, however, pornography has a more serious task attached to the profanatory intention. Drawing implicitly on Benjamin's observation that religion functions, like capital, through acts of separation, the remedial task is to profane that which the sacred has separated, or more precisely (and further into the essay), to render inoperative the relation of the sacred and the profane, to block the circuit. Yet in pornography, capital has produced something unprofanable, and leading into the section on pornography, the question is posed of how to profane something unprofanable, such as pornography. The question is answered by the system of pornography in its by now overfamiliar signature (in Agamben's oeuvre) of the star's look into the camera. But there is something more needed from Benjamin in order to unlock this particular argument and it comes in the idea of exhibition value (*Ausstellungswert*). Creating a third term with use value and exchange value, that which can be exhibited and whose features are given to an exhibitory mode, exercises a new value within a system of ceaseless circulation.

Agamben takes this idea into the sphere of pornography to unravel the meaning of the now 'brazen' look to camera, which extends his previous reading. Here its function is once again transformative, for the returned look is resonant of the value of exhibition. Its blankness is not expressive; it is neither defiance nor provocation but pure indifference, exposing the face as nothing but exposition. That is, the face of the porn star as it looks at the camera shows nothing but showing. The signature look of pornography becomes in this final account the feature that profanes the means to an end of pornography, or its instrumental purpose, by detaching erotic behaviour from its immediate outcome. Erotic behaviour, he argues, is left to idle. In this essay, Agamben has one porn star in mind whose modus operandi is at a considerable distance from the former utopian scenario of maids and nurses: Chloë des Lysses. He writes of de Lysses, 'Her impassive face breaks every connection between lived experience and the expressive sphere; it no longer expresses anything but shows itself as a place without a hint of expression, as a pure means,'[38] ushering in de Lysses as the perfect model of indifference. Her face is a revelation of profanatory intention because it communicates a serene calmness, 'the most stoic ataraxy'. The stakes here are high, as Agamben posits that in this one signature look resides the power to arrest the flow of the film, a radical blocking of pornography's function as a means to an end. The implication of such detachment of erotic play from its immediate end is, moreover, the opening for 'a new collective use of sexuality' to take place that diverts pornography from its prescribed and prescriptive ends. Of course the danger of this utopian finale is that the porn star's look of indifference is reappropriated and diverted by the industry as the latest fashionable erotic style, a brazenness that may well appeal to the viewer as an erotic challenge. This Agamben acknowledges in the possibility of the apparatus capturing desire once again, thus diverting the profanatory impulse from the collective to the individual and from play to consumption, the 'solitary and desperate consumption of the pornographic image'.[39]

Making an example of Chloë des Lysses

If pornography is key to the formulation of Agamben's analysis of the profanatory potential of the image under the sign of the commodity, it is not without problems. The sense of an overworked and overstated argument permeates the various writings on pornography as it strains to make the returned look a signature that signs for the promise of a new potentiality. It would seem in the multiple approaches to the topic that Agamben attempts to force this small and ambiguous gesture into a key position in the vanguard of political tasks, but in a way that is ultimately unconvincing. 'If the inexpressive and indifferent face of a porn star can be seen as the key figure of liberation,' writes Catherine Mills, 'it is hard to know what one can make of this as a mode of political transformation'.[40] Moreover, his mentions of pornography display in all but one case, a surprising lack of attention to the different nature of the bodies exhibited. Benjamin Noys notes that porn stars 'are presumed to be female by Agamben', a presumption that remains silent on the significance of the male star's body. Noys continues, 'the female body, especially the prostituted and exposed sexual body, is problematically and stereotypically the bearer of the weight of the absolute alienation of the present'.[41] In Agamben's accounts of pornography, 'sex', we might say covers over and assimilates the category of sexual difference. The failure to address the power relations pertaining to sexual difference as a critical component in the scenario of the returned look, a look that is only ever returned by the woman in the genre of pornography, displays a disregard that is repeated in more detail in his discussion of Chloë des Lysses. Agamben writes with an uncomfortable distancing from her performance when he introduces her, for example, as a porn star 'who passes off her efforts as artistic performances' [*che spaccia le sue prestazioni per* performances *artistiche*], as though performing in a pornographic film could never be considered 'art' (although perhaps artful).

And yet when he writes that, 'She has herself photographed in the act of performing or submitting to the most obscene acts, but always so that her face is fully visible in the foreground,' she appears to be attributed directorial control as indeed an artist might.[42] Yet there is an ambiguity to her being in control of how she is photographed, for she then appears to take responsibility for her own submission to what Agamben calls obscene acts. In this circling of questions of agency and indifference, submission and control, the discussion omits to mention the most striking feature of pornography, which is the carnal detail: the body fluids and emissions that make regular appearance in pornography, punctuating its form. This matter of the 'real' exchange between bodies, which is also a guarantor of the 'real' taking place before the camera, takes various forms, but the most prized within the genre is the male actor's ejaculation onto the face of the woman. Indeed, the face of Chloë des Lysses is routinely covered in semen in the final close-up of a sequence, an act to which, her expression would suggest, she is not indifferent. There is, at least, an ambivalence towards thinking through de Lysses as anything other than a sign of indifference.[43]

It might be argued, in support of Agamben's reading, that the 'money shot' is only the reverse side of the indifferent stare. The image of ejaculation closes one sequence so that it will start over again in the relentless promise of yet more images (underwriting the infinity of the commodity system). This repetitive system is precisely broken by the look to camera that reveals its empty functionality. But in extracting this single look from a context that he neglects to attend to, Agamben fails to account for the specific nature of pornography. The pornographic as genre most potently produces and commodifies the real. The returned look, I will argue, is one shot on a continuum of what Lúcia Nagib, in a different context, has named physical realism.[44] The particularity of pornography is neither its faux-narrative appeal nor the hermeticism of a fictional world whose spell is interrupted by a look. Its particularity is the physical enactment of sex in front of a camera, a physical realism that the returned look can only support as a dramatization of a lack of fictionality.[45] That Agamben sanitizes pornography in his account is evident, but a more serious charge is that the edifice upon which he builds an argument for the profanation of the unprofanable is not stable. The conclusion to which this leads is that the signature look of the porn star, far from jamming the machine of an otherwise endlessly playing film, is only a banal feature of a commodified act that must at all costs preserve itself on the territory of the real.

That the exhibition of emptiness is not the same in these two different contexts becomes further evident if consideration is given to the history of the returned look in pornographic images. Agamben, in the essay on profanation, draws a sketch of the history of erotic photography, albeit a story conforming to a heteronormative set of practices in which the figure in the image is always a woman. He finds that where early photography romanticized its coy subjects, who were caught in the boudoir apparently unawares, such poses of 'indiscretion' changed 'quite soon' in line with the development of an absolute commodification of relations. The transformation wrought the new brazen expression in place of dreamy states, a moderate version of what 'in our time... arrives at its extreme stage',[46] a position of which the expressionless face of Chloë des Lysses is the most radical designation. Yet whilst this history traces a shift from a romanticized avoidance of the camera to a brazen stare towards it in the early years after photography's inception, it raises the question of why this look of indifference did not effectively disrupt the encroachment of a commodification of all relations during this period.[47] The argument also fails to account for the slow emergence of a returned look in image forms that predate or coexisted with photography. As those familiar with painting will know, Velázquez's *La Venus del espejo* (c. 1652) featured a naked woman whose back is set towards the viewer but whose look engages the viewing subject via a mirror. She is emphatically not admiring herself but conversely the specular relay allows her an entry point into the exchange of looks. Similarly, Goya's *La Maja Desnuda* (c. 1800) has the *maja* stare at the viewer as she reclines elegantly upon a bed, and most famously Manet's *Olympia* (1865) looks defiantly back.

The predominance of the look in these images testifies to something more specific than a general alienation. The ornamentation of the model's body (Victorine Meurent) in *Olympia* extravagantly displays the signs of a female sex worker of the mid-nineteenth century no longer hiding her occupation: the details of her pearl earrings, bracelet and the flower in her hair signal her work.[48] Her white body dazzles and with the white bed clothes provides a luminescence that obscures all else, including the black maid in attendance but barely visible. The white female body is at the centre of spectacular relations, whilst the black body, tilted slightly sideways, almost off balance, moves around it.[49] The white woman's positioning of her left hand is the second most striking feature of her pose, placed across her pubic area it effectively blocks visual access to her groin. The gesture of her hand is in a manner as confrontational as her expression. The hand in refusing revelation of the body in full suggests that this body is part of an economy of exchange in which further visual access is granted through payment, a metaphor for the practice of sex work itself. But this gesture is also a taking hold of the erotics of hiding and display, secrecy and revelation, that features in more covert form in representations of erotic play across the centuries. If one were to assemble a constellation of images of this kind, from Velázquez's model to Victorine Meurent and Chloë des Lysses, the animating feature would be the display of an eroticism played through a relay of looks whose inventory includes the return stare. It arrives as a challenge to the viewer and opens questions of desire and desirability that are always implicated in looking, and that are implicit to the choreography of sexual intimacy precisely as a question. Read from this direction, Chloë des Lysses is paradigmatic, not of the ultimate alienation from the capitalist machine, but rather of the interpellation of the female figure, designated both subject and object in this scene, into the codified field of visual exchange. In this sense, pornography is the site where exhibition value and exchange value unite to exemplify the smooth workings of the machine under the sign of the most fabricated desire. And the returned look is but one more gesture captured by the capitalist sensorium.

The example of Soad Hosny

It is not unlikely that Agamben has, at the back of his thoughts at least, Walter Benjamin's brief feuilleton 'A State Monopoly on Pornography' (1927), and it is worth exploring this short text as it offers a key to what Agamben is trying yet failing to do with pornographic film. More importantly, I will argue, it is possible to channel Benjamin's thought towards a different outcome in the treatment of film and community. Written in the period shortly after Benjamin's doctoral thesis was deemed unsuccessful, the piece was one of many articles that he wrote in a turn from more scholarly research to journalism.[50] The subject of language presents no surprise as it was at the centre of Benjamin's concerns from his earliest writings. In 'A State Monopoly on Pornography' the concept being elaborated is the force of language, and at the limit of this is pornographic language with its 'excesses of communicative energy'. This fragment extends Benjamin's thesis of language as transformative matter, that is, language is not a neutral transmitter of thoughts but an active participant in the world. Pornographic language resides at the edges of official or lauded discourse, like the discarded and lowly objects that attract his attention on the streets of the city. Yet what makes it obscene and therefore effective is 'the striving for instant, unambiguous communication through a liberating, suggestive mode of expression'.[51] The language of pornography exhibits what Benjamin has elsewhere named as the magical effects of language, releasing an energy not unlike Warburg's engrams. The image that he presents in this article is of water, a not entirely unerotic image of a mass that glides until it is suddenly discharged over the edge of Niagara Falls. Benjamin argues that this potency lingering in pornographic description should not be blocked or banished but in fact harnessed by the State: 'It is society's duty,' he writes, 'to put these natural – not to say profane – processes in the life of language into service as natural forces'.[52]

When Agamben turns to pornography in the many places alluded to, he does so for reasons that are aligned with those of Benjamin; pornographic film is a marginal genre discarded at the outer edges of thought, and it is unprofanable. Yet where for Benjamin obscenities function almost magically to bring language to life, to make language itself appear, the returned look in pornographic film is not the equivalent. For Benjamin, obscenities dissolve the separation between language as form and the content of language. But in the case of pornographic film, when the porn star turns her gaze directly towards the camera the effect is to enhance the separation between what we are looking at (acts of sex) and the medium in which it appears (film). It merely produces another level of fantasy involving the oscillation of the real and the fictional; is the viewer investing in the reality of the scene or the fiction of its reality? Is the actress who looks back at the camera recognizing a fantasized viewer or the apparatus of recording? Perhaps she is merely doing as she is told. In singling out this well-rehearsed manoeuvre, Agamben here mistakes the tropes and clichés of performance for a profanatory impulse.

The question of how to interpret cinema's relationship to the system of commodity images without losing sight of cinema's ethical dimension as Agamben defines it requires a return to the analysis of gesture and to the example to iron out the convolutions here. If we recall, in Agamben's terms cinema's element is gesture rather than the image, that gesture exhibits a common means as such, yet over the course of the twentieth century a culture of spectacle has appropriated this potential. Gesture has become itself a commodified form. In a short article on the ethics of cinema, Agamben glosses this change, arguing that today the film star or *divo* 'constitutes a parodic realization of the Marxian "generic being" in which individual practice coincides immediately with its genus'.[53] The article ends, 'In the twilight of post-cinema, of which we are seeing the beginning, human quasi-existence, now stripped of any metaphysical hypostasis and deprived of any theological model, will have to seek its proper generic consistency elsewhere,' he writes, continuing, 'no doubt beyond the ethico-theatrical person, but also beyond the commodified seriality of the type and unigeneric being of the divine star'.[54] Where in cinema's history the star fused the *whatever* being of singularity and the collective form or genus, the *divo* is now a generic being in its pejorative sense, a serial type. Gesture then loses its force as the element of cinema that Agamben has valorized; cinema becomes only one amongst many forms of image production.

What brings us closer to an exhibition of cinema's language, or the 'instant, unambiguous communication' desirable to Benjamin as the language of pornography, is a different form of registration that nonetheless acts as an example in Agamben's use of the term. This is the appearance of cinema as such, apparent in the marks and scars, the sparkle and scratch of images. For it is amongst the rags and scraps of film as Benjamin might have said that the idealized surface of the spectacle is eroded and the image is returned to common use. This is not to be mistaken for a form of 'spoiling' commodified perfection; rather, it is the registration of all that is present and yet rendered unintelligible in cinema. As the voice is to language, these 'deformities' are to the image: the signature of all that is banished from representation. The significance of these forms is to be located in their exemplary status as individual marks, each a historical inscription of a particular kind occurring on a particular day, and each referring to a group beyond itself, to the materiality of cinematic form as a collective or generic substance. The further implication of these signatures, which are also exemplary marks, is this: the material imperfection of the image renders inoperative the distinction between recording and transmission. In the disclosure of material imperfections, cinema draws attention to itself; it ceases to appear as a frozen record of a past moment, communicating instead its capacity for transmission. And when cinema reveals its basis as celluloid, electronic signal or plastic tape, it exposes the degradation inherent to every act of transmission. It is a moment, like Don Quixote's slashing of the screen, in which the revelation of means breaks the spell and the image is cast from the sphere of the sacred (and untouchable) into the every day. The image loses its lustre as commodity, but gains its historical and imperfect dimension.

When the Egyptian actress Soad Hosny appears in Rania Stephan's film, her appearance is conditioned by and inseparable from the medium in which she appears. The rhythm of the film is determined not only by the movements of the body of the actress as they were recorded, and the duration of shots controlled through Stephan's montage. It is also produced by the horizontal rhythmic green or white lines of electronic signal that move up and down the screen, a condition of VHS tape. Illuminated by the colour of video more than celluloid, Hosny's face is often saturated with greens and blues, and at other times, a curious technicolour flare of pinks, oranges and blacks. The image ignites with sparkle that dances like fireflies across the screen, flashes here and there, and then becomes geometric in a sudden squaring of shapes. The medium of videotape is inseparable from the figure of Hosny, captured here in her many gestures. The film operates as a location in which Agamben's dual axes of cinema converge: cinema as the site of a common dwelling in gesture comes into contact with the profanation of the film image as spectacle. For in *The Three Disappearances of Soad Hosny*, Hosny is not only a star of Egyptian cinema whose gestural figure displays its communicability, but she is also the means through which cinema exhibits its common means of transmission. The point here is not simply that cinema displays or reveals its own status as a recording apparatus (the aim of many avant-garde film works of the 1970s), but rather that this film profanes the separation of recording and transmission. Cinema is always sent, communicated, in transition.

In a study of Arab cinema, *Hanan al-Cinema*, Laura U. Marks attends to the politics of the glitch and notes how in Stephan's film certain objects that were negligible in earlier, possibly celluloid, iterations of the film become marked out, artefacts that the representation of the film in effect rerecords.[55] The sea is a case in point in *The Three Disappearances*, where it has become a busy surface of patterns and blocks of colour, suggestive of swarms and creaturely life rather than liquid. Similarly the soundtrack comprises a rewriting of speech and music through the addition of interference, of crackle, hiss and the distortions of Hosny's voice as though the sound wave bends as it travels. Stephan's choice of VHS tape as her medium for reassembling Hosny's celluloid films carries the materiality of film as transmission rather than representation. In other words, the historical form of film as materiality, rather than platonic ideal, is manifest in the images that exhibit the film's transfer to and use as video. Hosny's films cannot be detached from this history in Stephan's practice, a history that registers the circulation of the films as an affective quality. The screening of these films in domestic environments is registered in the effects of the demagnetization of tape as it has been worn moving through the rollers of a VHS player. The life of these films on video is also connected to the politics of Arabic film circulation in the post-war period, during revolutions, upheaval and the dispersion of communities who carried with them or sent films to friends relocated to various diasporas. At one point in the film, there are French subtitles visible beneath English subtitles that testify to an improvised distribution practice across more than one border. In addition to this history is the effect of the commercial transfer of celluloid to VHS, with the concomitant compression of the image that is entailed, and the further transfer of VHS to digital stock in the making of this film. These material effects are critical components to a film that brings gesture to the fore in a form that gives dimension to the ethical apprehension of film.

In the prologue to the film, we see Hosny running away, stopped, arrested in some sense by the question 'Are you Egyptian?' She answers 'maybe', and her expression is one of uncertainty. In another sequence, she speaks on the telephone; the screen splits and she is doubled, speaking to herself in an image from another film. More than once we see her win a race, running in shorts, white top, long socks, to collect a cup that she holds high above her head in a gesture of jubilance. Yet the detail that I notice here, and when it appears again, is that her knees are moving backwards and forwards, with excitement, with nerves, with the need to keep running. Hosny's tremor seems to prefigure the jumps and glitches that are to come, and in turn the electronic fallout that is to recalibrate the rhythm of the image. The gesture stands out, and yet when we see it again it is different, lifted out of a stream of story; it rides the currents of an electronic storm and opens itself to us.

Notes

1   Giorgio Agamben, *Means without End: Notes on Politics*, trans. Vincenzo Binetti and Cesare Casarino (Minneapolis: University of Minnesota Press, Minneapolis, 2000), 72.
2   Leland de la Durantaye, *Giorgio Agamben: A Critical Introduction* (Stanford, CA: Stanford University Press, 2009), 157.
3   Jean-Luc Nancy, *The Inoperative Community*, ed. and trans. Peter Connor and Lisa Garbus (Minneapolis: Minnesota University Press, 1991).
4   Maurice Blanchot, *The Unavowable Community*, trans. Pierre Joris (Barrytown: Station Hill Press, 2000).
5   Alphonso Lingis, *The Community of Those Who Have Nothing in Common* (Bloomington and Indianapolis: Indiana University Press, 1994).
6   Leland de la Durantaye, *Giorgio Agamben: A Critical Introduction*, 159.
7   Giorgio Agamben, *The Coming Community*, trans. Michael Hardt (Minneapolis: University of Minnesota Press, 1993), 9.
8   Agamben, *The Coming Community*, 10.
9   Giorgio Agamben, 'Dim Stockings', in *The Coming Community*, trans. Michael Hardt (Minneapolis: University of Minnesota Press, 1993), 46–49.
10 Ibid., 46.
11 Giorgio Agamben, *Stanzas: Word and Phantasm in Western Culture*, trans. R.L. Martninez (Minneapolis: University of Minnesota Press, 1993), 38.
12 Agamben, *Means without End*, 79.
13 Karl Marx 'Part 1 Commodities and Money. Section 1 'The Two factors of a Commodity: Use-Value and Value (the Substance of Value and the Magnitude of Value', in *Capital: A Critique of Political Economy Volume 1*, trans. Samuel Moore and Edward Aveling, ed. Frederick Engels (Moscow: Progress Publishers, 1887 [1867]), 27–30.
14 Giorgio Agamben, 'Marginal Notes', in *Means without End: Notes on Politics*, trans. Vincenzo Binetti and Cesare Casarino (Minneapolis: University of Minnesota Press, Minneapolis, 2000), 73–90, 86.
15 Antonio Negri and Michael Hardt, *Empire* (Cambridge, MA and London, England: Harvard University Press, 2000).

16 Thomas Levin, 'Dismantling the Spectacle: The Cinema of Guy Debord', in *Guy Debord and the Situationist International: Texts and Documents*, ed. Tom McDonough (Cambridge, MA and Cambridge, England: An October Book for MIT Press, 2002), 321–454, 324.
17 Levin, 'Dismantling the Spectacle', 328.
18 Agamben, 'Marginal Notes', 78.
19 Jonathan Crary, 'Spectacle, Attention, Counter-Memory', *October*, 50 (Autumn 1989): 96–107: 98.
20 In citing *The Jazz Singer* (1927) as the first definitive transition to sound, however, Crary reproduces common lore film knowledge that has since been discredited. Michael Slowik argues, 'According to many accounts, *The Jazz Singer* was the first feature-length sound film and the movie that singlehandedly convinced Hollywood to shift to sound film production. Neither claim is accurate, however. Not only did feature-length sound films like *Don Juan, The First Auto* (June 1927), and *Old San Francisco* all precede *the Jazz Singer*, but ... *The Jazz Singer* was only a second-tier hit. It was instead the "one-two punch" of Warner Bros' *Lights of New York* (July 1928) and *the Singing Fool* that convinced Hollywood to shift permanently to sound film production.' In *After the Silents: Hollywood Film Music in the Silent Era 1926–1934* (New York: Columbia University Press, 2014), 57.
21 Siegfried Kracauer, 'The Mass Ornament', in *The Mass Ornament: Weimar Essays*, trans., ed. and introduced by Thomas Levin (Cambridge, MA and London, England: Harvard University Press, 1995), 75.
22 Ibid., 76.
23 Ibid.
24 Agamben, *The Coming Community*, 47.
25 Ibid., 49.
26 The transfiguration of Christ appears in Matthew 17: 1–8, Mark 9: 2–8 and Luke 9: 28–36.
27 Giorgio Agamben, *The Idea of Prose*, trans. Michael Sullivan and Sam Whitsitt (Albany: SUNY Press, 1995), 73.
28 Peter Stallybrass and Allon White, *The Politics and Poetics of Transgression* (Ithaca, NY: Cornell University Press, 1986).
29 The deactivation of class difference he returns to twenty years later in the essay, also mentioning pornography, 'In Praise of Profanation': 'The classless society is not a society that has abolished and lost all memory of class differences but a society that has learned to deactivate the apparatuses of those differences in order to make a new use possible, in order to transform them into pure means,' *Profanations*, trans. Jeff Fort (New York: Zone Books, 2007), 87.
30 Leland de la Durantaye, *Giorgio Agamben: A Critical Introduction*, 193.
31 Agamben, *The Coming Community*, 48.

32 Ibid., 49.
33 Ingmar Bergman cited in Agamben, 'Difference and Repetition: On Guy Debord's Films', in *Guy Debord and the Situationist International: Texts and Documents*, ed. Tom McDonough (Cambridge, MA and Cambridge, England: An October Book for MIT Press, 2002), 313–320, 319.
34 It is interesting that Agamben focuses on this returned look as shameless, when shame is the feature of humanity that he finds in the concept of testimony and its impossibility. See Libby Saxton's *Haunted Images* (London and New York: Wallflower Press, 2008), 95–104, for a discussion of this.
35 Agamben, 'Difference and Repetition', 319.
36 Giorgio Agamben, 'The Face', *Means without End: Notes on Politics*, trans. Vincenzo Binetti and Cesare Casarino (Minneapolis: University of Minnesota Press, Minneapolis, 2000), 91–101, 93.
37 Giorgio Agamben, 'Parody', *Profanations*, trans. Jeff Fort (New York: Zone Books, 2007), 37–52, 48.
38 Giorgio Agamben, 'In Praise of Profanation' *Profanations*, trans. Jeff Fort (New York: Zone Books, 2007), 73–92, 91.
39 Ibid., 91.
40 Catherine Mills, *The Philosophy of Agamben* (Stocksfield: Acumen Publishing Limited, 2008), 128.
41 Benjamin Noys, 'Film-of-Life: Agamben's Profanation of the Image', in *Cinema and Agamben: Ethics, Biopolitics and the Moving Image*, eds H. Gustafsson and A. Grønstad (New York, London, New Delhi and Sydney: Bloomsbury Academic, 2014), 95.
42 Agamben, 'In Praise of Profanation', 90–91. In Italian it reads 'Essa si fa fotografare nell'atto di compiere o subire gli atti **più** osceni, ma sempre in modo che il suo volto sia ben visibile in primo piano', in *Profanazioni*, 105.
43 This ambivalence makes an appearance again in a passage in the essay 'The Face', where Agamben writes of the erotics of the face-to-face encounter and the possibilities open to us at the moment of its occurrence:

> I look someone in the eyes: either these eyes are cast down – and this is modesty, that is, modesty for the emptiness lurking behind the gaze – or they look back at me. And they can look back at me shamelessly, thereby exhibiting their own emptiness as if there was another abyssal eye behind it that knows this emptiness and uses it as an impenetrable hiding place. Or, they can look at me with a chaste impudence and without reserve, thereby letting love and the word happen in the emptiness of our gazes. (Agamben 'The Face', 92)

One may return the look or not, and if the path taken is the former, there is the possibility of a return look that is to all intents, another version of the inexpressive face of Chloë des Lysses, the face that looks 'shamelessly', or a look of 'chaste impudence'. The choice of terms is telling, revealing in the abstract exchange of looks a sexualized yet impenetrable emptiness or an idealized look deracinated from its erotic potential.

44 Lucia Nagib, *World Cinema and the Ethics of Realism* (New York: Continuum, 2011).
45 The failure of pornography to conform to the conventions of either fiction or documentary and its location in versions of liveness and the real has lengthy documentation in discourses of film, feminism, censorship and law. See, for example, Judith Butler's *Excitable Speech: A Politics of the Performative* (London and New York: Routledge, 1997).
46 Agamben 'In Praise of Profanation' 89.
47 The photographers of early erotic pornography named in the essay on profanation are Bruno Braquehais, Louis-Camille d'Olivier and Auguste Belloc, who were working predominantly in the 1850s.
48 Coincidently, Manet's model Victorine Meurent went on to become 'an artist in her own right' as de Lysses (born 1972 in Toulon, France as Nathalie Boët) has also done.
49 See Lorraine O'Grady's famous critique of the painting in 'Olympia's Maid: Reclaiming Black Female Subjectivity', in *The Feminism and Visual Culture Reader*, ed. Amelia Jones, 2nd edn. (London and New York: Routledge, 2010), 174–186.
50 Alexander Gelley points out that journalism of this kind was not as distant from scholarly research in Germany in the 1920s as it was in America. Siegfried Kracauer's diagnostic treatment of social phenomena including film and photography was published in a Frankfurt newspaper. See Alexander Gelley, 'Epigones in the House of Language: Benjamin on Kraus', in the journal *Partial Answers*, 5:1 (Baltimore, Maryland: John Hopkins University Press, 2007): 17–32.
51 Walter Benjamin, 'A State Monopoly on Pornography', in *Walter Benjamin: Selected Writings Volume 2 Part 1 1927–1930*, trans. Rodney Livingston (Cambridge, MA and London, England: Harvard University Press, 2005), 72.
52 Walter Benjamin, 'A State Monopoly on Pornography', in *Walter Benjamin: Selected Writings Part 1 1927–1930*, trans. Rodney Livingston and Others. Michael W. Jennings, Howard Eiland and Gary Smith (Cambridge, MA and London, England: The Belknap Press of Harvard University Press, 1999), 72–74, 73.
53 Giorgio Agamben, 'For an Ethics of the Cinema', in *Cinema and Agamben: Ethics, Biopolitics and the Moving Image*, trans. John V. Garner and Colin Williamson, p. 24, eds H. Gustafsson and A. Grønstad (New York, London, New Delhi, Sydney: Bloomsbury Academic, 2014), 19–24, 23.
54 Ibid., 23.
55 Laura U. Marks 'Algorithm, Decryption, Glitch', in *Hanan al-Cinema: Affections for the Moving Image* (Cambridge, MA and London, England: MIT Press, 2015), 239–274.

4

Cinema as Laboratory: On Insects and the Anthropological Machine

Flight

In the history of cinema there is a fly, and in the history of biology a tick. The tick is critical to the theories of biologist Jacob von Uexküll who from studying the tick, develops the concept *Umwelt* as a description of the perceptual environment in which an organism exists. The implications of this theory are that creatures perceive selectively, inhabiting radically different 'worlds' simultaneously. As a result the field of biosemiotics is established. The theory of the *Unwelt* ripples out to influence Heidegger and the tick enters philosophical history. The fly, in comparison, is reduced to an obscure footnote in the history of cinema.

This chapter explores the investment and disinvestment in the figure of the fly in the emergence of cinema, a phenomenon connected to what Agamben calls the anthropological machine. This is the term for a mechanism that imposes a separation, a machine for sifting matter into binary form: inside/outside, society/nature, included/excluded. Most significantly for our purposes, the mode of operation serves to cleave the human from the animal, passing first of all through man, to produce a definition of *humanitas* through an exclusion. Man's animality, Agamben argues in a work that has become one of his most well known, must be separated from himself in the first instance, followed by a radical deployment of this injunction across various sites. It is an operation that, in pre-modern times, worked in inverse form; that which the human wished to expel was produced as a form of animality without, projected onto those 'animals' that served as slaves for example, whilst in modern times, humanity is something that can be removed from humans who exist at the border of death and life in camps. The question of whether cinema is complicit with the anthropological machine invokes a further question of whether cinema is founded upon and necessary to the production of *humanitas*. The answer to this question, this chapter suggests, is provided not only by attending to the productions of the machine, (the cinema that we have), but to that which is situated external to it (the ex-centric).

The term 'insect' carries within it a perceptual history, derived from the Latin *insectum* and the Greek word *éntomon*, meaning to cut into sections. The insect has appeared to the human eye as a machine without covering, a set of organs without skin, and perhaps for this reason it fascinates. Insects occupy an interesting place in the history of cinema. They are critical to its development, I will argue, as the progenitors of the human close-up. A fascination with insects propels Lucien Bull's early experiments with high-speed cameras, which in turn produces large-scale stereoscopic images of creatures in flight. The method pursued here is simply stated: 'Follow the flight pattern of a fly', instructs the French philosopher Michel Serres, 'Doesn't time sometimes flow according to the breaks and bends that this flight seems to follow or invent?'[1]

Types of machine I: The lottery machine

The object on the table is octagonal in shape and at its broadest, about half a metre wide and tall. The main body of the thing is a box made of wood, perhaps a light oak whose surface is stippled and striped, its darker marks prominent against a pale yellow background. The wooden hexagon sits upright upon a metal base, which has four feet that splay out at the corners to cover a surface area great enough to stabilize the upper part. Attached to the metal base on each side of the hexagon are metal A-frames. At the apex of the A-frame is a circular electronic motor that drives a rotating drum at forty revolutions per second inside of the hexagonal wooden box. The box is secured by two metal hook clips. When undone, the top half of the box lifts back, supported by a brass hinge that runs the width of the box, revealing a metal drum inside of the hexagon. Attached to the drum and situated in two channels are strips of film. On the front of the box is a square wooden cube of relatively small proportions. Attached to this is a brass plate securing two brass-coated camera lenses situated in proximity to each other. This object is the stereoscopic spark drum camera made by Lucien Bull in 1904.

The octagonal shape is striking in its symmetry and its rarity outside of the pages of geometry books. It is a regular polygon and often appears in architecture. The box shares its geometric features with the standard umbrella, the UK Stop road sign and Japanese lottery machines. There is something handmade and artisanal about the large, cumbersome camera. The oak wood is familiar from its use in furniture from the early twentieth century, its texture and tones reminiscent of the solid tables and chairs with padded seats that now appear, unwanted and unloved, in thrift shops. The brass is a different matter. With its distinctly nineteenth-century appeal, it evokes the image of dark evenings lit by brass gas lamps and the assuring sound of brass clocks. The splayed feet suggest a hybrid of clawed furniture designed in the 1930s and the more industrial hardware of factories. Lucien Bull was a craftsman who made many of his own designs. Running your fingers over its surface evokes the soft rub of sand paper smoothing the contours of the box, rounding its edges.

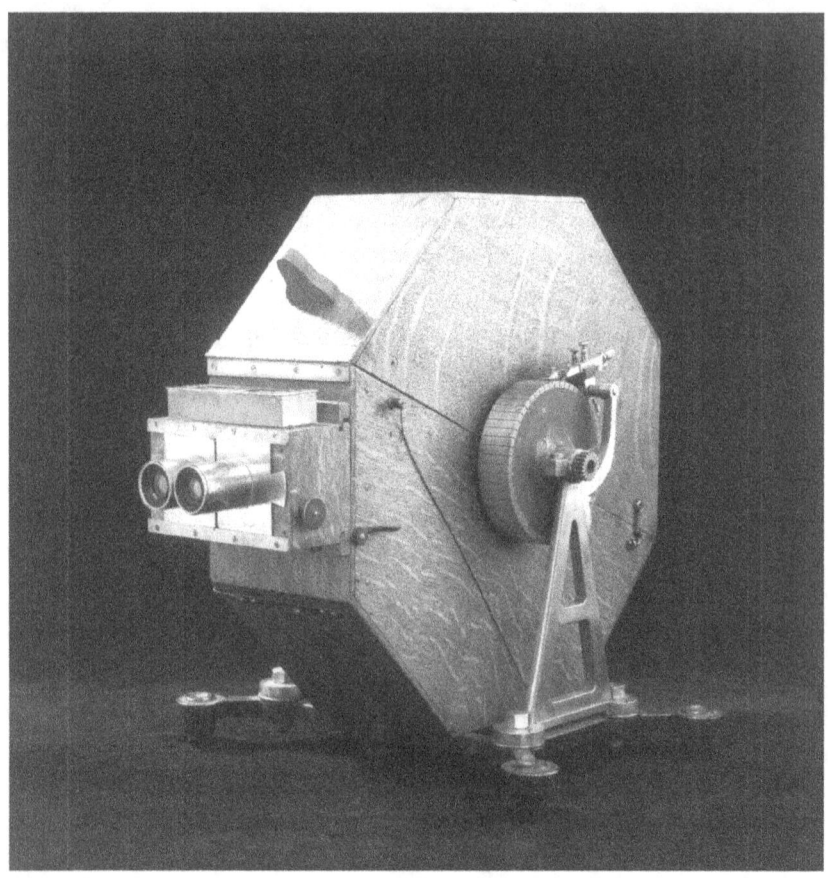

Lucien Bull, The Spark Drum Camera (1904)

Interval

One of the clearest explanations of high-speed film recording is offered by Lucien Bull delivered in a presentation of his work to the Royal Institution of Great Britain on Friday 30 May 1924.[2] In the course of this description, he provides a definition of early cinema as that through which we may analyse movement and reproduce its form in the projection of film, using the instrument of the cinematograph, the apparatus combining film recording, printing and projection. '[T]he cinematograph, as everyone is aware, is used, firstly, for analyzing motion – that is to say, registering photographically the different phases of movement.'[3] Movement is not one phase but several. The camera responds to the nebulous phases of movement by calibrating the trajectory of a thing as a calculation of movement in time (or speed). In 1900, the speed of the average camera recording at sixteen frames per second, adequate for social dramas, is ineffective for scientific research. We should note from this synopsis that for Bull, operating from a perspective of science, all other film productions (amateur film production, slapstick, actuality films and social dramas) inhabit the same category of slow film.

Bull, like Marey, sought to analyse not only movement, but movement of an object or creature at a speed that eludes the human eye. This form of movement is liable to take place 'in the interval between two pictures, and to leave no record at all of its occurrence'.[4] This fine description of the elusive nature of movement draws our attention to the black leader, to the absence that underwrites film in the necessary production of gaps between frames. Cinema is predicated on the coupling of image-absence, fleetingly repeated and dependent on the persistence of vision. There is an interval, a gap in information, that subtends the system that is called the cinema, but as an absence it is overlooked. It is seemingly unproductive space, a darkness that refuses semiotic meaning and in this sense it stands for all that is ex-centric, unlived and underdeveloped in cinema. Attuned to the interval, Bull turns to the process of its exploration to retune human perception to an other modality: that of the insect. The interval requires exploration, not only to reveal the anthropocentric limitations of human vision that fails to register life forms of different scale and speed, but the unlived of history and the ex-centric of cinema.

What is needed to obtain clear images of an insect-subject moving at high speed is a camera that can operate at rates far exceeding fifteen or twenty frames per second. Bull speculates on the taking of a thousand photographs per second, but no mechanical shutter can operate this rapidly and natural light would not be powerful enough to register an image. One could move the camera at the same speed as the object but the apparatus to enable this is flawed. The method that Bull promotes finds a solution in the electric spark, produced by an induction coil and a Leyden jar to create both 'extraordinary brilliancy and extreme instantaneousness'.[5] The brilliancy here is the intrinsic brightness per unit of surface, which is more than ten times the brightness of the sun. A yard of film is wrapped around the circumference of the drum, which turns inside of a wooden box, passing in front of two lenses. The spark occurs in front of a glass condenser, which concentrates the light into the photographic lenses. The camera does not operate a shutter speed but runs the film continuously through the gate. The framed image is created by the intense momentary illumination of the film with the absence of light declaring a border between the images. With this system, Bull reports that he has been able to obtain pictures at a frequency of 3000 pulses per second. Analysis of the interval produces a division of the interval into minute, spark-illuminated slithers.

Mon Maître Marey

Lucien Bull was an assistant to Étienne Jules Marey, from 1895 to 1904. When Marey died in May 1904, Bull went on to become sub-director of the Institut Marey. Born in Dublin to a French mother and a British father whose trades were carpentry and merchandizing, at the age of eighteen he moved to France. A year later, as a result of his practice of amateur photography, he became Marey's assistant. Bull was also a craftsman in wood and metal. Marey, a physiologist, influenced Bull's development and perhaps Bull's passion for wood rubbed off on Marey. Part of Bull's remit was to develop and print the chronophotographic negatives of Marey's physiological studies. In addition, the assistant was dispatched to the streets of Paris to record scenes with the chronophotographic camera. The main feature of this camera was its use of non-perforated film stock, which Marey sought, unsuccessfully, to project.

Bull appears in one of Marey's physiological studies. Dressed completely in white, he leaps into the air and over a hurdle. Bull is prepared or perhaps even grateful to test, try out and model his master's inventions, to play second fiddle to Marey whom he referred to years later as 'mon maître Marey' (my teacher Marey). It is after Marey's death that Bull excels with the non-perforated film stock and more. Bull refers modestly to the Institut as the place where 'we continue a good deal of Marey's original researches on motion'.[6]

Mon Maître La Grosse Mouche Bleue

The flies were kept in small glass containers. They were attached to a small clasping device with pincers that delicately held a part of the insect. When the insects were released they triggered the start of the camera and the electric motor, which in turn generated the sparking gap. Bull used blue dragonflies (*agrion puella*), large blue flies or 'bluebottles' (*la grosse mouche bleue*) and bees (*apis mellifera*) in his laboratory. The insects offered a range of flight patterns, wing shapes and wing beats. In the series of short films, *Stenographics*, that run for no more than a few seconds, the creature takes off from what appears within the frame as a launch pier, the insects moving from left to right in front of a static camera.

The fly is held and then released. The moment of its flight trips the system into operation. Sparks fly, 1500 per second. The static images are produced by the series of sparks illuminating the scene, sparks in turn started by the release of the fly, or by the fly's first movement. What is captured in this operation is the distribution of agency across a system, a human-fly-fire-machine. It is perhaps less that the fly 'plays its part' in an anthropomorphic sense of the fly as performer and more that the whole system has been constructed around the capability and capacity of the fly. The fly commands Bull by its propensity to fly at 2000 wing beats per second. Bull's assembled apparatus, like many other cinematic machines, have not until now been up to the job. The cinema needs to be adjusted to comply with the demands of the fly, which of course are not demands but the entry fee to closer observation of the life-world of the *grosse mouche bleue*.

Types of machine II: The animal machine

In 1873, Étienne Jules Marey published his studies of animal movement, *La Machine Animale*. Chapters one and two are dedicated to the flight of insects and the mechanism of the flight of insects, respectively, whilst the third book describes its subject as aerial locomotion. The creature is now brought into focus through the optic of the mechanical age; epistemologically deconstructed, fragmented into parts and reassembled for flight it becomes machine.

The metaphor works imperfectly precisely because the animals are not mechanical but operate according to different rates and resistances. Marey deploys the tools of the industrial age to bring the creatures to account, introducing a method of the trace. In one set of experiments, the creature (a fly, a wasp) is held in proximity to a sheet of paper blackened by candle wax smoke and attached to a revolving cylinder. The cylinder is then turned at a rate of one revolution per second and a half. Marey writes:

> The insect, the frequency of the movement of whose wings is to be studied, is held by the lower part of the abdomen, in a delicate pair of forceps; it is placed in such a manner that one of its wings brushes against the blackened paper at every movement. Each of these contacts removes a portion of the black substance which covers the paper, and, as the cylinder revolves, new points continually present themselves to the wing of the insect.[7]

The result, as Jussi Parikka notes, was a graphic representation of 'various kinds of movement resembling beautiful abstract lithographic art'.[8] The marks on the darkened paper are at one and the same time the performance of an attempted flight, a repeated pattern like those found in fabric, a code open to translation into information about the movement of insect wings. Marey produced a table of these expressions of wing beats per second according to the different insects:[9]

Common fly	330
Drone fly	240
Bee	190
Wasp	110
Hummingbird moth (*maeroglossa*)	72
Dragonfly	28
Butterfly (*pontia rapae*)	9

What the human eye cannot see is retrieved through a different sensory route: touch (the beat of the wings on the paper) and sound (the high pitch of wing motion in flight). Earlier in the century, natural historians had suggested a method of determining the number of wing beats per second by attending to the musical note produced by the wing membranes cutting the air and by the vibration of the thoracic plates which move in response to the wing muscles. This method Marey draws on in his experiment. It is uncertain whether the sound produced correlates exactly to the beats of a wing: '[I]t must be clearly established', he writes, 'that the sound produced by the wing depends exclusively on the frequency of its movements, in the same manner as the sound of a tuning fork results from the frequency of its vibrations'.[10] The method cannot clearly establish this fact as the fly may encounter other sonorous vibrations whilst in flight, or wings may not operate identically to each other resulting in different acoustics on each flight. Nonetheless, Marey combines the blackened paper method with the tuning fork. A chronographic tuning fork registers marks on the blackened paper near to the line made by wing beats to produce a second type of trace. The success of this experiment in producing data sets pertaining to insects, however, returns sight as a significant tool to the scene of experiment. Coating the tips of the wings of a fly with gold leaf and setting it before a sunbeam, it was possible to record a trace of movement as a trail of luminous figures of eight.

'Marey stands as one of the early pioneers of insect media,' Parikka writes.[11] Marey's experiments, according to Parikka, bring Bergson's division between intuition and intelligence into operation.[12] The intuitive model of experience represented by the fly's engagement with the world as an open system of vibrations, currents, temperatures, sounds and so forth meets the intelligence of Marey's model of abstracting experience as information. Both intuition and its abstraction combine to produce a version of agency that is relational rather than voluntary. The movement of the fly through the air depends on the resistance that the wings meet, forcing their efforts into a torsioned figure of eight rather than a simple ascending and descending motion. The fly in flight rides the currents that in turn produce its support.

Insect temporality

The dragonfly is slowly released and left to glide across the screen, the line of its form hanging at an angle. The slowing of the film is an adjustment that the human subject must make to partake in this insect world. Is the dragonfly less like itself when slowed and more like the human observer? Does slow motion adapt the creature to the observer, or the observer to the creature? In Bull's view, it is clear that the human must adapt in order to inhabit the interval that is otherwise lost. The first version of the film that was presented that night to the audience of the Royal Institution, Bull projected at standard speed, serving to underline the limited capacity of human sight as the insect all but disappeared in a blur across the screen. The second slowed projection released the audience into the exquisite presence of the dragonfly as a phenomenon. The third projection was a repeat of the second, so that the audience could experience again, yet fleetingly, the motion of the insect. In this demonstration, Bull crafts the cinema as a prosthesis for the human creature. For in this apparatus, the human body has a support, or a supplement, revealing of course that the human body was never *complete* in the first place.

The system that Bull presents to his audience and dutifully explains is neither the provenance of the fly nor the human viewers. It partakes of the miniature and the gigantic; the fly's microcosmos is enlarged to enormous proportions. In terms of looking into tiny worlds, this was not at all an isolated hobby in Bull's lifetime. 'When Alice took her size-shifting journey into the hole of the white rabbit,' writes Charlotte Sleigh, 'she was following a well-established path for late nineteenth century readers into the world of insects'.[13] Entomology was part of the century's passion for 'natural history', a history detected through the bodies, habits and behaviour of creatures, with Jean-Henri Fabre's *Souvenirs Entomologiques (1879–1907)* a widely translated popular text. This fascination with small things has implications for time, recalling Susan Stewart's interpretation of the 'other' time of the miniature. 'The reduction in scale which the miniature presents skews the time and space relations of the everyday lifeworld, and as an object consumed, the miniature finds its "use value" transformed into the infinite time of reverie.'[14] Whilst Stewart is speaking of commodities, the model of 'use' versus 'reverie' maps onto the insect world in terms of an entomological interest in 'worker' insects (in particular the bee and the ant), which in its cinematic rendition transforms into a wistful musing.

A fascination with scaling down was also part of an Edwardian obsession with childhood and time, as Carol Mavor writes, a sustaining of the time of childhood into 'adult' years.[15]

The proximity of humans and non-human creatures in literature and in cinematic experiments stirs up and disrupts conventional notions of time as uniform. In Lewis Carroll's work, time stretches, bends and speeds up. In Bull's cinema, time seems to have become slowed to the point of near suspension, the flies somnambulant. In the work of German biologist Jacob von Uexküll published in 1934, there is the story of a tick that, whilst being kept in a laboratory in Rostock without nutrition or stimulus, fell asleep for eighteen years and, when it was woken up, continued to function in the same manner as it had eighteen years previously. This extraordinary story raises a number of questions, of why the tick was left to sleep, of how the tick was monitored during the interval, and perhaps most of all, it raises the question of what is the time of the tick when time can seemingly be suspended. Can we think of this as a cinematic freeze-frame? But this is to get ahead of ourselves.

Divine insects

Bull allows us to anticipate the fly in flight over and over again, a repetitive pleasure. We first see it run at 'standard' speed, the standard a gesture to human perception. The second and third runs of the film are repetitions with a difference (as though repetition must always incur a difference of some sort, no matter how small). The film is projected at a far slower speed. The slowed fly on film is a different prospect altogether. The viewer no longer strives to catch the fleeting figure but is allowed to contemplate the possibility of the fly's passage. The viewer, like the fly, is preparing for take-off, is suspended and has fallen into a lull in this sink before the launch.

Walter Benjamin famously wrote of cinema in 'The Work of Art in the Age of Mechanical Reproduction' that 'Space expands in the close-up, slow motion extends movement.' It might appear that if space expands in the close-up, then what is expanded in slow motion is time, yet the enlargement is of a different order. Pursuing this theme, he continues:

> slow motion not only presents familiar qualities of movement but reveals in them entirely unknown ones which, far from looking like retarded rapid movements, give the effect of singularly gliding, floating, supernatural motions.[16]

What is expanded by slow motion is an apprehension of movement as a qualitatively diverse field. It is not simply a change of speed, but a revelation; slow motion reveals the micro-world of different forms or worlds within worlds. Benjamin, like Epstein in his passion for cinema's photogénie, found the world changed by this technological rendition of a second nature, a nature that is not available to the naked human eye. That Benjamin names this *supernatural* refers us both to nature and the beyond of nature. From the nineteenth century onwards, according to Marina Warner, the supernatural refers to a life or force beyond life, the spectral presence, a sign of life that is at once outside of our comprehension but within a human sensory register of visions, sounds, vibrations and so forth.[17] Yet wrapped within this term is the medieval meaning of *supernaturalis* as divine, above nature in the sense of that which is given by God. Cinematic slow motion, we might say in following Benjamin's train of thought, involves a transfer of the natural into the supernatural. The fly in slow motion appears as a figure of grace, defying or making use of gravity's pull in the lightest of choreographies. Whilst Benjamin famously declared the cinema a departure from the auratic culture of singular artworks, the slow-moving fly re-invokes an aura of kinds.

Whilst Benjamin's ambivalent and complex reading of cinema as a cultural technology is well documented, the question of whether cinema could expose the limits to a human-centred model of perception is less clear. According to Esther Leslie, Benjamin may be seen to anthropomorphize cinema, investing the apparatus with human-like agency in his attribution, for example, of an optical unconscious.[18] Yet, if the machine of cinema may be said to partake of human qualities, it in turn changes the *physis* of human perception.

Air

The fly inaugurates a cinema of anticipation that begins with stasis (the stillness of the creature on the perch) and has no end (the film runs out). It is pure middle, medium, media. The flight begins and continues. It is only the film stock that runs out, that cannot keep up with the energy of the fly that runs on and around the confinement in which it has been placed. The fly launches delicately. It first leans into the direction of the flight, its wings move forward in front of its head, the longer rear legs stretch to lift the back of the body which is now higher than the head, whilst the wings move back and forward three times. At lifting point the creature tilts so far forward that it seems that it must surely fall and that the round body must defy the injunction of the delicate wings to lift and be up. The legs push away from the platform, the body tilts, head down and then seems to pivot about the middle as its rear half drops, recovering its direction. With head up, it moves forward.

The fly in the laboratory of cinema is like a messenger or a translator, making connections within what Donna Haraway names 'shared conditions of work'.[19] Its passage here in this scenario creates connections between the human world, the world of the machine and the world of insects. Its flight pattern cannot in this instance be complex for it operates within the constraints of a cinematic laboratory, but its presence is nonetheless affecting. 'People and animals in labs', writes Haraway, 'are both subjects and objects to each other in ongoing intra-action'.[20] The fly, that is, trains the human in this experimental scene as much as it is determined in advance by the apparatus in which it finds itself. Placed upon this platform, the fly also moves between its figural presence in which it flies through stories, myths and legends, and its presence in the entomological register in which it is classified, pinned down and labelled. In classical mythology the fly is the creature that Zeus sends to bite the winged horse Pegasus, and in the Bible flies swarm as a plague. In the laboratory of cinema, flies are brought closer in order to be observed and annotated, and yet the entomological desire does not exhaust the fascination here, for cinema attempts also to be with (to accompany) the fly in flight.

Echoing the two principles strongly associated with cinema at its beginnings, the fly has a direct line to both magic and realism. In the moment of its launch, the fly becomes a magical entity, for it brings into play the substance of air. Air, as Steven Connor writes, is unlike the other elements in that it appears not to have form; to us it is invisible. 'Take away air', he writes, 'and the empty space you have left still seems to retain most of the qualities of air'. Air appears to be there and not there, and we cannot discern the difference: 'The air is unique among the elements in having this affinity with nothingness, in signifying the being of non-being, the matter of the immaterial.'[21] The fly rides the air and, in using the air, makes it manifest. In this it is magical in its transport, demonstrating the invisible matter that moves under its wings to lift it, which will, in other circumstances, fiercely resist it or push powerfully behind it.

A connection linking the fly to the practice of realism as an artistic style may also be found in Connor's work.[22] A story of the fly in renaissance times marks the style of realism in the work of the young Giotto, writes Connor, noting the reference in Giorgio Vasari's *Lives of the Painters* (1550).[23] Giotto, so the story goes, arrived at the studio of his instructor, Cimabue, to find a portrait on an easel, and finding himself with time on his hands, so to speak, he added a fly to the end of the nose. On his return, Cimabue tried to brush away the fly several times, mistaking it for the creature itself at which point, notes Connor, the skill of Giotto and the style of realism are recognized in a moment that takes the order of a revelation. Interestingly, the fly inverts expectation. When it is most ordinary, gliding the currents of air, it appears most magical, and when it is most fabricated on the surface of a painting, it appears most real.

Accident

In 1962, during the filming of a scene with Jeanne Moreau and Henri Serre, who are playing the characters in the film *Jules et Jim* (François Truffaut, 1962), a fly presents a third character to those present. Crawling on the pane of glass behind them, the fly moves towards Jeanne Moreau's open mouth just as she is about to be kissed. The fly perhaps extends the moment of anticipation before the kiss, something that takes our attention away from the path of the two mouths or holds them in suspense as we notice something else, some other movement in the frame. 'Truffaut caught the insect by surprise', writes Dudley Andrew, who then corrects the statement 'or, rather, the insect caught Truffaut by surprise'.[24] The fly moves upon the pane of glass saturated in sunlight, its body caught in silhouette just as the human creatures are silhouetted in the foreground. As it moves, time bends and enlarges to take in this other activity that reframes what is in the foreground. The accident recomposes cinema in the moment. Accident, from *ad* (to) *cadere* (fall). The fly and the actors fall together in this accident which exposes the non-essential characteristic of a thing.

Carriers of significance

In a chapter entitled '*Umwelt*' in Agamben's work, *The Open: Man and Animal*, the fly, the dragonfly and the bee are figured as creatures surrounding us on a summer's day. They inhabit the ether but 'do not move in the same world as the one in which we observe them, nor do they share with us – or with each other – the same time and the same space'.[25] This assertion is borrowed from Jacob von Uexküll (1864–1944) and his notion of the *Umwelt* (the environment) which is to lead Agamben to Heidegger's concept of the open.

The concept of the *Umwelt* developed by Uexküll is of an environment that functions as a closed unity within the wider environment of the *Umgebung*, the 'objective space in which we see a living being moving'.[26] The fly moves in an enclosure that is not spatially constrained, but rather selectively constructed from elements drawn from the *Umgebung*. The *Umwelt* is the environment formed of a number of elements that Uexküll calls marks, or carriers of significance. These are the features that attract the creature and that constitute its world. For the biologist, the task of the researcher is to identify these carriers of significance for each subject of investigation. Famously, Uexküll described the passionate attunement of the tick to its world, that is to the environment registered through its olfactory perception and temperature sensitivity. The environmental cues to which the tick responds amount to three: the odour of butyric acid that is carried in the sweat of mammals, liquid at the temperature of thirty-seven degrees (the temperature of the blood of mammals), and mammalian skin constituted by hair and blood vessels. The responses of the tick are to these particular carriers of significance, and through the example of the tick it is possible to comprehend how selective is each creature's engagement with the environment. Yet the model of the tick's attunement to its surroundings raises the question of how, if at all, different 'worlds' or *Unwelts* correspond. One of Uexküll's most referenced metaphors in this regard is that of a musical score. He notes that the markers and the sensory system of two separate creatures can be composed of heterogeneous elements, which nonetheless function together like notes within a symphony. The possible blindness of one creature to another does not detract from the overall composition. The unintended synchronization is a surprising feature of the non-communicating lives of insects, but the startling principle is the following claim: 'no animal can enter into relation with an object as such',[27] but only with its own carriers of significance.

In his explication of the non-relationality of the *Umwelt* in which the creatures that are 'blind' to each other's carriers nonetheless intra-connect, Agamben turns to an example of a spider and a fly. The spider is busy stitching its web, but with no knowledge of the specific details of the fly. Yet the web is created to the correct proportions, the threads being of appropriate distance and strength to detain the fly. And to capture the fly totally, the spider differentiates between the radial threads and the circular threads. The circular threads are covered in a viscous liquid to remain elastic enough to respond to the fly's weight and pressure and thereby retain the captive. The radial strands remain dry to enable the spider to move across them swiftly and to wind in its prey. According to Uexküll, the web is constructed without the fly in mind, and the fly is blind to its existence. Yet the two perceptual worlds of the spider and the fly, which are 'absolutely uncommunicating', meet here, in this fragile silk textile through a 'reciprocal blindness'.[28]

It remains to ask what features of this account bring us closer to an understanding of cinema, both as an anthropological machine that has historically manufactured a divisive distinction between humans and animals and also as a benign assemblage of heterogeneous elements without essence, but put into relation. In the first instance, we may find the framework of the *Umwelt* is one that may be transposed onto the cinematic screen and, as Anat Pick argues, its revelation of life-worlds to which we remain external.[29] We may, in the suggestive mode of Akira Lippit, find these worlds magnetic, so mesmerizing that the human world is by comparison (and through a reversal of Heidegger) a poor world.[30] Yet in the instance of the non-relation between systems, which leads Uexküll to conclude that 'no animal can enter into relation with an object as such', the task is more demanding. If we consider ourselves the animals of this formulation, we do not relate to things, but only signs.

Stones

In a series of lectures delivered at the University of Freiburg in 1929/30, entitled 'The Fundamental Concepts of Metaphysics: World, Finitude, Solitude', Heidegger considered the principles of first philosophy through a broad enquiry into the relationship between the animal and its environment. The thesis to be set out in part two of the lecture series famously is this: 'the stone is worldless (*weltlos*), the animal is poor in world (*weltarm*), man is world-forming (*weltbildend*)'.[31] Agamben reports that Heidegger quickly set aside the stone as a thing not capable of captivation in its environment, moving on to the second aspect, of the animal and the concept of poor of world. His analysis here was, as he acknowledged, influenced by the biological and zoological thinkers of his day, including amongst them Jacob von Uexküll. In *The Open*, Agamben draws attention to the extent to which Heidegger's ideas and terminology are borrowed from Uexküll.

When Heidegger speaks of the poverty of world in relation to the animal, he is working in great proximity to Uexküll's terms; speaking of the animal's disinhibitor, or carrier of significance, Heidegger uses the term *das Enthemmende*, and for the *Umwelt*, he uses the term *Enthemmungsring* (disinhibiting ring). The world of the animal is this enclosure of a disinhibiting ring, which in Uexküll is comprised of the small number of carriers that define its perceptual or sensory world. The extent of the world is limited to these markers, and all other elements and events remain outside of this ring, unable to affect the creature. Heidegger departs from Uexküll, according to Agamben, when he defines the animal's relation to the *Umwelt* as captivation (in German *Benommenheit,*).

This is no simple term. Heidegger plays on the relationship of *benommen* which means captivated, stunned, taken away or blocked, *eingenommen* meaning taken in or absorbed, and *benehman* meaning behaviour. The rich sense of the term 'captivation' is used to the full in the account that Heidegger gives of the animal's relation to its disinhibitor. Unable to take up a position over and against it, the animal is absorbed by its disinhibitor which has two significant implications. The animal 'can only behave insofar as it is captivated in its essence',[32] he states, describing a state of being in which the animal is responding only to that which captivates it, which in turn is defined by its predetermined sensory motor scheme. The second implication to be drawn from this path of thought is that the animal '*behaves within an environment but never within a world*'.[33] The nature of this distinction made by Heidegger is that in being captivated, the animal is unable to relate to something other than a carrier, a sign within its own creaturely system. The animal's behaviour is not constructed through encounter and contingency but motivated, and delimited, through its instinctual capacity. To underscore this point, Heidegger refers to an experiment described by Uexküll in which within laboratory conditions a bee is placed in front of a cup of honey. Once the creature starts to suck the substance, the experimenters cut away the insect's abdomen only to find that the bee continues sucking at the honey in spite of the fact that it simply pours out of the opening where its abdomen had been. For Heidegger, the experiment demonstrates that the bee is taken by the honey and that in being taken, the bee cannot take up any position over or against it. The bee, that is, does not apprehend the honey as honey, but responds instinctively to a carrier.

What Agamben does at this point is trace the steps through which Heidegger arrives at the conclusion that animals are poor of world. These include the proposition that beings are not closed off from animals, nor disclosed to them but animals have no relation to the potentiality of either of these positions. The animal does not apprehend beings, either in terms of itself as being or others. In what way then can the animal be said to be open? Through its relation of lack, precisely a poverty in world, the animal may be described as open. 'Being open in captivation', writes Heidegger, 'is an *essential possession* of the animal'.[34]

Muteness

Heidegger introduces the term 'open' with reference to the series of ten poems that make up Rainer Rilke's *Duino Elegies*, yet contra-Rilke. Rilke's verse uses the open to cleave a distinction between man and animal. In the eighth poem, the animal achieves ascendency through a reversal of the traditional hierarchy, whereby it is the animal that is 'seeing' in the open, and man whose eyes are turned inwards. The animal enters the open, man merely looks on; the animal in the open 'mutely, calmly is looking through and through us'.[35]

In Heidegger's address, the animal environment is conditioned by a paradoxical ontology, as the animal is neither open nor not open. It is spellbound by its disinhibitors but unable to recognize them as such which is why the animal inhabits an environment and the human animal a world. The reversal that Heidegger enacts in order to counter Rilke's turn is to posit a moment in which the animal, in becoming human, 'has awakened *from* its own captivation *to* its own captivation'.[36] What allows for this awakening is the capacity of the human to catch hold of its own being captivated, a capacity that is typically shielded from view but that arises under the conditions that Heidegger names as mood. Matthew Calarco writes: 'This is a topos that, while typically hidden, comes explicitly to the fore in certain moods such as anxiety and boredom, moods where the tight grip of captivation that binds a human being to other beings in its world gives way to the malaise and uncanniness of the indifference of other beings'.[37] This ontological difference from the non-human animal that gives rise to the definition of the human places *Dasein* in the arena of the 'not-open'; the animal remains captivated within the open whilst the human is defined by a suspension of that captivation in a state such as boredom. This relation to the open is dependent upon the human animal's ability 'to remember captivation an instant before the world disclosed itself'.[38]

Yet the ontological prioritizing that subtends Heidegger's account, where not only man rises over animal, and animal over stone, but also world soars above environment, is open to question. As Pick writes 'one could just as easily turn this evaluation round and ask whether man's ontological apprehension of the being of things is not infinitely poorer than the animal's embeddedness in her environment'.[39] There is a sense that Agamben's orientation is swayed momentarily by this thought when he writes, concerning Uexküll's tick and its relationship to the elements that form its environment, that this is 'an intense and passionate relationship the likes of which we might never find in the relations that bind man to his apparently much richer world'.[40] The tick's passion for its *Umwelt* is exclusive and, moreover, defining of its ontology. Agamben continues his trajectory, 'the tick *is* this relationship; she lives only in and for it'.[41] If the stone is readily disinvested and discarded by Heidegger for its inability to experience captivation by its environment, that is, if the relation of captivation is a measure of ontological differentiation and complexity, the tick in this regard exceeds the human animal. The tick is not only involved with its carriers of significance, but *is* that relation, which is also 'an exposure without disconcealment'.[42]

'But here everything becomes complicated', writes Agamben, for 'here' is the place where Heidegger's inclusionary-exclusionary logic becomes most evident. Man's capacity to awaken from captivation imposes the separation from the animal that remains captivated in the open. Agamben reads this scene as the necessary suspension of his *animalitas* that Heidegger posits as the ground of man's *humanitas*. This brings us to the place where the distinction between man and animal in Heidegger's thinking is exposed as a (re)production of the anthropological machine. Forever seeking the proper of the human (in Agamben's reading), Heidegger replays the animal as that which is external to a definition of the human, yet guaranteeing the excluded background against which the human may appear. Therefore the animal emerges as the excluded term, abandoned to the zone of indistinction whereby the terms of animal and man become used and reversed to support the ascendency of the latter over the former. He writes:

> Indeed, precisely because the human is already presupposed every time, the machine actually produces a kind of state of exception, a zone of indeterminacy in which the outside is nothing but the exclusion of an inside and the inside is in turn the inclusion of an outside.[43]

Given this critique, why does Agamben give Heidegger's animal-human philosophy such detailed treatment, patiently moving from 'The Fundamental Concepts of Metaphysics', to the Parmenides lectures and the text *An Introduction to Metaphysics*? Agamben's biographical history as a student of Heidegger leaves a mark on the text but does not answer the question. More convincingly it is because of Heidegger's reputation as one of the foremost critics of posthumanism that Agamben finds it necessary to establish that in the philosopher's work posthumanism, in fact, continues to rotate around the figure of man. So where does it all end?

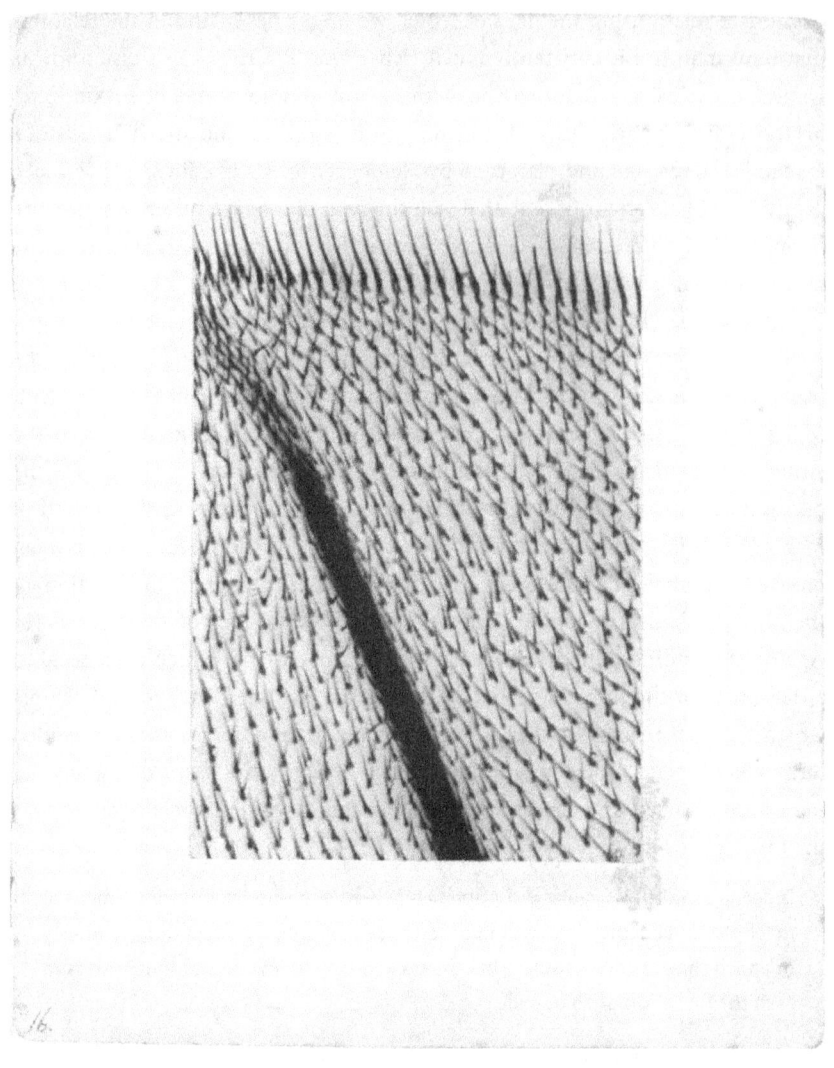

Hairs on wing of a fly, George Hook Rodman (1900)

Incubators

Agamben turns away from Heidegger and, in a familiar move, embraces Benjamin in the final instance. But this is not our ending. What commands attention here precisely through its critical neglect is the laboratory, the setting within which all of this activity takes place: not only Uexküll's working space, but that of Marey, Bull and Muybridge (to reserve until later amateur ethnologists and photographers). The laboratory functions as a site of experimentation in which the environment is radically pared down, its semiotically rich variation reduced and standardized to that of a blank canvas. It has been noted that Muybridge set up his studio as a laboratory, that is, as an environment stripped of its carriers of signification with only graph paper as a background. It is also the case that for a significant portion of his image sequences, Muybridge stripped his subjects of their apparel in order that they may appear in as simple a form as possible. Whilst 'locomotion' was the title collectivizing the sequences of photographs of human animals and non-human animals in motion, the project effectively established differences in accordance with Linnean principles of taxonomy. It is possible to read the sequences as an evolutionary table with the higher species performing more complex tasks until finally, as clothed beings, the human animals enter a new category that definitively breaks from the other species. Yet in placing humans at the centre of his studies in tandem with non-human animals, Muybridge subjects all species to the same treatment, an effectively levelling practice.

At about the same time that Muybridge set up his studio at the University of Pennsylvania, George Hook Rodman, a medical doctor based in London, built his own apparatus in order to photograph 'scientific subjects'. Rodman photographed flies, stick insects (*Bacillus Rossi*), spiders and fleas, as well as algae (*Diatoms*), plants and minerals outside of their 'natural' context, relocating them to a studio and presenting them against plain backgrounds. His apparatus consisted of a camera placed on a rotating table top in front of a magnifying lens that in turn amplified the subject or object before it. His detailed notes and diagram provide precise accounts of the strength of magnification, the source of light, length of exposure and the width of the aperture. Rodman, a member of the Röntgen Society and who suffered a skin condition as a result of practising radiography as a photographic art, exhibited these works at the Annual Exhibitions of the Royal Photographic Society between 1904 and 1915. Shown in the elaborately titled section, 'Scientific and Technical Photography and Its Application to Processes of Reproduction', Rodman's images of algae reveal intricate patterns like those of exquisite lace or wallpaper. His photograph of the hairs on the wing of a fly produces a planer landscape, an aerial view of a field with crops, or a fabric surfaced by dark threads. In the makeshift laboratory that Rodman sets up, the micro-worlds of creatures at the periphery or outside of the range of a human *Unwelt* captivate.

In the hybrid studio-laboratory, in which experiments of various sorts (photographic, filmic, ethnological) assume a momentum at the beginning of the twentieth century, the environment (in Heidegger's sense) is withdrawn and the animal and non-human animal are suspended without disinhibitors, without world. The situation resonates with Uexküll's observations about the sleeping tick in the laboratory in Rostock, a story that Agamben tells earlier in *The Open*.[44] Returning to this story some twenty pages later in his discussion of Heidegger, Agamben notes first of all that Heidegger could not have known of this experiment at the time of writing 'The Fundamental Concepts of Metaphysics', as Uexküll did not publish this finding until 1934. However, he speculates that had Heidegger heard of the laboratory tick, he might have enquired after it. For the endurance of the tick without environment is a puzzling fact for Heidegger's thesis: does it demonstrate that the creature is not after all fully dependent on its environment for its survival and may harbour another form of world inaccessible to the philosopher? Or does it suggest that the tick has some capacity to respond to its lack of captivation? Where the human awakens from his captivation to his captivation, the tick, in a state of withdrawal, goes to sleep. Agamben writes that within special circumstances, 'like those which man creates in laboratories', an animal may suspend its relation to its disinhibitors without either surrendering its animality or becoming human. This section of the text (*The Open*) ends with the following statement, the implications of which are then dropped: 'Perhaps the tick in the Rostock laboratory guards a mystery of the "simply living being", which neither Uexküll nor Heidegger was prepared to confront.'[45] The sleeping tick, we might say, falls into an interval, between recognizable states. This raises the question of what state the cinema-as-laboratory induces in the creatures that are brought there.

Teleporting the interval

Cinema demonstrates a certain reflexivity concerning laboratories and creatures. Another makeshift laboratory, this time in the home of a brilliant scientist Seth Brundle, is the site of an anxiety about insect-human cross-pollination in the film *The Fly*[46] (Cronenberg, 1986). The history of the story takes us recursively back to the post-war moment of *Playboy* magazine's zenith; the story written, by the British writer George Langelaan (who had acted as a spy during the Second World War), was first published in the magazine and was adapted into a film version the following year.

The story is an encounter between Seth Brundle, a scientist, and Veronica Quaife, a journalist. The journalist is taken back to the scientist's apartment in order to continue a conversation about a project that will change the course of life. Quaife is taken back to the warehouse that is Brundle's apartment. The fact that the apartment also operates as a laboratory does not unduly concern the journalist. Her interest is in the experiment that Brundle conducts for her benefit with his two teleportation pods (telepods). An inanimate object is teleported from one pod to another, creating a mode of instantaneous transmission that eliminates a temporal and spatial interval. Flushed with success, Brundle attempts the experiment with a living creature, a baboon. The baboon does not survive.

The scientist and the journalist begin a relationship and Brundle is inspired to reprogramme the telepod system, leading to the successful teleportation of a second baboon. Brundle is keen to share the news with Quaife, but her unavailability is read as a rejection. Consumed with feelings of rage and having consumed a large quantity of alcohol, the scientist strips naked and teleports himself from one pod to another. The experiment appears to have been a success, but Brundle begins to exhibit curious behavioural symptoms and shortly after his body begins to change. Referring to the records of the telepod, the scientist discovers that a fly was present during the teleportation process and that his DNA has been reconfigured with that of the insect. The infection of humanity does not end there as the journalist discovers that she is pregnant and dreams of giving birth to a giant maggot. The film concludes with the destruction of the hybrid human-insect.

The cross-species co-constitution that takes place in the film can only be envisaged as a horror story whose final play-out reinforces species purity, denying the stickiness of their muddled history.[47] The fly is once again notable for its furtive and unwanted presence that spoils rather more than the surface plane of representation. The fly, it seems, is forever in the human ointment.

Types of machine III: The anthropological machine

The anthropological machine manufactures divisions in the absence of demarcation, where ontological distinction is indeterminate. Underpinning Agamben's account is the sense of the terms 'human' and 'animal' as performative nouns whereby the human is brought into being through a performed exorcism of the animal iterated uniquely at each historical juncture. The anthropological machine works optically and is driven by a mirror relation between man and animal: 'It is an optical machine constructed as a series of mirrors in which man, looking at himself, sees his own image always already deformed in the features of an ape …,' writes Agamben towards the beginning of the text, continuing, '*Homos* is a constitutively "anthropomorphous" animal … who must recognise himself in a non-human in order to be human.'[48] The shifting figure of the human, lacking any essential quality to guarantee his humanity, depends on such an expulsion to secure his difference and status. At its most pronounced, the anthropological machine is productive of the state beyond the categories of the human and the animal, the zone of indistinction where bare life exists. And yet even whilst Agamben in *The Open* registers this critique of the anthropomorphic practice of becoming human, elsewhere in his work he is somewhat equivocal about the value of distinguishing man from the non-human animal. In the lecture on Debord most poignantly, he argues:

> Now man is an animal who is interested in images when he has recognised them as such. That's why he's interested in painting and why he goes to the cinema. A definition of man from our specific point of view could be that man is a movie-going animal. He is interested in images after he has recognised them as such.[49]

Cinema appears here as a critical component in the manufacture of a distinction between man and animal as the image displaces language as the standard bearer of humanity's defining quality. As a purely optical machine that produces virtual images, the cinema partakes in this drama of anthropological distinction.

Yet to attend to the cinema solely as image is to neglect the conditions of its emergence as an assemblage of heterogeneous elements, not least with animals and insects. Through a prolonged dalliance with animals and insects, an imaginary version of cinema as a sequence of ambulatory images takes form. In the studio-laboratory of Marey and later, Bull, in the campus studio of Muybridge, various men, women, insects and animals walk, crawl and climb. In the laboratory of

Uexküll, and in the home of George Hook Rodman, creatures are captured and bred. In all contexts, a complex, often makeshift apparatus is constructed around the subject in order for it to be seen and photographed. Through a series of studies, a momentum gathers (that will be named later as cinema), at first through still images fashioned staccato (but nonetheless suggestive of serial viewing). Later, in the studio of Lucien Bull, the question is not simply how motion is broken down and serialized, but rather, what is being produced in the series of relations between the human, the insect, and the arrangement of glass lenses, brass plates, screws, clasps, a wooden casket, a Leyden jar and a motor. Who or what is captivating whom, and who or what is doing the adapting?

Animal. Mineral.

The case against this proposition would find in favour of a set of experiments that involved humans and animals, potentially with a remit to stage human evolution in a direct line of ascent evidenced through motion studies. Yet, if anthropogenesis is an underlying discursive current, the everyday contingencies that characterize the laboratory effectively upend, subvert and redirect such a rational project. The laboratory (that of Muybridge, Marey, Bull, as well as the famous Black Maria enclosure of Edison and Dickson) in practice provided an effective focus for mixing categories of species and things, including the mineral properties of stones. Since the stone has been cardinally dismissed philosophically as a simple thing, it is instructive to recall part of its history in the processes of photographic image-making, beginning with the compound mixes of film stock developed through combinations of silver salts that turned black when exposed to sunlight, followed by silver-plated sheets of copper treated with iodine vapour followed by mercury vapour (the Dageurrotype). The collodian mix that supplanted this introduced properties of the animal, combining albumen (egg white) with gun cotton soaked in ether. Each of these chemical mixes effectively stabilized the image upon various surfaces, whilst a further set of mineral and vegetable elements were used to create the cellulose nitrate, acetate (short cotton fibres or wood pulp) and polyester (petroleum).

The laboratory offers a scene of experimentation involving materials, ideas and human and non-human actors that collectively contain a potentiality unknown and unknowable in advance. The insects that fizz and buzz in Lucien Bull's studio are lively in their suggestiveness. Their small forms, for which instruments are crafted and assembled in order to contain without injury, compel the project through a human desire to see the creature more clearly, more closely. There are years of labour undertaken in order to deliver the final films of insects in flight. Bull, the modest showman as well as the inventor and co-creaturely collaborator, sets up the projector. The audience watch, perhaps stupefied or spellbound, as the tiny creatures at the edges of everyday life appear here, centre stage and in gigantic form, on the screen. Their anatomy is visible as interlocking components that move unexpectedly, but assuredly into flight, a motion slowed so that their bodies move as though through water. Flying insects now move like fish, like Hieronymus Bosch's giant human-carrying fish operating like a gravity-defying aircraft mid-flight, yet curiously also like gigantic domestic animals swimming across the screen with a slow grace reserved for ballet. The experiments deliver this, the possibility of the close-up, of the radical shift in human perception brought about by this apparatus and these creatures. The close-up, a shot that is not introduced properly into human dramas until years later, but is to become the most mesmerizing feature of cinema, begins here. The history of cinema may be rewritten as this: the intense desire to watch an insect in flight.

That the body of the insect has been overwritten by the human face is exemplary of cinema's combinatory powers of abstraction and intensity.[50] The human face is enlarged and fetishized until, in Epstein's graphic description, it 'swells with an extraordinary intensity'.[51] The close-up parades the human face, putting it on display through its extraction from narrative and context, or for Deleuze, from spatio-temporal co-ordinates 'in order to call forth the pure affect as the expressed'.[52] Its potency has invoked an extended commentary from film theorists and philosophers enthralled by its stature and potency. Mary Ann Doane, in an essay that summatively gathers together the presence of the face as close-up in many theoretical accounts of cinema, demonstrates how this image illuminated, from the earliest discussion of its form, an understanding of the specificity of the medium. She writes, 'For Balázs, the close-up was "the technical condition of the art of film", Epstein described the close-up as the "soul of the cinema". Writing in 1916, Hugo Münsterberg naturalized the close-up, reducing its potential danger by aligning it with the mental act of attention.'[53] Perhaps most significant, in its emphatic appeal to texture through extreme proximity and expanded scale, the close-up of the face presents the image qua image. 'The image becomes, once more, an image rather than a threshold onto a world,' writes Doane, 'Or rather, the world is reduced to this face, this object.'[54] Cinema also is reduced to this face, this object, in a theoretical account that makes the face integral to an understanding of the medium and sequesters its history for humanity.

The passion for insects evident in the first decade of the twentieth century can be regarded as an essential component in an account of cinema as an aggregate form. Bull's films inspired film producers such as Charles Urban who had a passion for scientific, educational and documentary films. In 1903, he presented at the Alhambra Theatre in London a show entitled 'The Unseen World', which ran for nine months. Its trope was microcinematography, screening works such as those by the filmmaker Francis Martin Duncan, whose film about cheese mites was fantastically popular. Urban also worked with the filmmaker Percy Smith. Smith constructed his own laboratory replete with miniature furniture to which he delicately attached insects including flies, blue bottles, ants and fleas. Famously, he presented them with objects, such as matchsticks, which the insects examined, in the process seeming to juggle, balance and play with the things. First screened in 1908, the films caused furore as the public demanded to know whether the films were tricks and whether the creatures had been harmed during their making.[55]

Worlds

If insects present part of the ex-centric history of cinema, and as such are occluded and suspended as an outside, they nonetheless reside with us as a pressure pressing in on the contemporary. In foregrounding the pressure of the thing that cannot be made intelligible from the inside, the machine that produces the distinction between inside and outside begins to falter. The outside begins to look like the inside, the cinema takes on the appearance of a laboratory, the human begins to resemble the insect and we may ask again what state the cinema-as-laboratory induces in the creatures that are brought there.

If the philosophical legacy inherited from Heiddeger marks the animal as poor in world and the human as world forming, the cinema readily bends to this description as exemplary of the world-forming capacity of man. Troubling the exemplary instance of cinema however is the spectre of cinema as a laboratory through which the human was attuned to an environment. The cinema in this instance operates a privation, removing sensory effects as it becomes an institution in the second decade of the twentieth century. Sounds, smells and lighting are excluded from the scene of projection, fixed seating is installed and the experience is standardized across Europe and America. The experience of watching moving images becomes, that is, the suspension of carriers of significance and a version of laboratory conditions. Facing uniformly forward, the audience attends to the screen. The experience may be one of passionate attachment, like the bee to honey, and it is notable that descriptions of cinema audiences in this decade utilize terms of creaturely life: audiences are constituted as a mass that 'swarms'. A social anxiety accompanies the idea that audiences are passionately attached to images rather than world-forming creatures, that the cinema may be a laboratory of sorts and that the distinction between the fly and the viewer may not be so clear.

The concealedness of cinema

Agamben turns away from Heidegger and, in a familiar move, embraces Benjamin in the final instance. At the end of *The Open*, Benjamin's concept of the 'saved night' (*Die gerettete Nacht*) saves Agamben from the ravages of the Heideggerian anthropological machine. In a letter to his friend and theologian, Florens Christian Rang, dated 9 December 1923, Benjamin speculated on the relation of nature and man (history): nature (including ideas) is a world of closedness and of the night, in contrast to history, the world of light and revelation. Where the anthropological machine attends to a distinction between man and nature in order to produce the human, or, in an inverse figuration the 'savage' animality of nature is seen to dominate man, the two terms constitute *humanitas* through their separation. The anthropological machine is the ongoing production of a conflict between the terms (man and animal, history and nature) that excludes one-half of the binary in the production of man. In contrast, what occurs in the saved night is closer to Benjamin's dialectic at a standstill. '[W]hat is decisive here', writes Agamben, 'is only the "between", the interval or ... their immediate constellation in a non-coincidence'.[56] In a state of suspension of man and animal, history and nature, something 'for which perhaps we have no name'[57] takes up the place between, in the interval, which is the saved night. The thing for which we have no name is also the thing of Bull's laboratory and the black leader of celluloid cinema, 'the interval between two pictures' that leaves 'no record at all of its occurrence'.[58] The saved night 'concerns the lost and the forgotten as such';[59] it is a relation to something unsavable.[60]

The open is a figurative term that shifts throughout the text as one of the terms through which world and being are invoked. But most explicitly towards the end it refers to a dialectic of revelation and concealment and it is here that the threads of insects, stones and machines converge and, if we are patient, where we move outside of a concern with *being*. The animal, if we recall, is open and not open. It is open to the thing that compels it despite the thing (disinhibitor) remaining inaccessible (opaque) to it, and simultaneously, the animal is not open as it remains spellbound in this relation of captivation. In Heidegger's terms, the rendition of the animal thus is the backdrop against which man's relation to a world-that-is-open may be revealed (and effectively his humanity produced). But if we step aside from the anthropological machine and tend to the machines of early cinema, we can for an instant inhabit the space of the interval. An interval before we became predisposed to melodrama, and before

Benjamin's bored spectator sat ruminating in the auditorium, it is a space in which a human passion for the creature is in play. The (human) experimenter is captivated by the creature to the extent that he creates a whole apparatus through which this captivation may be fed. In Lucien Bull's study, the human and the animal fold into one another. His machines and films were not the only ones of course, but they occupy a special space of creaturely non-distinction in the early twentieth century where art and science, or cinema and documentation, have not (yet) been set on their separate tracks. Later on, the fly is brushed aside, dismissed, a nuisance to the controlled environment of the sterile film set. But for a brief interval, the screen opens onto an environment that is not a revelation of human interiority, but offers us up to the pure relation of being captivated, albeit in a laboratory of our own making.

Notes

1 Michel Serres and Bruno Latour, *Conversations on Science, Culture and Time*, trans. Roxanne Lapidus (Ann Arbor: University of Michigan Press, 1995), 64–65.
2 The Royal Institution was founded in March 1799 with the aim of teaching science and introducing new technologies to a general audience.
3 Lucien Bull unpublished paper 'Recent Developments in High-Speed Cinematography', presented on 30 May 1924, to the Royal Institution of Great Britain: Royal Institution Library Holdings 245 (1924–5), 2.
4 Ibid., 2.
5 Ibid., 3.
6 Ibid., 1.
7 Etienne-Jules Marey, *La Machine Animale*, Book Three (New York 549 and 551 Broadway: Appleton and Company, 1873), 183.
8 Jussi Parikka, *Insect Media: An Archaeology of Animals and Technology* (Minneapolis and London: University of Minnesota Press, 2010), 14.
9 Marey, *La Machine Animale*, 185.
10 Ibid., 181.
11 Parikka, *Insect Media*, 13.
12 Ibid., 21.
13 Charlotte Sleigh, 'The Insects', in *Secrets of Nature*, ed. Tim Boon (London: BFI, 2011).
14 Susan Stewart, *On Longing* (Durham and London: Duke University Press, 1993), 65.

15 Carol Mavor, *Reading Boyishly: Roland Barthes, J. M. Barrie, Jacques Henri Lartigue, Marcel Proust, and D. W. Winnicott* (Durham and London: Duke University Press, 2007).
16 Walter Benjamin, 'The Work of Art in the Age of Mechanical Reproduction', in *Illuminations*, edition 1999, trans. Harry Zorn, ed. and introduced by Hannah Arendt (London: Pimlico, 1936), 229–230.
17 Marina Warner, *Phantasmagoria: Spirit Visions, Metaphors, and Media into the Twenty-First Century* (Oxford and New York: Oxford University Press, 2006).
18 Esther Leslie, *Walter Benjamin: Overpowering Conformism* (London: Pluto Press, 2000), 156.
19 Donna Haraway, *When Species Meet* (Minneapolis and London: University of Minnesota Press, 2008), 71.
20 Haraway goes on to describe intra-action thus: 'The parties in intra-action do not admit of preset taxonomic calculation; responders are themselves co-constituted in the responding and do not have in advance a proper checklist of properties.' *When Species Meet*, 71.
21 Steven Connor, *The Matter of Air: Science and the Art of the Ethereal* (London: Reaktion Books, 2010), 31.
22 http://www.stevenconnor.com/flysight, accessed 17 March 2014.
23 Giorgio Vasari, *Lives of the Painters, Sculptors and Architects*, trans. Gaston du C. de Vere, ed. David Ekserdjian. 2 Vols (London: David Campbell, 1996). Connor also notes in passing that flies have a long association with painters as creatures that mark an outside to representation:
> The fact that representations of flies are often to be found in the vicinity of artistic signatures, especially those which have the *trompe l'oeil* form of the rolled or torn strip of manuscript, seems to heighten the association between the fly and the making, even the maker, rather than the meaning, of the work of art. The fly that appears in the foreground of the New York Metropolitan Museum's *Portrait of a Carthusian* by Petrus Christus (1446) perches on top of the *trompe l'oeil* wooden frame, on which is carved 'Petrus Xdi Me Fecit', perhaps hinting that the fly aspires to be the referent of 'me' rather than the painting.

In the essay 'Flysight', http://www.stevenconnor.com/flysight.
24 Dudley Andrew, *What Cinema Is!* (Malden, MA and Oxford: Wiley-Blackwell, 2010), 19.
25 Giorgio Agamben, *The Open: Man and Animal*, trans. Kevin Attell (Stanford, CA: Stanford University Press, 2002/2004), 40.
26 Ibid., 40.
27 Ibid., 42.

28　Ibid.
29　Anat Pick, *Creaturely Poetics: Animality and Vulnerability in Literature and Film* (New York: Colombia University Press, 2011).
30　Akira Lippit, *Electric Animal: Toward a Rhetoric of Wildlife* (Minneapolis and London: University of Minnesota Press, 2000).
31　Martin Heidegger, *The Fundamental Concepts of Metaphysics: World, Finitude, Solitude*, trans. William McNeill and Nicholas Walker (Bloomington: Indiana University Press, 1995), 177.
32　Ibid., 238–239, cited in Agamben, *The Open*, 52.
33　Agamben, *The Open*, 52.
34　Ibid., 55.
35　Rainer Rilke, *Duino Elegies*, trans. Edward Snow (Berkeley, California: North Point Press, 2001), 79.
36　Agamben, *The Open*, 70.
37　Matthew Calarco, *Zoographies: the Question of the Animal from Heidegger to Derrida* (New York: Columbia University Press, 2008), 99.
38　Agamben, *The Open*, 90.
39　Anat Pick, 'Review: Agamben's *The Open*', *Bryn Mawr Review of Comparative Literature*, 5:2 (Winter 2006): 45–46.
40　Agamben, *The Open*, 47.
41　Ibid.
42　Ibid., 62.
43　Ibid., 37.
44　Agamben first tells the tale of the sleeping tick on page 47 of *The Open* and returns to it in relation to Heidegger on page 70.
45　Agamben, *The Open*, 70.
46　*The Fly* (Kurt Neumann, 20th Century Fox: 1958) was followed by two sequels, *Return of the Fly* (Edward Bernds, 20th Century Fox: 1959) and *Curse of the Fly* (Don Sharp, 20th Century Fox: 1965). The first film was remade by David Cronenberg: *The Fly* (David Cronenberg, 20th Century Fox: 1986). George Langelaan's short story 'The Fly', originally published in *Playboy magazine* in 1957, was the inspiration for the films. The story continues to resonate; it was adapted by Howard Shaw into an opera in 2008.
47　This phrase is a version of Donna Haraway's description of cross-species becoming in *When Species Meet*, 42.
48　Agamben, *The Open*, 26–27.
49　Giorgio Agamben, 'Difference and Repetition: on Guy Debord's Films', in *Guy Debord and the Situationist International*, ed. Thomas McDonough (Cambridge, MA and Cambridge, UK: an October Book for MIT Press, 2002), 314.

50 The question of whether film can constitute a language has a long and vexed history within Film Studies. Christian Metz, writing in the 1970s on the relation of cinema to language, insisted that there is no equivalent unit within cinema to the word in language. The close-up is merely a tone of expression, a forceful pointing towards a thing rather than a term in itself. See Christian Metz, *Film Language: A Semiotics of the Cinema*, trans. Michael Taylor (New York: Oxford University Press, 1974).
51 Jean Epstein, *Magnification and Other Writings*, trans. Stuart Liebman. 3 October (1977): 9–25: 9.
52 Gilles Deleuze, *Cinema 1: The Movement Image*, trans. Hugh Tomlinson and Barbara Habberjam (London: Athlone Press, 1983), 96.
53 Mary Ann Doane, 'Scale and Detail in the Cinema', *Differences: A Journal of Feminist Cultural Studies* 14:3 (2003): 89–111: 92.
54 Mary Ann Doane, 'The Close-up', *Differences: A Journal of Feminist Cultural Studies*, 14:3 (2003): 92.
55 Jenny Hammerton, BFI *Screenonline*, 'The Strength and Agility of Insects' (1911), accessed 5 May 2014.
56 Agamben, *The Open*, 83.
57 Ibid.
58 Bull, 'Recent Developments in High-speed Cinematography', 2.
59 Agamben, *The Open*, 82.
60 The saved night occurs again at the end of the essay 'Genius', in *Profanations*, at a similar apex of a loss of mystery and an ability finally to live an earthly life. It is a reference to Prospero's injunction to Ariel to 'be free'. Agamben says about this: 'This is exhausted and suspended time, the sudden penumbra in which we begin to forget about Genius; this is night fulfilled' ('Genius' 18).

5

When the Assistants Profane Cinema

Do it yourself: Instruction or description?

When André Bazin writes in the mid-twentieth century about the origins of cinema, he sees a history in which the idea of cinema was set against its material form. The idea of cinema, he argues, existed in people's minds for centuries as a platonic form waiting for its moment of emergence. Writing against a simplistic tale of technological determinism, Bazin reverses the situation, imagining that technology actively delayed this venture, a case of an 'obstinate resistance of matter to ideas'.[1] Matter is nonetheless granted some agency as a resisting form, but what is more striking than this dismissal of materials as a driving force is his disregard for cinema's 'begetters':

> Its begetters are in no sense savants, except for Marey, but it is significant that he was only interested in analyzing movement and not in reconstructing it. Even Edison is basically only a do-it-yourself man of genius, a giant of the *concours Lépine*. Niepce, Muybridge, Leroy, Joly, Demeny, and even Louis Lumière himself, are all monomaniacs, men driven by an impulse, do-it-yourself men or at best ingenious industrialists.[2]

The repetition of the term 'do-it-yourself' drives home the point that cinema, for Bazin, was born in the hands of amateurs. Whilst this is useful for his argument that the idea long preceded the actual realization of cinema in the hands of these 'in no sense savants', Bazin also introduces the concept of amateurism to the scene of cinema's becoming. The term 'amateur' designates a space external to the legitimate sphere of work and productivity, where play, extemporization and experiment are the unofficial rule. Contingency governs the modality of amateur production, or rather the amateur one might say is open to the possibilities presented by chance and accident. Amateur productivity short-circuits the direct line attributed to human agency through an immersion in worlds of materials and things. For all of these reasons, the amateur is a discredited figure in the histories of making.

In an interview with Leland de la Durantaye, Agamben is asked to comment on why he writes about what are often considered unserious and discredited things. He has this to say:

> Walter Benjamin once wrote that the Messianic Kingdom can be present in the world only in forms that appear low and discredited. For this reason in his great book on Paris he concentrated his attention on things that historians had hitherto neglected: the scraps and refuse of culture. For me this is a fundamental methodological principle. What is more, we live in a society where the most beautiful things can only exist in distorted form, can be expressed only through parody.[3]

More than simply finding value in what is discarded and discredited by a culture, the work of parody takes us further into the methodological principles of an archaeology that hones its practice in unexpected and neglected places. Its tools describe a repertoire of devious practices that lead, through acts of doubling and copying, to a place on the border of legitimate production. In this space we find the amateur who sets to work in the downstairs parlour taking apart the machine to see how it operates or the assistant who muses and meditates in boredom outside of the offices of power. The amateur is kindred spirit to a figure who recurs in Agamben's texts and who we can trace recursively through the writings of Walter Benjamin to the stories of Franz Kafka: the assistant. Amateurs, assistants, inventors and artists people this chapter as indeed they do in Siegfried Zielinski's accounts of media history, whose proximate entanglements with material forms can lead to ruin as well as creation.[4] They are to be found off to one side of any official version, occupying a space external to the factory, the film production studio, the great artist's studio and the office; they exist in spaces that are thresholds such as hallways, cloakrooms, corridors and closets and often find themselves to be lacking visibility. Despite their determined or lack-lustre efforts (their activity subsumes both practices), they are regularly overlooked. Each has the capacity to work alongside the main narrative, absorbed in the activity of the moment with little regard for ends that qualify means, and in this they are like children, for they suspend instrumental reason and take back into common use what has been separated into the sphere of professional production.

Amateurs, assistants, inventors and artists have a particular relationship to the materiality of forms, to the opulence of matter that comes before the idea, or more accurately, they co-create the idea in its multiple forms of suggestiveness. The matter to which these figures are attracted is not simply the materials of the scrap heap, however heterogeneous they may be. These figures take from the sphere of officially sanctioned or sacred things to decompose them and in this they perform acts of profanation. This chapter unearths the practices, objects, materials and figures through which a profane cinema may be glimpsed. This troop of peripheral figures leads us through digression and detour to the place of the para-text, the parody or the parable, to the side of or a commentary upon a principle text. The mimetic principle of parody is instructive here, for through the act of copying or rehearsing, the contours of the 'original' are thrown into relief. The principle text in question here is of course a cinema that has become a sacred, spectacularized religion of commodified bodies and desires whose relationship to materiality is buried. This chapter draws on three ideas from Agamben's work in order to draw out and make intelligible the complex nexus of matter and people that constitute cinema at its various moments of inception. First, the concept of the assistant as the invisible yet highly productive figure who mediates worlds, and second, the idea of parody as a threshold between worlds 'stubbornly suspended between reality and fiction, between word and thing'.[5] The third concept is profanation, a term that comes to describe a principle of transgressing official borders and deactivating the mechanism that separates cinema from its form and, in Agamben's work more broadly, life from its form of life.

Lively matter

The film *The Way Things Go* (*Der Lauf der Dinge*, 1987, Peter Fischli and David Weiss) opens with a shot close-up on the surface of a moving piece of plastic. Something dark grey turns anticlockwise and as the camera retreats from this object, we are able to see that it is a rubbish sack, tied at the top and suspended in the air by a piece of string. As the bag turns, it simultaneously lengthens the piece of string, thereby lowering the sack almost indiscernibly until we see a car tyre beneath it. The space between the bottom of the sack and tyre contracts and becomes narrower, and eventually, after almost sixty seconds and many twists, a lower corner of the bag brushes against the top of the tyre. On the eleventh rotation, the rubbish sack is low enough for its weight to properly make contact with the tyre and with a scuff against its surface, the object is propelled forward, down an incline and into the path of a trestle table. The tyre rolls beneath the table to brush up against a barrel which rolls under a table, lifting its surface to send a tin rolling along the top of what is in fact a plank. As the tin rolls, it shifts the centre of gravity and one end of the plank lifts into the air whilst the other end swings under the table and smacks into the stationary tyre. This is once again sent on its way, heading into another scene of seemingly haphazard but actually meticulously planned encounters of objects, materials and chemicals.

The suspenseful nature of the opening minute of the film as the rubbish sack slowly descends as it unfurls is also the descent of the viewer into the realization that this is a film about things and the properties and interactions of things that roll, brush, collapse, rub and ignite. These are the characters and this is what they get up to. When the rubbish sack makes contact with the tyre, and the tyre with the barrel, we begin to figure that the characters here form a paradigm; routinely discarded objects from quotidian life create a group, a collection from what is usually collected and taken away by a refuse service, after which we are absolved of responsibility for its future life. The relationship between each of the singular items is in the process of being demonstrated in spectacular display. In the second minute, and as the camera pulls back, the wider shot reveals the *mise en scène* as a concrete enclosure, perhaps a garage or warehouse, featuring a run of pipes along the wall. The colour palette is predominantly muted greys. But what is the most surprising disclosure, and the register of this film is discrete disclosure rather than revelation, is that the interaction of these various objects in this particular arrangement is spellbinding. It continues to be so for the film's duration of thirty minutes.

The film could be read as either a piece of cinema or an artwork. As the former, it could be read as parody. It is a film that seems to belong to another dimension, another sphere that in all appearances is like ours, but for a few minor differences and distortions. It is not a satire, nor a pastiche, but it enters the register of these literary forms. The term 'parody' carries its root from the ancient Greek παρά, or *pará*, meaning beside, next to, near, from, against and also contrary to. A modern definition of 'parody' (modern in the context of late European culture of the sixteenth century) may be found in the work of Giulio Cesare Scagligero, who wrote in his book *Poetics*: 'Just as Satire derives from Tragedy and Mime from Comedy, so does Parody derive from Rhapsody ... Alongside and in addition to the serious argument, [Parody] inserted other ridiculous things.'[6] In Agamben's essay on parody, he proposes (following Scaligero) that there are two canonical features to parody. The first is the dependence of a parody on an existing model that may be changed from the register of serious to comic. The second feature is a parody that maintains the formal elements of a work to which 'new and incongruous' contents are inserted. What then might be the rhapsodic form of cinema that is parodied by *The Way Things Go*, and is it possible to deduce from the film itself the cinematic model that it parodies?

The Way Things Go conforms to the principles of events unfolding over a duration, which may or may not take place in real time. A sequence of events begins with an inciting incident of sorts, the setting into motion of one of the elements and its collision with another. This acts to progress a movement that we may loosely call a narrative as one thing follows another. The characters respond variously to the inciting factor and their complex interactions create the twists and knots of the story. The film breaks these elements down into a number of scenes or sequences that are later stitched together. These are the principles of screenwriting established early on in the industrial system of film production and at its peak perhaps in the studio system of the mid-twentieth century. Let us take Charles Vidor's film of 1954, *Rhapsody*,[7] as a fine example of the structure of narrative melodramatic cinema in a film that is at the top of its game. Starring Elizabeth Taylor and Vittorio Gassman, the film is adapted from the novel *Maurice Guest* (1908, Ethel Richardson), in which a wealthy woman follows the object of her love, a musician, to a conservatoire in Switzerland. In the new location she becomes the object of another's desire, culminating in her forced choice between a husband who loves her more than his music and one who loves his music more than her. The drama plays out through a series of inversions and doubles (her pursuit of a lover whose focus lies elsewhere is a theme repeated), whose repetitious logic recalls the interplay of the objects in the other film. We could say that *Rhapsody* shares something else with the Fischli and Weiss film; in these encounters, the push and pull of desire acts like magnetic forces operating below the radar of language, as though the chemical properties of characters are at stake.

In *The Way Things Go*, the structure of drama is reproduced in the arrangement of a series of sequences that act like scenes. In place of characters, there are objects, chemical liquids and elements that each bring a singular quality to the encounter and therefore produce drama. In certain scenes, objects or fluids blend and infuse, literally setting one another alight. In another encounter, water pours from one thing onto another with the force of a channel whose flow propels the second object into motion. The film takes the model of drama produced through the impact of different identities and inserts new, ridiculous and somewhat incongruous components. The ensemble of characters includes dustbins, tyres, ladders, bottles, tin cans, planks of wood, plastic bags, candles, balloons and various liquids and foams. With some of the elements, their potential to interact in a given situation is evident, whilst for others, such as the liquids and foams, the possibilities are not marked in advance; the viewer must be patient. The handheld camera tracks along the line of interactions, its proximity to or distance from the scene about to take place anticipating what is about to take place; our perspective is set up and we need only attend to the movement of a thing and wait.

The linear drive of narrative cinema, and its complicating devices of plot, is parodied through two means: in its citation of causality, the principle is overstated, made grotesque, and second, the principle actors are ostensibly, perhaps perversely, without agency. There is something spellbinding to this world of things, something of the animistic about objects 'magically' moving. They reveal through reflex the affiliations between diverse matter and, simultaneously, the secret singular identity of each thing. The title invites the viewer to approach all of this activity casually, as though the drama that ensues is the result of an unstoppable course of action, said with a shrug *that's the way things go*. Yet in earnest, the labour of calculating the impact of objects, weighing things, experimenting with explosive chemicals and rehearsing the many scenes of collision suggests, on the contrary, that this is a highly constructed event. It is a gag that might be told about many high-budget films where continuity of action provides an appearance of simplicity that belies the meticulously detailed work that brought it into being. This film, the film of Fischli and Weiss, in fact lightly disguises the many edits that were necessary when the action misfired and contingencies intervened, yet they are there. The cuts and joins are markers of the unruliness of objects, which, despite extensive planning on the part of the directors, threaten to upend the project and always leave a trace. Weiss likens the preparation and rehearsals for the film to the work of training animals for a circus act.[8]

Assistants assisting

David Weiss and Peter Fischli are two figures who might have stepped from the novels of Franz Kafka or more likely Robert Walser, figures belonging to the category that Agamben terms 'Assistants'. There is something ambulatory about the way that the artists set about their work, which has a quality of playfulness and even childishness. *The Way Things Go* is an assistant's parody of what, over time, has sedimented into an apparently mature cinema of the dramatic. But their film achieves more than an inversion of the lofty ambitions of a melodramatic cinema; more pertinently and profoundly, it reveals a cinema beside the other, created for a different purpose, or indeed a cinema of the waiting room, lacking what would elsewhere be recognized as purposeful. For *The Way Things Go* demonstrates a cinema of digression that entices as it waylays us into the path of its story, as though we were travellers not quite trusting where the small yet friendly stranger is taking us. In this sense, the artists belong to the paradigm of assistants whose task is never quite clear, whose bearing appears to reside in a brilliance that is often idle, but who seem to know or retain something that we are lacking.

In an essay published in the collection *Profanations*, there is a celebration of the various and paradoxical characteristics of these creatures that appear in fairy tales and in the works of Kafka and Benjamin. Assistants regularly feature in children's stories as helpers, sometimes as animals, or as genies in bottles or inanimate things, beholding magical powers that open doors onto a new vista or reveal an escape route. Assistants are helpers, but 'help seems to be the last thing that they are able to give'[9] in any direct way. They indulge in childish games, they can be pests, idle company and sometimes lecherous, and yet also they are intelligent and gifted, supple of limb, mathematically bold, and most appealing of all, they act with an 'unforeseen grace'.[10] And yet, he writes, by the end of the story, these 'helpers' are discreetly forgotten. These assistants are, in Agamben's account, in-between figures, translators of other languages and mediators between worlds. Assistants undo what needs to be undone, and in this they retain a relation to play and its reconfiguration of ritual time and mythical telling. In the other direction, and in the end, they bring forth the possibility of a messianic redemption, for it is only in distorted things of this world that the possibility of hope resides. This proposition is of course deeply inflected by Benjamin's figure of the little hunchback, a diminutive creature whose chin rests on his chest, who is between Kafka's assistants and the Sufi *wazir* (helpers to the messiah). The key to Agamben's definition we find in the recursive movement of Benjamin's reading of Kafka's assistants.

In the essay 'Franz Kafka: on the Tenth Anniversary of his Death' (1934), Benjamin writes a memorial of the writer through the structure of four subheadings which it is worth laying out in some detail here. Written in a deceptively plain, free-associative style where the correspondences are permitted to emerge from the writing itself, Benjamin presents four stories, starting with

'Potemkin', and followed by 'A Childhood Photograph', 'The Little Hunchback' and 'Sancho Panza'. Each story (or section) entails a scenario beholding an assistant or many assistants. In the first, Benjamin draws on a story not by Kafka but by Alexandr Pushkin, a tale of Prince Grigori Potemkin, chief in the Russian army and a senior figure in the court of Catherine the Great, to whom he was also a lover. Potemkin, the story runs, who was given to fits of depression and extreme melancholia, once retired from court for weeks, failing to sign official documents and frustrating the business of congress. Overhearing the problem, a minor official in the court by the name of Shuvalkin took it into his hands to approach the general, and to the stupor of those around him, took the papers into his chamber to be signed. Potemkin duly signed each paper and the junior official returned triumphant. Yet when the more senior assistants checked the papers, the signature read 'Shuvalkin' on every paper.

In the second scenario, the assistants are the actors of the Oklahoma Theatre whose fate it is to perform a series of gestures for which a code has not yet been found. In the third, the hunchback, kin to the assistants, features as a portent of some kind, whose presence is attached to the clumsy deeds of children. The last section features the rotund assistant to Don Quixote, Sancho Panza. Whilst diverse as a set, the four parts attain a sense of balance as pairs: the protracted life of waiting in the first is countered by the gestural energy of the actors in the second, whilst the menacing figure of the hunchback in the third meets the paunchy and familiar figure of Sancho Panza of the fourth, 'a sedate fool and clumsy assistant'[11] who nonetheless removes the burden from his back and enjoys a 'profitable entertainment' to the end. These various facets of the assistant demonstrate that the in-between place that they inhabit can be a site of sinister affect (the failure of Shuvalkin, the deformity of the hunchback) or joyous revelry and nonconformity (the theatre performers, Sancho Panza).

For Benjamin, Kafka's assistants are those who have escaped the family circle, and the family circle is a descendent of corrupt and corrupting institutions that may yet cast their shadow over those in its antechambers. There is a direct connection between the family and Kafka's world of officials. The correspondence, carried by the father, involves 'filth', a literal pollution that extends from one sphere into the other, as 'dullness, decay and dirt'. Benjamin continues: 'The father's uniform is stained all over; his underwear is dirty. Filth is the element of the officials.'[12] The offices that administrate matters of the modern world in as obtuse a manner as possible are peopled by men who are lost to themselves; they are the falling and fallen, who nonetheless hold power.[13] Significantly the assistants of each sphere hover at the edges, but do not cross the threshold into familial and institutional circles, remaining untainted by 'filth'. Expelled from, or never in the familial frame in the first place, assistants do not belong to and will not inherit from the patrimonial line. And what the assistants have to offer is not of value there. Their minor position and relative powerlessness however registers inversely for Benjamin. 'It is for them and their kind', he writes, 'the unfinished and the bunglers, that there is hope'.[14] Of their many attributes, it is as clumsy fools that they are linked to redemption, and in this they are related to the figure that has personal resonance for Benjamin: the hunchback.

Benjamin names the hunchback cryptically the 'prototype of distortion'. But the hunchback is sketchily drawn, an elliptical reference in the essay on Kafka; it is in another text that we find a fuller account, towards the end of the autobiographical fragments, *A Berlin Childhood*,[15] where the crepuscular figure appears in the final pages. The reminiscence runs thus that whenever one of the countless little catastrophes of childhood had taken place,[16] Benjamin's mother would say, as was the tradition in Germany, 'Mr Bungle sends his regards.' The sinister and yet infantile nature of the character of Mr Bungle holds in tension the dualism that Benjamin traces between this world and another, between profane time and messianic time. For, if Mr Bungle spells the disaster of the accidental, the dismal effects of contingency and failure, he also signals another moment when these features would be redeemed. The hunchback's physical distortion signals that, within profane time and within this world, he is 'the representative of the forgotten',[17] a sign of all that has been cancelled out and pushed into oblivion. His presence stands as an inversion of the profane, wherein the messianic resides in all that is cast aside as shameful or defunct, and where everything 'that now appears debased and worthless to us, is the currency we will have to redeem on the last day'.[18] It is upon this reading of the hunchback that Agamben draws in his elaboration of the angelic and gestural assistants, whose 'look, whose very posture "seems like a message", and who represent our unfulfilled desires'.[19]

Benjamin's interpretation reverses the fate of the fairy-tale hunchback; this omen of failure is in fact a sign of success. For to *not* succeed in the political context in which he was writing, where the growing 'success' of fascism in Germany defined the landscape, failure was a position to be reclaimed. To fail was, in Benjamin's terms, to be out of time with the contemporary.[20] The only hope ('but not for us'[21]) is the unfolding of this moment onto another, familiar from Benjamin's description of the dialectic at a standstill. This is a phenomenon in which movement, time and progress are arrested by the potency of the dialectic, which can reveal the forgotten and the present together, in the time of the now. The assistants have an indirect line to this space and time that runs parallel to the quotidian, and the hunchback is a conduit. Yet, if these creatures are manifestly strange, far stranger still is Kafka's creation, Odradek, described by Benjamin as 'the strangest bastard which the prehistoric world has begotten with guilt in Kafka'.[22] Odradek 'looks like' a spool for thread, yet is star-shaped, has an extending part and a crossbar, and is found in the many places where discarded objects and persons convene: the attic, hallways, corridors and staircases. 'Odradek is the form which things assume in oblivion,' writes Benjamin, of the misshapen, unrecognizable thing that has no home.[23] It also appears in one of Agamben's early works, *Stanzas*, where it features in the title to the second part of the book ('In the World of Odradek').[24] Tellingly, in this text, which addresses Marx, commodity fetishism and the aura, Odradek references the things that have moved beyond use value and exchange value, that have lost all purpose and identity, but nonetheless have a haunting presence and retain a potentiality. In *Stanzas*, Odradek is cited as the ancestor of the Angel of the Bizarre, a creature from one of Edgar Allen Poe's stories whose physicality is constituted by utensils joined together. Like the Angel, Odradek's presence disturbs the order of things, the classificatory precisions that command the arrangement of a household, or office space. Odradek is a thing out of place and out of time, and for this it shares with the assistants the capacity to create a relationship with what is lost.

In order to understand how the assistants function to undo what needs to be undone, it is necessary to enquire further into what it is that the assistant mediates and to ask what worlds are they that this figure in some sense bridges? If we start with Kafka's stories, they provide a key to the schema, a key that Benjamin finds in the detail of spatial features, of where assistants are located. In corridors, hallways and even in attics the assistants loiter, wait, and find themselves suspended in a place *between*. The placement of assistants is between the world of officialdom, whose rooms they wait outside, and the world of the defendant. By the same measure they are outside of the law of the father polarized in the dispute with the son. Assistants, in their playful idleness, are suspended between the sphere of work and that of non-productivity; in their lecherousness they eschew both imperatives of chivalry and reproduction. It would seem that they remain external to a binary system that mechanically reproduces its counterpart (persecutor/victim, powerful/powerless, corrupt/innocent), but they exert a greater force than might at first seem evident. The 'work' of the assistants effects a digression from this power play, and in so doing, their activities begin to release the potency of the dualism in other directions. Whilst the assistants might present a parody of work, of adulthood, or thoroughness, they are also connected to another movement of *para*, or beside: the parable.

The fact that Kafka had a predilection for parables is picked up by Benjamin and replayed in the form of the homage essay; the four stories that structure the essay present a series of parables requiring interpretation and opening a new route in the process. The particular potency of the parable for Kafka, according to William S. Allen, is this digressive function that threatens to debunk the status and singularity of a 'main' text. He writes: 'This aspect of the parable is what appealed to Kafka, insofar as the parable suspends its own significance as a tool by refusing to be interpreted unambiguously.' The parable sets the scene for the reader to anticipate a meaning to come, yet 'any clues that it offers are also held in question by the fact that in offering them it also diverts the reader into further questions, perhaps unrelated to the initial question'.[25] Indeed, Kafka's short story, 'On Parables', is a reflexive play on the demand for parables to deliver a truth or meaning that may be mechanically applied to everyday life; the man who questions the relevance of parables, who reads the answer to his question as yet another parable, wins in the world of 'reality', yet loses in the domain of the parable.[26] Kafka's work manifests this re-routing of the binary apparatus, of reality versus interpretation, and of power versus revelation, by voiding the centre of the world of meaning or conspiracy; for there is no person, or no knowable persona at the heart of this system, and no final interpretive key. There is a secret that ultimately no one in these stories can know, but the assistants are not at all interested in its revelation and this is why they remain a critical figure of thought.

The assistants mark not only an exteriority; they represent a different ontological register, their diversionary behaviour deceptively redrawing the boundaries of permissible thought and practice. In the time of waiting outside of the offices of power, in the space that remains *para*, they are busy with other things. As eternal students, their learning is never done, which conspires with other of their features to ensure that they remain incomplete beings. In their idleness, they neglect to comply with the work ethic; their time is another time, like that of Playland, in stark contrast to the commodified temporal units of capital. And their play, of course, refuses the demands of productivity, routing activity back to a state of distracted absorption. They have, in fact, much in common with another figure familiar from the nineteenth century: the amateur. The term, originating in the late eighteenth century, borrowed from the French *amateur* (lover of), and derived from the Latin term *amatorem*, describes a passion that propels the amateur's activity, distinct from both the motivations of money and status in the world of work, and the casual nature of leisure. The amateur has a passion for things that may, in the terms of the conventional criteria for success, be going nowhere.

Amateur practices: Birt Acres makes the Birtac in conditions of dissent

Some years after the emergence of cinema, in the mid-1950s, Roland Barthes identified the amateur as one who approached painting, music, sport or science 'without the spirit of mastery', and furthermore, one who 'renews his pleasure', who comes again, as it were. There is a certain limitlessness to the amateur's practice; unconstrained by the demands of productivity as work, the amateur is at liberty to create or make to excess. Barthes also suggests that this lover, who 'loves and loves again', is not in search of recognition, nor does he steal an idea or an image to achieve an attribution. Rather, his practice is established graciously, 'he is – he will be perhaps – the counter-bourgeois artist'.[27] Barthes lifts us from the darkened passages of Kafka's work into a breezy workroom (his own) where the amateur passes through amidst brief paragraphs on stupidity, the love of an idea, Brecht's criticism of Roland Barthes and the middle-class maiden (*La jeune fille bourgeoise*). Class, stupidity and love are stirred around together.

A hundred years earlier, and these features are traceable in the rush for amateurism. Self-directed learning burgeoned across the subjects of natural history, botany and archaeology throughout the nineteenth century. At the same time, in sport the amateur signalled an activity undertaken by those unencumbered by work, the mark of a gentleman's status, which was to turn again of course in the twentieth century with working-class young men exercising their bodies in order to rise to a professional sporting life.[28] Photography, as Barthes notes elsewhere, had its share of amateurs, those who shared knowledge through channels such as *Amateur Photographer* magazine, first published in 1884. The forging of unofficial knowledge produced without the constraints of economy characterized both the work of the amateur and a related figure, the inventor. Both the amateur and the inventor have an enigmatic relation to authority; they prefer, it would seem, to trust in their own capabilities to act creatively than to enter the world of officialdom and patronage. Yet, if this is the starting point, their trajectories diverge when the inventor enters the system of patents and copyright, desiring the legal stamp of recognition and exchange (at times, prior to the invention at the stage of the idea alone). The inventor is involved in the transitioning of ideas across a threshold, from amateur to professional, from hobby to financial gain, whilst the amateur is not. The amateur institutes a sense of freedom that violates the demands of a work-based culture and commercial gain. Writing of its evolution through the nineteenth century, Patricia Zimmerman comments on amateurism:

> The professional was controlled, committed to an institution rather than the self, possessed reproducible skills, and functioned as an interchangeable part. The concept of the amateur, on the other hand, evolved as an antidote to the enervation of the professional, bureaucratized cog… [Amateurism] emerged as a zone for all that corporate capitalism expelled from the workplace: passion, autonomy, creativity, imagination, the private sphere, family life.[29]

What is extended in this description is the breadth of the amateur, who is not simply aligned with a class position, or a counter-identity, but furnishes a *zone* with activities expelled from the workplace. Interestingly the amateur is repeatedly aligned with an affect (of love, of passion) that is not captured by capital but circulates in a separate place, perhaps within the corridors and interstices of official institutions.

Cinema, in step with the practice of photography, emerged as an amateur form during the first part of the twentieth century. The variety of film stock and equipment was paralleled by micro-cinemas, like that of small gauge cinema, around which a culture of inspired and divergent film practices emerged.[30] The broad characteristics of amateur film during the 1920s and the two decades beyond are, according to David James, threefold: films of domestic leisure activities and rituals, individually produced documentaries, and narrative paradigm films emulating an industrial model on a lesser scale.[31] James foregrounds a period during which amateur films exceeded the first category of home movies but were not formalized as an avant-garde of any kind, which was to come later in the 1950s (with Maya Deren as the most lucid advocate of amateur film production).[32] Amateur filmmaking in the interwar years, he writes, proliferated the idea of film, whilst the recognition of these creators as a 'market segment' produced a terminological trauma as 'blundering novices' were pitched against 'true amateurs' in the trades press. This was effective until 1933, when the *American Cinematographer* removed 'amateur' from its lexicon and added 'cine' to a number of practices associated with 16-mm gauge film: cinematographer, cinegrapher and cinegraphist.[33]

Yet earlier still, amateur activity was integral to the development of the objects of cinematic production, the technical devices and labouring machines of the late nineteenth century that, like assistants and amateurs, remain in the corridors outside of the debating chamber of film history. Birt Acres was interested in the dreamy subject of clouds. An American by birth, Acres was working in London at the photographic materials company, Elliot and Son, in North London in 1892. Acres was interested in photographing clouds and this is what he did in his spare time, constructing time-lapse studies of changing formations. But in viewing them, Acres found the blousy or mercurial formations, wonderfully kaleidoscopic as they change shape, were rendered static by the process of photography. To solve this problem, Acres developed an apparatus named a rapid lanternslide changer, which he patented in 1893, a device that facilitated some degree of motion in the transitions between slides. Photography, it seems, was an art that opened the possibilities for change and transformation of the apparatus itself as well as its effects.

In December 1894, Acres was approached by Robert Paul, an electrical instrument maker, to collaborate on a project to develop a moving image camera. The canny Paul had discovered that Edison's Kinetescope (allowing a film to be viewed through a small aperture at the top of the device) had not been patented within Britain.[34] In dismantling the Kinetescope, he was able to copy the machine. His reproduction of the machine was effective, but what Paul lacked was the films themselves to advertise the apparatus as an appealing device for exhibition and viewing, and a workable, cost-effective camera. Approaching Acres as a person with a reputation for a keen knowledge of film and a flair for invention, Paul required a camera and the experience of how to take and process film stock. The camera was designed within two months, and a number of experimental films were shot. In March 1895, the apparatus went into commercial production with an actuality, 'The Oxford and Cambridge Boat Race', followed by a number of other comic and dramatic films. The camera was a success, yet the ownership of the invention became a subject of acrimony and wider controversy. Each of the pair was different in their attitude to risk, or commitment, depending on how one views the situation. Acres patented the camera in his name, resigned from his job in June in order to devote his time to a film, whilst Paul continued with his business and partitioned off an area for film. Acres left the country to explore commercial potential of cinematography with a German company, whilst Paul, in his absence, advertised himself as the sole European manufacturer of the films.

The two entered dispute upon his return, and the partnership was dissolved by July of that year. Three years later, Acres set up the film coating, developing and printing business, the Northern Photographic Works Limited, Barnet. In this story, one of many in the history of cinema's inventors and assistants, there is a blurring of the line between the original and the copy, the inventor and the assistant to the inventor, as though invention itself is put into play through parody.

Charles Musser in his work on early cinema suggests that the period pre-1907 was characterized by 'collaborative pairings'.[35] In addition to William Dickson in the United States, Thomas Edison partnered with Thomas E. Murray, William Unger and George Harrington.[36] There were other pairings from the same studio, such as James White and William Heise, or James White and Frederick Blechyenden. Working both with and against Edison were the businessmen Frank Gammon and Norman Raff, who sold the rights to projectors such as the Vitascope.[37] In Britain, there was the partnership of filmmaker George Albert Smith and performer Douglas Blackburn, and George Albert Smith and Edmund Gurney, although this also transpired to be an unhappy coupling. Smith was a magic lantern lecturer, a psychic and a filmmaker, who worked theatrically with Gurney to establish tests on the capacity of memory under hypnosis. It later transpired that Smith in all likelihood had faked the results and this damaged Gurney's reputation. Gurney subsequently took his own life. Smith also worked to develop a colour additive system, Kinemacolor, with Charles Urban. Collaborations included the fraternal, with the brother team Richard and Cherry Kearton photographing birds and wildlife more generally, standing on each other's shoulders to photograph a nest or disguising themselves as part of the landscape including as a cow, or sheep, and a pile of sticks.[38] In their disguise, the Keartons come to double and parody animals in the landscape. And of course, in France the Lumière brothers dominated the period. Whether one stood to the side, or on top of the other, professionally, the pairs suggest the potential *para*-text of parody, the version that is to the side, as well as the doubling of possibility. 'Twofold', 'double', 'twinning', the terms describe a mirroring function that may go awry with dismal results, as it did with Acres and Paul. The mirror created something of a distortion, perhaps with chin dropped to the chest like Benjamin's hunchback; they took departure of each other but continued to be tied together through rivalrous competition in the field of film.

Acres considered film to be an extension of photography; that is, he considered film to be principally a photographic art and, like photography, to be widely available as a practice. In a lecture to the Hackney Photographic Society in

December 1898, he delivered his vision of the cinematograph, which would take back cinema from being 'the instrument of the showman' and return it to its proper place, as a popular photographic form.[39] For cinema to have the wide appeal that he envisioned, it required an affordable and simple apparatus to be available at a reasonable cost. These were the parameters that he set himself in developing the Birtac, a small substandard gauge machine that combined the functions of a camera and a projector, widely known as a cinematograph. To change its function, one had to remove the photographic Ross lens and place a different lens into the top part of the box camera for projection, with the positive film fitting into the film holder attached to the underside of the top panel, formerly occupied by the negative. The movement was driven by an eccentric cam mechanism. The camera was lightweight, portable and 'essentially suited to drawing-room displays of small proportions, designed for a disc not greatly exceeding two or three feet, and depending upon the usual supply of house gas for its illuminant'.[40] Acres, keen for his invention to gain the popular use that he imagined for cinema as a

The Birtac camera projector (Birt Acres, 1898)

home entertainment, or a cinema of the every day by the every person, marketed the Birtac at ten guineas. The owners of the device could also develop and print their own film stock by purchasing the 'simple and compact printing and developing outfit' at a small additional price of two guineas.[41]

The camera took a film with a gauge of 17.5 mm, with perforations along one side of the stock only, the magazines holding 20 feet of film, sufficient for a projection with a duration of 40 seconds. In the file that accompanies the Birtac camera at the Media Museum in Bradford, there is a handwritten note running to two sides of A4. It is dated 1946 and would appear to be information accompanying the gifting of the camera. It opens 'This instrument, patented by Birt Acres in 1898, was designed for use with film 17.5mm wide, obtained by dividing standard 35mm film into two parts.' This is written in a neat hand using a pencil. Over the top of this, a different handwriting crosses through some of the words in pencil, such as 'dividing' and 'into two parts'. This hand has annotated the script in black ink, crossing through these terms and writing a different version which reads: '... designed for use with film 17.5mm wide, obtained by *splitting* standard 35mm film *down the middle*'. The reason for this annotation is not entirely clear but perhaps it corrected the potential to misunderstand how the filmstrip was divided. What is clear, unequivocally so in this clarification of a detail, is that the film stock was made by dividing one length in two, creating a twin from a single entity. And the written text that was one has also doubled or twinned; there are two anonymous authors, who may or may not be the gifters (there is no further information in the file to anchor the writing). Certainly these inscriptions are not by the hand of Birt Acres, who died in 1918.

The Birtac was not subtly marketed. The advertisements carried by *The Amateur Photographer*, and similar magazines, promote three things about it. The first is the accessibility of the apparatus: 'At Home Animated Photography within Reach of Everybody'. The second point made is the combined functions of the item as a camera and projector, whilst the third is its simplicity and lack of danger 'No danger, Perfectly Simple. A Child Can Work It'.[42] The last feature is not absolutely the case. When used as a projection device, the Birtac depended on house gas to produce the illuminant. In the first demonstration at the illustrious Anderton's Hotel on the Strand, the gas supply was deficient and Acres had to abandon his demonstration. Not one to be troubled with humility, Acres publically announced the failure to be on the part of the hotel gas supply rather than his machine. At the second demonstration (before the Hackney Photographic Society), the gas flowed sufficiently well for Acres to call it a success and an image of about six feet in height was projected onto a screen. Despite, or because of, the denial of danger, the whole system of attaching the device to a domestic gas pipe would appear to hold a tenuous relationship to safety. Examination of the camera in the archive offers no signs of burning, scalding or heat of any sort. But the carry case, a fine tan leather box with white stitching and a red velvet interior, shows signs of wear. The shape of the camera is embossed in the inside of the box as a flattening of patches of velvet; like a shell, the case reveals a previous life that has long since deceased. There is also a leather flap at the side, fixed by a brass stud, which swivels to reveal a keyhole shape for the lens to peek out of if needed. On the side is another hole for the winding key, which has left a dark line tracing the circumference of the key's path. The camera could then be used without removing it from its case, in tune with a Victorian taste for 'discreet' photography.[43]

The ambitions of Acres were to take the cinema back from the hands of entertainers and return it to the domain of serious documentary photography, testifying to the appeal of forms of cinema that were not classified as fictional entertainment, and simultaneously to wrest it from 'professionals' and industry folk and place it within the realms of the amateur. This figure is not, we may note, the general populace, but a person attached to learning and innovation, a figure inhabiting the grey area between the domains (and demands) of industry and leisure, work and play. Acres himself traversed this zone. In resigning from his position at Elliot and Son, he became an 'independent amateur' from 1894, compelled by the prospect of an educational cinema. He toured the country, giving lectures and presentations to scientific and photographic societies, yet the remuneration of this was paltry and in 1909, Acres became bankrupt, a fate he met again in 1911. His reputation was further damaged during this time by a publication by F. A. Talbot, *Moving Pictures*, which relied on an account of cinema history provided by Acres's rival, Robert Paul. According to Richard Brown, a volume of Talbot's book is kept in the BFI library, London, that was the copy read by Acres. In the margins are his notes providing an acerbic and dissenting commentary on Talbot's version (the amateur's notes in the margins of the professional text).[44]

Parody: A literary digression

There are many innovators and experimenters in the annals of cinema history and many cases of bankruptcy and failure.[45] They appear by turns inspired figures, illuminated by the vision of a thing not yet in existence, and also deluded individuals whose judgement of a 'real' prospect was deficient. The volume of patents applied for (and often granted) during the second half of the nineteenth century is suggestive of the great swelling of invention and inventors and their precarious economic footing, aiming through patents to secure future returns for an idea in the making. Their precarious footing straddles the realms of reality and fiction, to recall Agamben's definition of parody, which is also the line between the word and the thing. In the struggle to magic the thing from the word, the real from the fictional, the integrally parodic inventor is always in a process of becoming and simultaneously at risk of disappearing. '[P]arody is a notoriously impracticable terrain', warns Agamben, 'in which the traveler constantly knocks against limits and aporias that he cannot avoid but that he also cannot escape'.[46] The inventor, perhaps unwittingly parodic in his practice, reappears or perhaps doubles his form in 'reality' with an appearance in fiction in Robert Walser's novel, *The Assistant* (1907).

In this tale, Walser brings together both the master and the sidekick: the marvellously deluded and volatile inventor, Carl Tobler, and his shadowy assistant. Walser, who was never able to support himself from his writing, worked as a clerk and copyist, jotting down ideas and stories on tiny scraps of paper, written in a tiny hand and the novel is thought to draw on his experience. He finished *The Assistant* in 1908, a novel that is narrated from the position of the titular subject, Joseph Marti. His employer, Tobler, previously a factory worker, has at the start of the novel used a small inheritance to move to the provinces and set up business as an inventor, yet his patented inventions have little to recommend them. The task of Marti, the assistant, is to believe in these creations and their potential, a task that becomes more urgent as Tobler moves further into debt. In exact proportion to the difficulty of Tobler's financial predicament is the rising pitch of Marti's indignant rhetoric to debtors. The assistant, that is, is burdened with the problem of belief and rebuttal, as though his job is to will the thing into existence as a success and for his demeanour to reflect its value. Here are Marti's admonishments, and instructions to self, on the promotion of his master's Advertising Clock, this being an instrument for display in public forums, lavishly decorated by eagle wings and able to carry advertisements:

> The Advertising Clock is sprawled on the ground in defeat, wailing for a bit of solvent capital. Go to it and give it your support so that it may gradually, one limb at a time, rise up again and successfully imprint itself on people's opinions

and judgments once and for all, a task that is worthy, if you will, of your mental abilities, and useful to boot.[47]

Marti has to inhabit a land of fiction as though it were fact. He also, like Kafka's characters, has to suffer inept father figures and is closely tied to Agamben's observation that 'assistants are our unfulfilled desires'.[48] His work is caught between his master's imagination and the tools of the workshop. Emotionally, he is situated within the home and yet his 'place' wavers somewhere between the servants and the family members, both belonging and external to each. Similarly he moves between the province and the city in his time off, between a failed love affair and a new passion for his master's wife, and between states of exertion and inertia as an assistant. The novel drew on Walser's own experiences as a clerk. He was admired within his own time by both Franz Kafka and Walter Benjamin, and more recently, by Giorgio Agamben and by W.G. Sebald, who calls him wistfully a 'clairvoyant of the small'.[49]

If Walser, discreetly and gesturally, fills out the painstaking trials and half-realized desires of the assistant, Gustave Flaubert flamboyantly exercises the figure of the amateur in his unfinished novel, *Bouvard and Pécuchet* (1881). Flaubert, however, was not so empathic with his subjects, stating that he set out to write a novel in which he could 'vomit back onto my contemporaries' the disgust he felt for them, an exorcism as well as an exercise. Possibly influenced by Barthélemy Maurice's story, *The Two Court Clerks* (1841), which tells the tale of Andreas and Robert who retire on pension,[50] the novel is a satire of aspiration and conformity, the pursuit of knowledge in encyclopaedic form, the mechanical rote learning of the modern age. In this, the novel compelled Flaubert to repeat, or to parody (we cannot be sure), the errors of his two characters: the thorough approach he took to researching the work led him to read over 1500 books. Yet the story of *Bouvard and Pécuchet* is simple in structure, following the adventures of two copy clerks who are both living and working in Paris. They meet by chance, rapidly developing an intimate bond. Sharing a passion for learning and a fatigue with city life, the characters move to the countryside after Bouvard inherits a fortune that enables their fantasies to become material.

It is here that the pair move through an educational arc incorporating agriculture, gardening, food, chemistry, anatomy, medicine, biology, geology, architecture, history, literature, grammar, politics, love, religion, theology, philosophy, education, music and gymnastics. 'Six months later', chapter six announces, 'they had become archaeologists, and their home looked like a museum'.[51] There are no limits to their appetite for learning, yet the acquisition of knowledge as an amateur occupation reveals all of the weaknesses of this method; without context and depth, learning mutates into its opposite, the reproduction of received opinion. The characters speak an endless discourse of banalities and inane observations passed off as critique, whilst their outputs, experiments in everything from gardening to liquor making, are dismal failures. Amateurs in all things, but specifically in learning itself, the characters are derided by the novel's tone, shifting between distant description to a more satirical engagement with their pursuits. Their experiments, their enterprise and their capacity for application have strong affinities with the amateur practitioners of the photographic and cinematic arts.

Yet, it could be said that Bouvard and Pécuchet share many of the characteristics Agamben attributes to the assistants. '[A]like as snakes', they never do anything but engage in foolish behaviour and childish games, and in contrast to their childish ways, they have adult faces 'of students almost'.[52] They do not succeed in finishing anything. 'They embody the type of eternal student or swindler who ages badly and must be left behind in the end, even if it is against our wishes.'[53] And like Walser's assistant and inventor, they labour at their travails but have muddled this with domestic life and the space of the home. Yet they fruitfully prise open a gap between the idea of learning that leads to experimentation and even invention, and its output. Within this gap sits the spectre of the copyist in all of its different registers, the forlorn figure of Bartleby perhaps, as well as the copy clerks of Kafka's novels. Bouvard and Pécuchet become a parody of learning in their barefaced reproduction of the ways of others. They physically inhabit knowledge as a series of roles performed. And so the risks of learning include this possibility that one learns nothing other than how to reproduce the ideas of others, dismally. Learning, that is, may invoke a type of copying, a version that may, indeed, as it does in *Bouvard and Pécuchet*, result in serious comedy. The *Dictionary of Accepted Ideas* that the characters produce, appended to the main text, mixes the serious tone of aphorism with a wealth of disingenuous content. Alphabetically arranged entries reproduce the comedy of a randomness of connection between, part of Flaubert's satire of the encyclopaedic knowledge, but moreover, the dictionary mixes definition with badly observed social etiquette. The entry for the word 'Homo' is followed by the instruction 'Say "Ecce homo!" when the person one is expecting enters.'[54]

Copying and invention are notionally in opposing camps.[55] The dull reproduction of written texts, whether this is exercised by the clerk, the scrivener, the assistant, or Bouvard and Pécuchet, mirrors the mechanical reproduction whose rhythmic motion characterized industrial production. Invention, conversely, retains something of the romantic tradition of a creativity and vision emanating from a place beyond and surpassing rationalism; invention was seen to illuminate the dark corners of the long nineteenth century. Yet this polarity, when pressed, reveals that each of these positions is liable to become mobile in that the inventor, watching over the feats of others with a covetous desire, was prone to copying. In the experiments with cameras, projectors, processing systems and viewing apparatuses, many inventors simply took apart the instruments and, in so doing, got inside of their competitor's products. In this sense, the system of patents is an official exercise in the unofficial management of copying. To borrow from Bouvard and Pécuchet's lexicon of the *Dictionary of Accepted Ideas*, one might remark that 'copying is the best form of flattery'.

Importantly, in this account of inventions, mimesis and copying, the line dividing these practices from one another is crossed and rubbed out. In the material relations of things and people what is being exercised is use, which is separate from the question of ownership. Use, argues Agamben in an essay on play, is opposed to property; in fact it lays bare the function of property as a 'device that moves the free use of men into a separate sphere, where it is converted into a right'. As a form of use, copying overrides the prohibition of a legal discourse of rights and asserts a relationship to things as praxis. As such, it is the signature of a paradigm that includes doubles, partners, reproductions and mimetic forms of various kinds. Here, the machine that separates use from ownership, origin from copy and work from play is deactivated. Acres himself had come into the business through copying. In the earlier scenario, when Robert Paul had approached Acres, his task had been to copy an Edison Kinetescope. Equipment was disassembled in offices, factories and living rooms by inventors who wanted to know *how* through a process of copying, reproducing that which exists in order to produce a new set of relationships, a new assemblage. Imagination and diligent labour, the invention and the copy, were not in such polarized locations.

St Anthony patron of lost things

Flaubert's relationship to copying and to satire however is less straightforward than might appear through the prism of a pair of bungling amateur learners. Prior to writing *Bouvard and Pécuchet*, he had himself created a work of encyclopaedic ambition mining the treasures of a biblical story that became, in his hands, a work of dreams, phantasmagoria, theatre, spectacle, rhapsody and more. His extensive labours, like those of Orson Welles and *Don Quixote*, effectively doubled and redoubled the text. *The Temptation of St Anthony* was rewritten on three occasions over a thirty-year period and, according to Foucault in his essay on Flaubert's novel, 'Fantasia in the Library', it existed before any of Flaubert's books, was ritually repeated as an act of exorcism and was in fact Flaubert's own temptation needing to be overcome prior to the writing of his other major works.[56] 'Suspended over his entire work', writes Foucault, 'it is unlike all his other books by virtue of its prolixity, its wasteful abundance, and its overcrowded bestiary', offering a 'photographic negative' of the other novels.[57] *St Anthony* is the expansive, tumultuous and florid dream of a text that had to be thoroughly pushed down in order for the other novels to make their way into the clear light of literary life. St Anthony, the saint of lost things, retains Flaubert's passion for the book and all books. The story of St Anthony (prior to his canonization, Fernando Martins de Bulhões) is fittingly a tale of a lost book; when he prayed for its return, it was delivered back to him.

The novel is Flaubert's double that will not properly emerge nor depart, the shadow that compels him to work and retreats from him when it appears to be done. It is a multiplying work that will be neither reduced nor tamed, which refuses to stay within limits and leads, in the way of a temptation, to other works, more books, discourses and texts. It invokes an appetite for books that Flaubert cannot, with any seriousness, curtail. Giving way to its excessive demands allows a double to step forth, a double of the writerly persona, that is part serious and part comic grotesque. On the occasion of its first iteration in 1849, Flaubert, at the age of thirty, had finished what he believed to be his masterpiece after a period of labour lasting four years. Delirious perhaps at reaching this climactic end, he wished to share it with the two writers whose opinion he most respected, Louis Bouilhet and Maxime du Camp (another pair), by reading it to them aloud. In an excited state, Flaubert read the entire manuscript, page after page, although reading may have been more akin to a performance. The reading of 541 pages took eight hours a day for four days to complete. The effect however was not what Flaubert had envisaged. 'Bouilhet and du Camp would later remember it as the most painful days of their lives', writes Colin Dickey, 'as they listened to an endless morass of words that was alternately incomprehensible, banal, repetitive and childish'.[58] Reportedly, at the end of four days, Bouilhet and du Camp advised Flaubert to throw his novel onto the fire and never speak of it again. Flaubert of course was to do nothing of the sort.

Foucault finds in Flaubert's *The Temptation* a new excess of 'zealous erudition', new that is to the nineteenth century, an excess characterized by wakefulness, untiring attention and an unremitting vigilance.[59] The imagination was no longer a part of sleeping life and the world of night, but of the day. No longer in the realm of the boudoir, fantasy was to be found in 'the hushed library, with its columns of books, with its titles aligned on shelves to form a tight enclosure, but within confines that also liberate impossible worlds'. He continues, 'the imaginary now resides between the book and the lamp'.[60] *The Temptation*, according to Foucault, makes sense only in this context of the library, of other books. Indeed it partakes of a web of literary connections, but unlike the satirical literary intertexts such as *Don Quixote*, *The Temptation* is serious in its intent. It draws upon other works, not simply as Flaubert's fantasy project, but as a book dreaming other books.

In a remarkable passage, Foucault is himself feverishly exultant for this dreamwork. 'It dreams other books, all other books that dream and that men dream of writing', he announces, 'books that are taken up, fragmented, displaced, combined, lost, set at an unapproachable distance by dreams, but also brought closer to the imaginary and sparkling realization of desires'.[61] The gathering of books, that is a library, provides a location for the production of a new kind of knowledge, one that grows a fantasmatic reality in the network of its references, citations, plagiarisms and parodies. It grows by way of an accumulation of detail, the assembling of facts and reported speech, and by reproduction, or more accurately, 'the reproductions of reproductions'.[62] This is the new imaginative space that, for Foucault, Flaubert fleshes out in a gloriously repetitious and fervid manner in his writing and rewriting of *The Temptation*. With this text, he crafts an experience of the fantastic as a singularly modern imaginary located in the black and white signs of letters and words on a page. The fantastic has become at once subject to detail, location, fastidious attention, and electrified within the space of the library. St Anthony's temptation is the temptation of books no less, leading Foucault to announce, 'The library is on fire.'[63]

Bouvard and Pécuchet, writes Foucault, is the grotesque shadow and its double. It too is a book constructed through its relationship to and plundering of books. The characters are also tempted by what they read in books, and to be tempted is to believe. The pair, in their reading habits, is drawn into the power of an endless discoursing on the possible, and this is the site of their belief, not a belief to be tested, for failure means nothing in their world. Each time that an activity is frustrated, the episode is simply closed and the quest for knowledge moves on. The end of the novel marks a renunciation, but, according to Foucault, what 'they renounce [is] not their faith but the possibility of applying their beliefs'.[64] What Foucault's reading brings to Flaubert's works is the collapse of dichotomies that hold certain thoughts and actions apart: the patient and the frenzied, the scholarly and the imaginative, the ordered and the random, the singular and the multiple, the library and the inventor's studio, and most significantly, the saintly and the stupid. The essay ends with Foucault's celebration of 'the saintly stupidity of things', which is the final stop for Bouvard and Pécuchet, bound together at their double desk as they set about the occupation that characterized their former lives: copying. Copying signals their passion for the word, for books, without further exertion into territory of application. Copying also produces a text *beside* the original. As a practice, therefore, it carries within its form not only the copied text, but the mark of copying, that is, its relation as a double to the original.

By all accounts, Flaubert was inspired by a painting to write his book of books. In 1845, whilst visiting Genoa, Flaubert saw Breughel the Younger's artwork *The Temptation of St Anthony*.[65] Like the *Temptation* painted by Hieronymous Bosch, the work exudes a palette of grotesque occurrences amidst figures in rapturous states; the temptations, contemplations and their resistance are tendrils growing in and around each other. In a sense, Flaubert profanes the sacred in his telling, as do the paintings of Breughel and Bosch, for in the process of dispelling demons, one must first conjure them. In the conjuring, the distinction between them is lost. The saint is also a sinner; the serious novelist is also an amateur. The potential for doubling, joining and shadowing is infinite. The hard-working inventor accompanied at his side (next to, *para*) by his distracted or bored assistant may appear serious, or conversely, the diligent assistant by the side of his distracted master may carry the mantle of creativity. The positions are not fixed, but pairings and doubles are a relation before they are anything else and, as shadows, consistently threaten to invoke parody and its suspension of the laws of use and the comedy of play.

In Flaubert's practice we witness the operation of over-creation, an excessive production of one text, which seems in the writing to undo itself, to be unmade by the end of the work. In this bizarre act of writing and rewriting *The Temptation*, the actualization of the work appears to lead to its opposite, its de-actualization, until the final rendition. Flaubert's labours balance here, in the space between the eternal return, an endless repetition of lines that Benjamin likened to the punishment meted out to school children and the practice of decreation.[66] For most of his life, Flaubert harboured St Anthony as a potential project, and each approach to the writing seemed determined to end in its non-realization. Finally, the project steps out of the shadow of the famous (and published) novels to become a work in the full meaning that Barthes gives to that term, a mass of references and citations that refuses the delimitations of the novel. Flaubert, like Welles, preserved his own impotentiality.

Play and profanation

To take the passage that travels from parody to play, and that leads ultimately to profanation, is to follow a gossamer thread that connects the plentiful words of books, and plenitude of books in the library, with a storehouse of toys and mountains of discarded and obsolete things. The various figures of amateurs, assistants and children operate within the same paradigm. Just as Bouvard and Pécuchet work as bricoleurs, combing over piles of books in search of treasures that lie dormant, so children are 'humanity's little scrapdealers',[67] creating toys from everyday objects by suspending and re-imagining their use (as do amateurs), whilst the amateur takes things apart to reassemble differently and assistants make imaginative use of the scraps of information or knowledge that they have gleaned. Where Bouvard and Pécuchet labour in the library, the official archive of words, amateurs work at home or in outhouses, and assistants loiter in institutional hallways and corridors, children have a land of their own. Each of these vignettes commands a picture of activity that is off-centre, unproductively productive, which is to say without direct purpose. Each of these scenarios reorients our sensibility, not only in relation to things and their value, thresholds and their crossing, but to time and the historical. The path from parody to play, that leads ultimately to profanation, approaches the properly historical, kairological time. This is a time that opens up inside of the endless line of productive and progressive chronology, a line that makes of each one hundred years a *long* century. In play, as in parody, we step sideways, crossing the line or the threshold, and find ourselves in a place beside, a parallel track, a paraontology.

Agamben opens his essay, 'In Playland', with an account of Pinocchio's journey through the night on a donkey to this mysterious land, an 'infantile utopian republic'.[68] Populated by boys between the ages of eight and fourteen, Playland is the noisiest of places; with all the uproar and ruckus of games, it is necessary to stuff cotton wool into the ears to avoid deafness. The enigmatic feature of

Playland, however, does not concern the revelry and distractions, but the change that occurs in this place to time. In Playland, time is infinitely accelerated. Days, weeks and months fly past 'like lightening'. The demarcations of the calendar are made redundant by such activities, writes Agamben, and the year relaxes into one long holiday. Yet play has some secret connection to the sacred and to time, and for this reason it must be explored.

What is it that these privileged vectors, children, can accomplish in play that has such profound implications? The girl with the sleigh who beckons to us, and Dulcinea, belong to this group, and so do the children on the balcony of the cinema in the extract of *Don Quixote*. There are several moments in the 'Playland' essay and others where toys, fables and the like are threaded together in acts of profanation, the concept that is elaborated most powerfully in Agamben's more recent work and that is connected to time.[69] In the concept of play is gathered a number of ideas that effect a call for the reconstitution of the temporal. In the essay on play, the first of these is the relocation of the object, or toy, from the place of use to the domain of non-utility or experimental misuse. Through imaginative activity, everyday objects may become toys, suspending their relationship to the functional world. Play therefore is transformative, and part of its appropriative magic is to carry things across the threshold that separates the sacred form the profane. If we recall the sacred as the product of a categorical separation of things from human touch and human time, play inverts this process by contaminating the objects though handling, exploring and re-appropriating. The essence of the toy, writes Agamben, 'is something quite singular, which can be grasped only in the temporal dimension of a "once upon a time" and a "no more" ... The toy is what belonged – *once, no longer* – to the realm of the sacred or the practical-economic'.[70] The operation that children perform is either in the trafficking of things across this border between sacred and profane, or the rescue of those things that have dropped out of sacred or economic use, objects that (like Odradek) are made significant again in the reinterpretative practice of play.

The temporal dimension of play becomes visible in the renunciation of a singular time; the 'then' of an object's use is put into contact with the multiple times of other objects, producing a temporal montage or decoupage. Furthermore, in the extraction of the object from its 'real time' in the world, it enters another register, gathered into the 'remote adjacence of history'.[71] To get to this differential, Agamben draws on Benveniste's examination of play that started where anthropologists left off in the study of play and ritual. Comparing play and ritual to the structure of myth and ritual in anthropological accounts, Benveniste argues that where myth articulates history and ritual reproduces it, play performs the ritual without the myth. That is, play preserves the form of the drama but has forgotten what it is for. In so doing, play crosses the synchronic (the aspects of labour or play that operate in any one moment across all sites) with the diachronic (the aspects that operate across chronological time). Play takes something from its diachronic distance and places it within synchronic proximity; it mixes things from other structural wholes, whether these structures are material forms or temporal arrangements. Through activities that refuse the object's linear history, the toy is lifted from the diachronic into the synchronic 'now' of play, but at the end of the game, the toy becomes again the synchronic residue, yet always leaving a trace of the game.

Children not only release objects from fixed moorings, they are themselves unstable signifiers. Like the incomplete beings that are the assistants, children and ghosts are doubles, effectively troubling the boundary between the sacred and the profane, living time and dead time, birth and death. 'If the ghost is the living-dead or the half-dead person', he writes, 'the baby is the dead-living or half-alive person',[72] both ghost and child shaking the stability or certainty of signification, the accretion of time, and the definition of life. Ghosts and children may act 'inappropriately', out of alignment with common sense notions of deportment or logic, and it is here that Agamben locates the profanatory potential of play. Play liberates us from the sacred but without destroying it; it deactivates the power of the law, economics and politics by finding a new use for their language, tools or rites.[73] Indeed, one of Agamben's examples of profanatory re-appropriation comes from a film by Louis Buñuel, *The Discreet Charm of the Bourgeoisie* (1972), when adults at a dinner party are simultaneously seated on toilets excreting faeces; the new function of defecating as it is relocated to the domain of a dinner party is to change and charge the social banality of the ritual of the party. The ritual remains, but its purpose has been forgotten or written over.

When this becomes that

In the artist Simon Starling's work, we find an entry into the other end of the social spectrum, where the rituals and practices of a Berlin metalwork factory are appropriated and remade. In *Wilhelm Noack oHG* (2006), the metalwork factory becomes first of all a site of archaeological investigation and then transforms into a Playland. Starling worked at 'Wilhelm Noack' as a researcher of the factory's history, examining photographs and designs, displays and dismantled metalworks, and a number of prototypes of everyday objects such as lamps, gates, locks and keys. The discreet presence of metal in the world is made bold in his view of the factory's history, with attention to hinges, bolts, poles, girdles and brackets. What may threaten to commence as a history of industry, or a history of Berlin through metal, is usurped by the material itself, by the attraction of metal.

The piece of work that Starling makes in response to the factory is bifurcated: a film and something besides a film. The film, a four-minute loop in which it is difficult to identify a beginning and an end, combines archive photographs and documents with a camera roving through the space of the studios. Yet this is no steady-cam, rather it is a camera with an intense interest in the machines that manufacture metalwork, getting under lathes and clamps, moving around saws and under workbenches. It is shot from different heights, but most notably, from a low position, as though at the eye level of children or assistants. This effect is heightened by the activities that the camera is subject to; the bench is slammed hard by a hammer causing the camera to jump into the air, at another moment the trolley that the camera is travelling on is pulled too fast, and at yet another, the camera is attached to a pulley that has it swinging, suspended in air. The viewer of the film is aligned with the camera as a toy, a thing that is being made to exercise skills and conduct feats beyond recording. That is, the camera as an object of use has been transformed into a mechanism to explore a particular space. If the film begins in the spirit of Walser's assistant tasked with the chronicling of the factory's history, it is usurped by the agility and excellent judgement of Kafka's assistants, who 'give us help, even though we can't quite tell what sort of help it is'.[74]

If cinema has been defined as an experience of spectacle, famously the exposure of audiences to a large-scale image in the darkened space of a theatre, that definition is put to one side in *Wilhelm Noack oHG*. To enter the room in which the film plays is to enter a darkened room with a square of light on the wall opposite playing the film of the metalworks. But the room holds another, stronger presence; the outline of a spiral staircase is visible to the right, with water pouring from step to step. On closer inspection, the water is in fact slithers of film, and the whole structure is an elaborate support for the reams of celluloid moving from one level to the next, running through small plastic pulleys attached to the ends of each spoke. The enormity of this invention becomes apparent as

Film still from Wilhelm Noack oHG (Simon Starling, 2006)

Installation Wilhelm Noack oHG (Simon Starling, 2006)

the viewer realizes that this is not a staircase but a projector, projecting the film that is visible on the wall opposite and that the film on the wall opposite is a version of its making. In play, the projector has been stretched, elaborated and re-imagined as a staircase, or inversely, a staircase has been re-appropriated as a device for cinematic exhibition. The tension sustained by each threaded strip, creating a fine lattice of film moving through the multiple arms of this machine, testifies to the mathematical excellence of the assistants.

If Starling is an artist channelling the spirit of the assistants, it is a trope that he has used before, turning this into that, a shed into a boat, a car engine into a gallery energy system. In the transformation of a film projector into a sculpture, he has affected a further shift, perhaps of larger proportions. In moving the projector out of the back room of cinema, he has moved our attention from the image to the machine. The room that always sat behind the image, playing second fiddle, or assistant, to cinema's main act, has been placed at the centre of the event. The ritual of cinema has become an event of transformation, destroying the myth propagated by the cinematic image. For the image is perhaps the less interesting element in the room; representation has been shunted sideways by the fruits of an assistant's version of cinema, where the material properties of film, rather than its representational qualities, commands our attention.

Why might we applaud the shunting sideways of the image as spectacle? Because the image at its most extreme supports the separation of life and its capture as image, existing in a domain that is unreachable. The spectacle is cinema made sacred and untouchable, purified of its glitches and stammers. The cinema of the assistants returns the image to the realm of the profane; this is why there is a significant amount of noise and hammering and pushing and pulling, because a profane cinema is one that has been touched and handled, contaminated by human use. Its pure form has been mixed inexorably with the materials of other craft; its apparatus is made of the same elements as a staircase or a garden gate. But more than deactivation, this installation, which acts here as our figural assistants' cinema, mixes together parts from different structural wholes to make an event of bricolage. In its wake, it leaves the trace of an electrifying connection of historical moments, a hammer blow of one hundred years ago that operates on us now, of materials that were then 'this' and are now something else, of figures without names in photographs that look defiantly or expectantly back. In this room, where the assistants have been busy assembling, there lies an adjacent history, where *Wilhelm Noack oHG* operates in the differential between 'Once upon a time …' and 'no more'.

Notes

1. André Bazin, 'The Myth of Total Cinema', in *What Is Cinema? Volume 1*, selected and trans. Hugh Gray (Berkeley and Los Angeles, CA: University of California Press, 1967), 17–22, 17.
2. Ibid., 17–18.
3. In the online magazine *Bidoun* #28 http://www.bidoun.org/magazine/28-interviews/giorgio-agamben-with-leland-de-la-durantaye/ (accessed 19 September 2014).
4. Siegfried Zielinski, *Deep Time of the Media: Toward an Archaeology of Hearing and Seeing by Technical Means*, trans. Gloria Custance (Cambridge, MA: MIT Press, 2005).
5. Giorgio Agamben, 'Parody', in *Profanations*, trans. Jeff Fort (New York: Zone Books, 2007), 48.
6. Cited in 'Parody', 39.
7. *Rhapsody*, directed by Charles Vidor: MGM, USA 1954.
8. Interview with David Weiss and Peter Fischli in 'The Odd Couple', *Frieze Magazine*, 102 (2006): 102–103.
9. Giorgio Agamben, 'The Assistants' in *Profanations*, trans. Jeff Fort (New York: Zone Books, 2007), 29–36.
10. Ibid., 30.
11. Walter Benjamin, 'Franz Kafka: on the Tenth Anniversary of his Death', in *Illuminations*, trans. Harry Zorn (London: Pimlico, 1970), 108–135, 135.
12. Ibid., 110.
13. Benjamin uses this arresting image to describe official persons twice in the course of a few pages: 'now matter how highly placed they may be, they are always fallen or falling men' ('Franz Kafka', 109), and again 'We encounter these holders of power in constant, slow movement, rising or falling. But they are at their most terrible when they arise from the deepest decay – from the fathers' ('Franz Kafka', 110).
14. Benjamin, 'Franz Kafka', 113.
15. Walter Benjamin, *A Berlin Childhood around 1900*, trans. Howard Eiland (Cambridge, MA and London, England: Belknap Press, 2006).
16. Hannah Arendt, 'Introduction', in *Illuminations*, 12.
17. Ibid., 33.
18. Ibid., 34.
19. Ibid., 29.
20. Benjamin's interpretation of failure as a state of grace can be found also in his essay on Baudelaire, 'On Some Motifs on Baudelaire', in *Illuminations*, 152–197.

21 Kafka's comment to his friend Max Brod, cited in Benjamin's essay on Kafka. Although Benjamin uses the story to positive ends, his criticism of Brod's biography of Kafka, written in a letter to Gerhard Scholem, leaves no doubt as to his disdain for Brod's version of Kafka. See Benjamin's 'Max Brod's Book on Kafka and Some of My Own Reflections', in *Illuminations*, 136–143.
22 Benjamin, 'Max Brod's Book on Kafka and Some of My Own Reflections', 128.
23 Ibid., 129.
24 Agamben, *Stanzas: Word and Phantasm in Western Culture*, trans. Ronald L. Martinez (Minneapolis and London: University of Minnesota Press, 1993), 29–60. The Angel of the Bizarre appears on page 51.
25 William S. Allen, 'Melancholy and Parapraxis: Rewriting History in Benjamin and Kafka', *MLN*, 123:5 (December 2008): 1068–1087: 1069 (Comparative Literature Issue).
26 Franz Kafka, 'On Parables', in *The Great Wall of China and Other Short Works*, trans. Malcolm Pasley (London: Penguin Books, 1973): 184.
27 Roland Barthes, *Roland Barthes by Roland Barthes*, trans. Richard Howard (New York: Hill and Wang, 1977), 52.
28 A phenomenon captured by Lyndsay Anderson in *This Sporting Life* (1963).
29 Patricia Zimmerman, 'Morphing History into Histories: From Amateur Film to the Archive of the Future', in *Mining the Home Movie: Excavations in Histories and Memories*, ed. Karen L. Ishizuka and Patricia R. Zimmerman (Berkeley, Los Angeles, CA and London: University of California Press, 2008), 275–288.
30 Ryan Shand and Ian Craven (eds), *Small-gauge Storytelling: Discovering the Amateur Fiction Film* (Edinburgh: Edinburgh University Press, 2013).
31 David E. James, *The Most Typical Avant-garde: History and Geography of Minor Cinemas in Los Angeles* (Berkeley, Los Angeles and London: University of California Press, 2005), 140–141.
32 Deren's articulation of this position was, according to James, prior to the support of the avant-garde as amateur production that was later strongly associated with Jonas Mekas and Stan Brakhage. See Maya Deren, 'Amateur versus Professional', *Film Culture*, 39 (winter 1965): 45–46.
33 James, *The Most Typical Avant-garde*, 141.
34 John Barnes, *The Beginnings of the Cinema in England 1894–1901: Volume 1* (Exeter: Exeter University Press, 1988).
35 Charles Musser, 'Pre-Classical American Cinema: Its Changing Modes of Film Production', in *Silent Film*, ed. Richard Abel (London: Athlone, 1996), 85–124.
36 Gene Adair, *Thomas Alva Edison: Inventing the Electric Age* (Oxford: Oxford University Press, 1996).
37 Robert Allen, 'The Movies in Vaudeville: Historical Context of the Movies as Popular Entertainment', in *The American Film Industry*, second edition, ed. Tino Balio (Madison: University of Wisconsin Press, 1985), 57–82, 66–67.

38 Richard Kearton and Cherry Kearton, *With Nature and a Camera; Being the Adventures and Observations of a Field Naturalist and an Animal Photographer* (London: Cassell and Co, 1898).
39 John Barnes, *The Beginnings of the Cinema in England 1894–1901: Volume 3 1898* (Exeter: University of Exeter Press, 1996), 116.
40 Ibid., 114.
41 From the manual to 'The Birtac Animated Photography' (dated December 1898), courtesy of the National Museum of Media, Bradford.
42 These citations come from an advertisement collected by the Kodak Company and published in 1954 as *The British Journal Advertisements Highlights from the Kodak Catalogue*, published by Kodak Unlimited.
43 One of the most popular of these was Carl Stirn's waistcoat camera of 1886. The museum's note describes it thus:
> Disc shaped and all metal in construction, at first glance the camera resembles a cross between a frisbee and a hip flask. Thin enough to be worn unobtrusively beneath an ordinary waistcoat, it hung from the photographer's neck on a strap. The f10, fixed-aperture lens poked through a buttonhole of the waistcoat and, as a further aid to concealment, was designed to look like a button.

National Media Museum, Bradford, object notes, C.P. Stirn's Patent Concealed Vest Camera. Purportedly, 18,000 of these cameras had been sold by 1890.
44 David Robinson, 'John Barnes: Authority on the Early Days of Film Who with His Brother Created an Unparalleled Cinema Collection', in *The Independent Obituaries*, 30 June 2008.
45 For a more dramatic trajectory than Acres' life, see the biography of British photographer and inventor William Friese Greene.
46 Agamben, 'Parody', 50.
47 Robert Walser, *The Assistant*, trans. Susan Bernofsky (New York: New Directions Books, 2007), 141.
48 Agamben, 'The Assistants', 34.
49 W.G. Sebald, *A Place in the Country* (London: Penguin, 2014).
50 In Raymond Queneau's preface to the novel written in 1950, he argues that *Bouvard and Pécuchet* was influenced by Maurice's story 'consciously or not'. 'The Two Court Clerks' had appeared on 14 April 1841, in the Gazette des Tribunaux, followed by two further re-publications, the last of which was edited by a friend of Flaubert's, Eugene Delattre. See Raymond Queneau, 'Preface', in *Bouvard and Pécuchet*, Gustave Flaubert, trans. and introduced by Mark Polizzotti (Illinois: Dalkey Archive Press, 1881), xvii–xxxiv.
51 Ibid., 87.
52 Agamben, 'The Assistants', 29.

53 Ibid., 30.
54 *Bouvard and Pécuchet*, trans. and introduced by Mark Polizzotti (Illinois: Dalkey Archive Press, 2005), 304.
55 Although copying was in the late fifteenth century when Bosch was working, part of an artist's practice: see Laurinda Dixon, *Bosch* (London and New York: Phaidon Press Limited, 2003).
56 Michel Foucault, 'Fantasia of the Library', in *Language, Counter-memory, Practice: Selected Essays and Interviews*, trans. D. Bouchar and S. Simon (Ithaca, NY: Cornell University Press), 87–109, 88.
57 Ibid., 88.
58 Colin Dickey, 'The Redemption of St Anthony', in *The Public Domain Review: A project of the Open Knowledge Foundation*, http://publicdomainreview.org/2013/03/07/the-redemption-of-saint-anthony/ (accessed 15 August 2014).
59 Foucault's observations of the institutional production of states of attention recalls Jonathan Crary's work in *Suspensions of Perception: Attention, Spectacle, and Modern Culture* (Cambridge: MIT Press, 2001), and more recently, *24/7: Late Capitalism and the Ends of Sleep* (London: Verso, 2013).
60 Foucault, 'Fantasia of the Library', 90.
61 Ibid., 92.
62 Ibid., 91.
63 Ibid., 92.
64 Ibid., 107.
65 According to Bart's biography of Flaubert: B.F. Bart, *Flaubert* (Syracuse, NY: Syracuse University Press, 1967).
66 This detail of Benjamin's reading of Nietzsche's eternal return is made by Agamben in the essay 'Bartleby, or On Contingency', in the subsection dealing with decreation: 'Bartleby holds fast to this solution until he decides to give up copying. Benjamin discerns the inner correspondence between copying and the eternal return when he compares Nietzsche's concept to *die Strafe des Nachsitzens*, that is, the punishment assigned by the teacher to negligent schoolchildren that consists in copying out the same text countless times.' ('The eternal return is copying projected onto the cosmos. Humanity must copy out its texts in innumerable repetitions.') In *Potentialities*, 268.
67 Giorgio Agamben, 'In Playland', in *Infancy and History*, trans. Liz Heron (London and New York: Verso, 1993), 70.
68 Ibid., 67.
69 See, for example, 'Mme Panckoucke; or, The Toy Fairy', in *Stanzas: Word and Phantasm in Western Culture*, 56–60, or 'Fable and History: Considerations on the Nativity Crib', in *Infancy and History*, 125–132.
70 Agamben, 'In Playland', 71.
71 Ibid., 72.

72 Ibid., 82.
73 One might also locate on this map the cinema of Sadie Benning made through a playful engagement with the Fisher Price children's camera of the early 1980s, or earlier than this and of a different order, the cinema of Margaret Tait, located in the ordinary detail of domestic life. For further reading on Tait as amateur, see Sarah Neely, '"Ploughing a Lonely Furrow": Margaret Tait and Professional Film-making Practices of 1950s Scotland', in *Movies on Home Ground: Explorations in Amateur Cinema*, ed. Ian Craven (Newcastle: Cambridge Scholars Press, 2009).
74 Agamben, 'The Assistants', 30.

6

Ex-centric Cinema

Towards X

The writing of this book has been characterized by a progressive rolling away from the centre towards other definitions and possibilities of a cinema including those that are not yet, or not ever, to be actualized (a point to which we return). The mode of travel (rolling) is instructive as it is not possible to journey directly towards X, and there is no single point of departure; movement away from the centre can take any number of directions. When Nietzsce wrote that since Copernicus 'man has been rolling away from the centre towards X', the letter came to designate not a destination but a process of radical disorientation. Coincidently, it is the same letter that William Röntgen reached for when he noticed that a plate of barium platino-cyanide crystals glowed when the rays from his cathode tube were activated, naming them the X-ray. The figure of X, which gathers its momentum in Akira Lippit's description of it as 'x-space, an x-sign, a figure of representation no longer possible',[1] the unknown but deducible value of an equation in mathematics, is an unnamed point towards which we roll.

If this movement away from the centre of cinema towards other possibilities would appear to be simultaneously a decentring of man, as indeed Nietzsche suggests with his reference to Copernicus, the task is not at all that simple. For central cinema has never simply placed humankind at the centre of a representational world but has in its earliest productions cleaved a distinction. Cinema, that is, has to be understood as a machine that has separated out certain activities, practices, images and definitions of life from others. Its emergence in the nineteenth century is not coincidental in this respect, for cinema is one of the many apparatuses to document, record and fix behaviours within a culture in which, as Foucault notably amplified, the practices of auditing, taxonomy and statistical analysis had become standard practice. The running, walking, leaping figures that parade through Muybridge's studio are demonstrating this to us with their docile smiles and their obediently executed activities. As these figures stutteringly bring cinema to life, 'life' is increasingly brought within the domain of *zoe*, characterized by an official management and governance, which is simultaneously located within, and reduced to, a concept of the physical body (or in Agamben's terms, bare life). The familiar description of early cinema as an emergence of the human figure into a life-like form contains within its double articulation the ambivalent meaning of this term. What is being produced at this moment is not simply a sequence imitative of a coming-to-life of the still image but a concept of life captured, pinned and recalibrated in the process. In its nascent form, the cinema is complicit with this rendition of life as *zoe*, but its particular production is the relocation of bios as a truth internal to the subject. Therefore, the subject of collective communal law is finally figured in cinema as a subject turned inwards.

This chapter delineates, somewhat schematically, the preparations for a division between centric and ex-centric cinema or for what is to become cinema and non-cinema respectively. It is a division that surfaces in images prior to the first public showings of cinema and in figurations not necessarily associated with aesthetic interest. We begin then with three images each of which, when considered in relation, are key to an understanding of the shifts and splits that occur with cinema's emergence and proceed from here to chart the workings of cinema as it becomes a centric operator of exclusions in the first decades of the twentieth century. In the final part of the chapter, attention turns to what is excluded and its conceptual significance, resident in the term 'potentiality'.

Assembling the cinematic machine: Three scenes from the separation of life

Scene one: In 1838, on the Boulevard du Temple, Paris, on a day sunny enough to cast shadows from buildings and trees, a man stopped on the corner of the dusty street to have his shoes shined. Unbeknownst to him, Louis Daguerre had set his camera at the window of his room overlooking the street and on that day he was experimenting with the light-sensitive properties of silver salts, a process of chemical registration of the image on the thin copper plate inside the camera that would later be fixed by exposure to mercury fumes. The result was famously the first photographic image to register the human form. The lengthy exposure of the plate, requiring some ten minutes to absorb the effects of light, was in itself a process with selective properties. The crowds who would also have been present on the boulevard that day going about their business were not still enough to be chemically transferred. In an act that is suggestive of habit and routine, a man stopped to have his shoes cleaned, a communication of his intention to be well presented to the world, and possibly the pleasure taken in repairing the glossy leather to those particular boots. In this scene, the man is captured in his milieu, and in this smallest of tasks we read his status (above the one who kneels before him as he polishes) and possibly also a conversational attitude in his slightly forward-leaning posture. Crossing this axis of ritual is another axis, of contingency. The moment chosen by the man to stop was this and no other.

Boulevard du temple (Louis Daguerre, 1838)

Scene two: Some sixty years later, in 1896 the photographer Ernest Payne made an image, a gelatin silver print of a foot. The unusual aspect of this image was that the foot was visible despite its being inside of a shoe. Furthermore its representation was not the common surface area of skin and nail but the numerous bones that are the mechanical elements of the foot. A year after Röntgen's production of the inside of the body as image in the X-ray, Payne produced an album of prints that exposed various parts of the body in the new graphic form; feet, hands and more ambitiously the spine were all subjects to be revealed in their manifest structure, stripped bare of the disguise of skin and flesh. In this particular image, the top half of a foot including the toes is photographed wearing a shoe, although the two different types of matter are not obviously separate in the image. Indeed, in terms of pattern and tone, the foot and the shoe appear to be one textured object of lighter and darker shades. The image is set against a white background

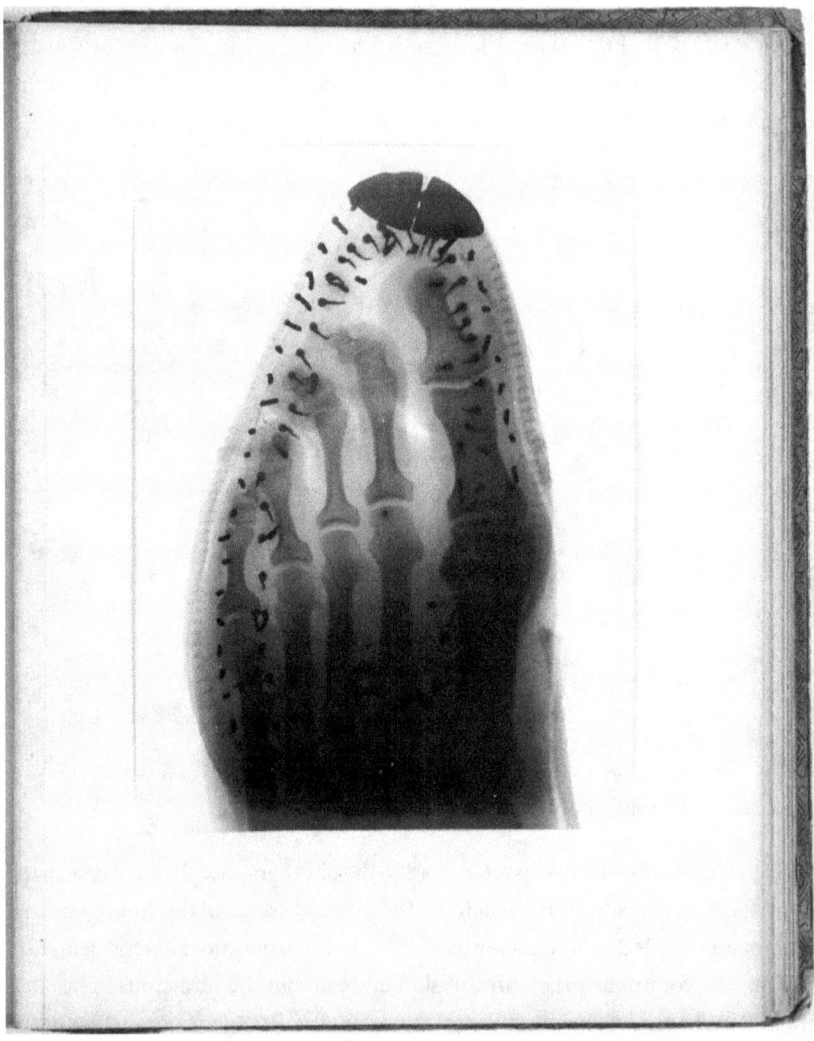

X-ray of a foot (Ernest Payne, 1896)

with the long shape of the foot and shoe central. Its border is speckled with the small bent lines of metal nails, whilst the very top of the shoe above the big toe is coloured a deep brown shaped as a half crescent, in all likelihood a metal toecap. A thin line of white suggests that the metal of the cap may be split or assembled in two halves. In a paler tone around the edge are regularly placed small lines like railways sleepers in miniature, in fact the stitches attaching the sole to the upper. Bulging into the seam of the shoe is the bone of the inner foot where the metatarsal meets the phalange. As the bone blurs into the fabric edge, there is the suggestion of the foot and the leather becoming mutually informed, a feature that appears again at the top edge of the shoe where the toes seem to press into the seam. In contrast, the whiteness between the toe bones describes space as small voids within the shoe. The toe bones themselves appear irregular and asymmetrical, their linkages showing as faint curved lines of light.

Scene three: The foot undergoes a different treatment four years later when George Albert Smith makes the short film 'As Seen Through a Telescope' (60 seconds, 1900). The film presents a man wearing a top hat and dark jacket, standing on a street corner holding a telescope to his eye. The instrument is pointed up towards some trees on the other side of the street, presumably where birds are nesting. In the background, we see what the man cannot at first see, a man and a woman walking along the street together, the man wheeling a bicycle. As they are about to disappear out of frame to the right, the couple stop and the man appears to be bending over to look at something, but we are too distant to see what is occurring. This is remedied by the following shot, a close-up in the format of a telescoped circular image; we are suddenly in the place of the first man who looks with the instrument. The close-up reveals the woman's foot placed on the peddle of the bike, her skirt slightly hitched to just above her ankle. The man's hands can be seen re-tying the lace of her right shoe. As he ties the bow, the woman subtly but provocatively raises her skirt in little jolting movements, imperceptible to anyone else on the street, with the exception of this voyeur whose special viewing instrument has made him privy to this intimacy. In response to the woman exposing more of her ankle and lower leg, the man gently pats the exposed leg, and as she raises it once again, he rubs the flesh in a discreet gesture of erotic fondling. The third shot returns to the full street scene where the man is hurriedly putting away his telescope and sitting down on the stool with his back turned to the approaching couple, gestures that disavow any interest in them. As the couple cross the street and walk behind him, the seated man is struck on the back of the head by the man pushing the bicycle so that he falls sideways from the stool and loses his hat.

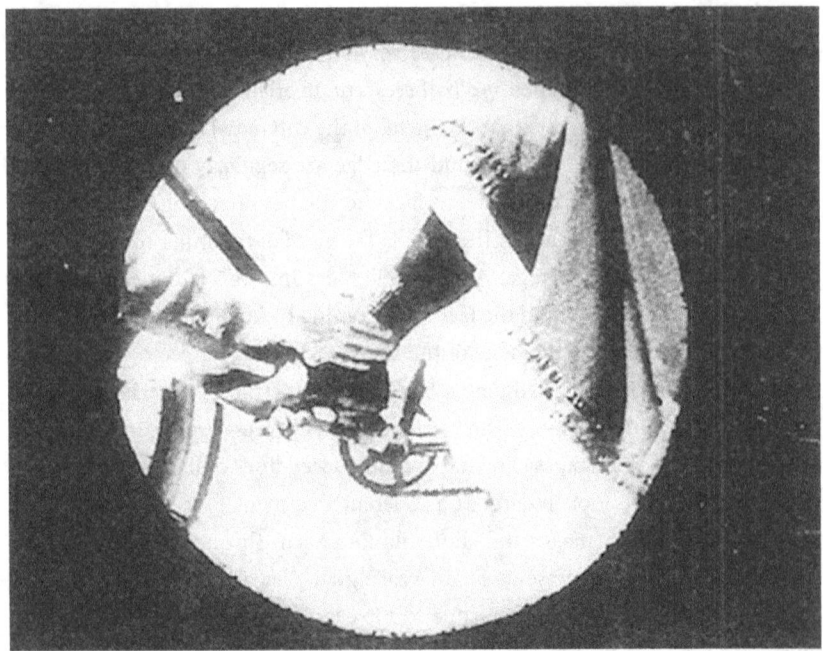

As Seen Through a Telescope (Albert Smith, 1900)

In the course of these three scenes, the concept of the human body is in the process of a transformation through which it is split. If the first photograph of a human being presents him in his singularity (this life and no other as Agamben writes, interpreting the image through photography's exigency), it is an extraction of sorts as the photograph throws a spotlight on the figure. The second image of the foot as X-ray moves inside of the body, separating the body as social entity (*bios*) from its biological manifestation (as *zoe*). The third sequence recuperates this division to a certain extent by framing the scene in which the body is fetishized as an intimate encounter that we remain external to. This final manoeuvre situates the body as an enigma that will become a fundamental focus and raison d'être of cinema, which is the question of how to access a subject's truth when it is rendered as interiority. If the cinema, for Agamben at least, reports a crisis of gestural communication, it nonetheless is tasked with the resolution of that problem. It is possible to read the ongoing oscillation between the semiosis of the body as surface and the internal enigmatic truth through the foot once again. By 1948, Powell and Pressburger had created a film-dance of this oscillation in *The Red Shoes*. The hypnotic, hallucinatory drive to read emotional and psychological 'truth' across the body becomes fixated on the feet as the possible site of an autonomous truth: the red shoes either separate the feet from the desiring subject or enable the subject's real desire to be expressed.

Selective exclusions

On the Boulevard that day Louis Daguerre imaged the human figure from a distance. It is a street scene almost prefiguring the high angle establishing shots that cinema would make its signature opening of a film some one hundred years later. The man having his shoes shined is a small figure in the larger picture, yet despite the distance of the camera from this figure, he is legible; his gestural quality and composure are communicable years later. Agamben writes about this image in his essay 'Judgment Day', where the 'secret relationship' between photography, gesture and eschatology is commented upon.[2] It is in the most ordinary, quotidian gesture, writes Agamben, that a man will appear on Judgement Day, that is on the day in which he will be figured across time in his singularity. Paradoxically in the stillness of the photograph the dynamic form of the gesture, or communication directed at no particular end, is revealed. Photography's potency is both to take us by surprise and to expose us in our most ordinary gestures. In so doing, the photograph captures what Agamben has called form-of-life (*forma-di-vita*), a mode in which the physicality of the body is inseparable from its social and aesthetic manifestations.[3] In this photograph we have less an image and more a gesture that communicates across time in the mode of Benjamin's historical dialectic. The gestural picture figures the detail of a man maintaining a form-of-life, by which I mean a life where his clothing, his bearing and his relationship to the other man and to the street are of a piece.

Although the difference between Louis Daguerre's photograph and Ernest Payne's X-ray of a foot appears retrospectively as one of category, at the end of the nineteenth century the two images were both considered to be part of the 'new photography', as Lisa Cartwright has argued.[4] During the first years of X-rays being performed, it was not unusual for high street practitioners to provide this service alongside the projection of the newly animated images of the cinematograph.[5] The X-ray in its infancy had popular appeal as a form of psychic reading of the body's interiority and as a serviceable high street appliance. The practice of X-raying feet with a machine named a fluoroscope during shoe fittings, for example, became standardized throughout a number of countries during the 1920s.[6] Early X-ray images provided for a mode of viewing the body in its local habitus, casually inquisitive about what kind of image can be produced of tissue and bones and what purpose it can be put to. But this enquiry into the experiment that was X-ray photography was curtailed by the use of the new imaging technology as an authoritative source of medical knowledge. This particular image is also the record of a loss of ease about the imaging of the body as the practice of X-rays became relocated from the commercial sites of the high street to the enclosure of medical institutions. The X-ray became a specialized method of producing knowledge of the body that could decode and render legible the various elements of physical matter. This X-ray of a foot effectively detaches it from its corporeality, isolates and delimits its significance, and renders it information, which in Agamben's terms, we need hardly be reminded, is the translation of life into bare life. The final feature to note of this shift from the photograph to the X-ray is the rendering of the body as interiority, which in turn creates a split, retrospectively designating an exteriority. It is a practice aligned with others, as Akira Lippit notes: X-rays, cinema and psychoanalysis emerge at the same time as 'phenomenologies of the inside'.[7] That the inside is the location of truth is increasingly significant, underpinning the opposition of an internal truth pitched against a dissembling external appearance.

If the foot surfaces in a scene in early cinema as the site of a discreet rapture observed from a distance-brought-close, it is a moment that conjoins the two former vignettes, if we may call them that. The film 'Seen Through a Telescope' brings together the habituated life of the street with a new instrument for looking, which is also an instrumentalization of vision. That this extension of the eye's capacity to see in detail what is distant is both voyeuristic and intrusive is fully recognized; the film's comedy turns on the punitive treatment of the surreptitious one who watches. With this caper, the comedy covers over the real trauma in this scene, which is the fragmentation of the body delivered by this new mode of telescopic seeing. Clearly this instrument for looking is a stand-in for cinema itself. Fetishistic disavowal is played several ways in this scene. The viewer is allowed to experience the fetishist's pleasure in regarding the foot in close-up, flirting with the knowledge that it is a part of anatomy situated at the end of the eroticized female leg (and of course, fetishism of the foot gathers momentum through the twentieth century as a trope through the coveting and collection of shoes). Yet this pleasure is disavowed by its displacement onto the man with the telescope, he who takes the rap. It is a scenario that Freud would have argued stands in for the disavowal and appeasement of a larger traumatic fantasy (castration). Similarly, the telescope, we may argue, stands in for the larger trauma that cinema presents in its cutting up of the human body, a psychic dismemberment that is just emerging as a critical component of cinematic language in the close-up exhibited by this particular film. Shot in the year of a new century, 'Seen Through a Telescope' inaugurated an imaging technology that could not only render the body in fragments, but effectively stitch it together again through the device of montage.

In each of these images there is a selective process at work that renders one part of the image visible and eliminates other aspects. In the photograph of the man having his shoes cleaned, the man and the blurry figure of the shoe polisher appear whilst other figures are made invisible. It is the product of an alchemy, literally of the chemicals as they interact with light on that particular day. But the photograph testifies to another kind of alchemy, of the relationship between a camera that observes the dynamics of a scene which remains beyond its control, open to chance. In the second image, the X-ray renders invisible the texture and form of the shoe as a worn artefact. The shoe disappears in a selective process dependent on the power of cathode rays. In the third image, the street and the human form in its entirety is screened out by an instrument that seems to have divided space and anatomized the scene. There is resonance here with Benjamin's analogy for the cameraman as surgeon in the artwork essay, who 'greatly diminishes the distance between himself and the patient by penetrating into the patient's body', and whose practice consists of the production of 'multiple fragments which are assembled under a new law'.[8] Whilst the analogy of the cameraman as surgeon is a comparison with the painter as magician in this section of the essay, it is instructive to take account of Benjamin's choice of profession; only a surgeon or a pathologist works beneath the skin of the human body. The surgeon enters beneath the skin and 'penetrates deeply into him',[9] destroying what he names a 'natural distance'. Whilst this 'unnatural' proximity in cinema's imaging of the body suggests a transgressive closeness, the threat identified by Benjamin is the crossing of a boundary between the exterior and interior. In short, the cinema comes to pose the question of what is inside the human being, a question that is being asked simultaneously in discourses of medicine and pathology, criminality and punishment, education and deviancy. The question is loaded and the answer that the cinema provides shores up anxieties about the nature of the human being. Inside of the human body, cinema answers, is the expressive soul communicating an inner world. In other words, cinema properly births human interiority as the location of meaning and the anchor of that new fangled concept, identity.

The machine at work: Producing centric cinema

If these three images serialize the body's capture and division, as I have argued, then what is it that the body is captured by? At the centre of a network of regulation and representation the body is a production of what Agamben calls a machine that performs separations and caesurae. These include but are not limited to the separation of the life of the physical body from political life, the animal from the human being and the profane from the sacred. In Agamben's work, the machines that render these separations are not simply political infrastructure; rather they are the basis from which the polis may take effect, that a political domain may begin to be thought. In this sense they are not only instructional but ontologically foundational. The machine is the description that Agamben affords for a number of critical separations, the anthropological machine sifting the human from the non-human animal (producing the human by banning its animality), being the most famous. Yet the mechanism that separates the sacred from the profane is equally paradigmatic for the realm of objects, matter, materiality or Heidegger's stones that are purportedly without world. The machine that separates the sacred from the profane enacts the removal of certain objects from common use and places them under a rule of prohibition. The division that cleaves bare life from form-of-life is a further operation of a juridical machine that operates an exclusion as the suspension of sovereign law. The common form of machines is their practice of separating and dividing in order to cleave distinctions that instrumentalize life and sustain its attitude towards what he names means and ends.

Cinema is a machine not only in terms of its apparatus, but in the symbolic sense as a processor of form-of-life and a facilitator of exclusions as it becomes standardized and nailed down. In the late nineteenth century the human body becomes the site of forensic attention, spectacularization and management. It undergoes what Didi-Huberman calls the tyranny of medical management in the realm of hysteria[10] (and more broadly in medical imaging), it is the site of the comparative study of species in evolutionary biology, and it is subjected to a wide-ranging set of tests of every faculty imaginable in Francis Galton's anthropometry. The body, that is, is matter to be tried, measured, presented and recorded, reduced to bare life by this system of governance. What this generates in its wake is the uncomfortable question of what exactly the human being is if it can be defined by such empirical measures. Perhaps more starkly, what if any is the remainder to this testing or in addition to the human-animal body? For a supplement that provides an *in addition* to the body is needed to create a margin in which humanity can be claimed against the pure animality of the body, and form-of-life against naked life. A critical feature of the supplement would be its opacity, precisely its resistance to anthropometric testing and interpretation.

If not exactly in response, it is certainly in dialogue with late nineteenth-century practices of administering the human body that the cinema provides a version of the human being in excess of this. In cinema as it becomes institutionalized in the first decade of the twentieth century in a form of studio production, the body becomes anchored by an enigmatic human interiority. There is less emphasis on slapstick comedy and more on the body as a manifestation of a feeling subject. In 1901, Charles Musser notes, the Edison Company opened a glass-enclosed rooftop studio at 41 East Street, New York,[11] with the ambition of making films that were longer and fictional, and not subject to the contingencies of the street. The studio in a sense performs an inwards turn, letting in the outside only in terms of the weather and the sky above. Edison's studio was not particularly prolific for a number of complex reasons, but the ambition that the studio presented was widespread. The notion of a cinema that was controlled, dramatic and expressive both drew from theatre and marked its departure from theatrical presentation; cinema could in the close-up scrutinize the emotional weather 'within' the character. The early acted feature films, still only running to six reels, were however to become the precondition for the popular nickelodeon culture of small, shopfront cinemas emerging a few years later in 1906, whose programmes provided a rapidly changing menu of films including these new dramas. As the experience of cinema began to become ritualized with this shift towards dramatic film, the move involved a simultaneous refinement in the apparatus; the adoption of the three-blade shutter in projection allowed a more comfortable pulsing of light. This gradual shift in film production and exhibition from short actuality films and comedies to fictional films conspires with a turn inwards and away from the bodily carking of early cinema comedies.

This is the cinema that Agamben writes of in the essay 'Notes on Gesture', that records bodies in their gestural mode and as they are about to lose this capacity and 'turn inwards'. For whilst the focus on interiority secures the division of human from animal, and civic identity from that of bare life, it also marks the end of an open gesturality between people, the manifestation of communicability itself. Human interiority is produced and coded in new forms of melodrama as a mystery that becomes attached to bodies as they perform the ineffable and the dramatic. Of course it is not the only form of cinema during this period, nor is it a transformation that occurs everywhere. It begins in local practices of planning and centralizing filmmaking as activities within a production line, appearing in pockets of America and Europe. It becomes consolidated as the American studio system by 1917. The story of the standardization of cinema is well rehearsed elsewhere; suffice to say that the standardization of a feature film (its duration, type of film stock, mode of projection and so forth) was later linked to a mode of distribution and exhibition that secured its presence well beyond the United States. This form of film became centric cinema, and whilst it was only one mode of filmmaking amongst many, its trajectory was set to ripple out in concentric circles across continents.

What happens to the *gestural* body as centric cinema evolves? We find that when the body is foregrounded as such, as sexualized star persona or the vehicle of action, it operates as a kind of rigid residue that cannot be eliminated, only displayed. The body as animal entity is paraded almost as a totem of the gestural body that has become, paradoxically, fixed. The fluid form calcifies in centric cinema in performances that are always already scripted, as film production gradually moves to pre-production and all aspects of the film are determined in advance of the making. The gestural body that is losing control of its gestures in 1895 mutates into the spectacular body that Agamben aligns with Guy Debord's society of the spectacle. 'We might think here of the hypertrophy of gesture in contemporary cinema', writes Benjamin Noys, 'no action star is without his, or more usually her, display of balletic assurance and combat proficiency', revealing 'a deadly conformity of gestures' that are both signature turns and interchangeable clichés.[12] Gesture, that is, becomes a means to an end that is always known in advance. Contingency is lost, along with the proficiency of an actor who can work out the meaning of a gesture in the process of its production. We might think of this form of display as another, more contemporary version of melodrama as action: in this bifurcation, cinematic melodrama is on the one hand the production of intense emotional affect as an interior state of the character, and on the other, the drama of a staccato sequence of actions devoid of interior motivation. The body in the history of cinema is something that cannot be properly and definitively defined, and for this reason, it must be articulated and divided over and again.

In summary, if we trace Agamben's thought into the realm of cinema, cinema comes under the sign of the anthropological machine to perform the task of a separation between man and animal. Cinema, I am arguing, is complicit with the ongoing separations in the production and articulation of humanity. Yet in so doing, man has produced cinema in his own image, simultaneously positing an outside to cinema, a zone of exclusion in which other versions are put to rest. The product of this separation and exclusion is ex-centric cinema. It is a cinema that is not redundant however, for it produces the cinema that we have.

A nameless science

When Agamben wrote in *Potentialities* about Aby Warburg's work, he called Warburg's practice the nameless science. Warburg himself had struggled to find a title to name what it is that he did with artworks, working through possibilities such as 'history of culture', and 'iconology of the interval', but coming to settle on none, stating that whilst his method exists, it 'has no name'.[13] The reason that Agamben proffers for this nameless approach is related to disciplinarity and boundaries. Warburg, he argues, did not recognize the territories of disciplines, the borders that sealed off certain areas of cultural study from one another. Warburg in fact transgressed demarcations of this nature. 'What is unique and significant about Warburg's method as a scholar', writes Agamben, 'is not so much that he adopts a new way of writing art history as that he always directs his research toward the overcoming of the borders of art history'.[14] Warburg's ambition as he moved between images was to create relationships with other disciplines, to link philology, religion and anthropology to the study of art in a manner that might be read as either disingenuous or genius. Agamben notes astutely, 'It is as if Warburg were interested in this discipline solely to place within it the seed that would cause it to explode.'[15] The study of images as transmitters was Warburg's intent, and disciplinary boundaries were merely obstacles to this pursuit.

The name that is given to the approach explored in this book of ex-centric cinema faces a different problem. The disciplinary borders that distinguish the study of film from other cultural objects and approaches present no more than a token obstruction. The difficulty of the name here concerns the transformation it enacts on the object. That is, film and cinema are less objects of study and more the nexus of relationships between differently constituted objects and practices. Ex-centric cinema is above all an aggregate. In Latin, the term draws on *grex*, meaning a flock, and *agregare*, to herd together. It is a term used for the mass of particles in soil, the mass of minerals in stone, and the Oxford English Dictionary suggests as an example of an aggregate the carpels of a flower such as a raspberry. It is a term that lends itself to multiple material forms and describes the relationship of parts as an assemblage or a collection. An aggregate has the feel of impermanence, like animals herding or rocks in a river gathering in a temporary sink. The ex-centric does not designate an ontology for cinema, a medium specificity, nor a material substrate that conditions its form indefinitely. The ex-centric designates a practice, a set of relationships and an outside to actuality.

In his analysis of experimental film and video as ex-cinema, Akira Lippit elaborates on the meaning of the exergue, the *ex* from Greek meaning outside, and *ergon* referring to work.[16] Ex-cinema, he writes, is simultaneously a space outside of the work and yet essentially part of it. Artworks which are films are ex-cinema in the sense of residing both within the frame of cinema and outside of its main body of reference as it were. The film which is an artwork exists in tandem, alongside cinema. The exergue, he writes, is also 'a thinking and excavation of the outside', and in this sense it has some relationship to film archaeology, to the practice of creating a description to that which is produced as an excess to the idea of cinema, always already a remnant or trace.[17] Another term for the excavation of an outside is 'paracinema', the name given by Jonathan Walley to the experimental forms of cinema characterizing films of the 1960s and 1970s. For Walley, cinema is not conditioned by its material properties, but it retains an essentialism of sorts, reminiscent of Bazin's appeal to the idea of cinema as centuries old. For paracinema, as for ex-centric cinema, contingency marks the assemblage of materials that provide for cinema at any one time. He writes that film is constituted by 'a cluster of historically contingent materials that happens to be, for the time being at least, the best means for creating cinema'.[18] In contrast to Walley, Pavle Levi advocates for medium specificity as a way of redefining cinema. Yet the focus on film's materiality, attached as it is to histories of experimental practice, to an outsider understanding of film as praxis, and to the transition from celluloid to digital materials, fails to engage with the multiplicity of relationships that constitute what we take to be cinema at any one point.

The iterations of ex-centric cinema that I want to draw out as concepts in this final chapter are the outcomes of the preceding chapters. The first of these is a cinema of transmission. The second is an aggregate cinema, produced through encounters, enactments and cross-species practices. The third modality of the cinematically ex-centric is a cinema of the impotential, a form of cinema that challenges the automatic privilege of that which becomes (or is actualized) over that which remains potential. It provides for a cinema that is both once upon a time and never, for its purpose is not to accede to a linear account of time, from conception to realization. Rather, its effect is to demonstrate to us that the past is only one of many possible futures. If each of these conceptualizations is in its synoptic form necessarily abstract, what follows is an elaboration of each as an example, recalling Agamben's recommendation for this concept that 'escapes the antinomy of the universal and the particular'.[19]

Ex-centric cinema as transmission

To conceive of cinema as a transmission is to attend to its capacity to communicate across time, but not simply this. What is transmitted as cinema is not determined and fixed by the act of recording, for the time of the image and its resonance exceeds its inscription. The image, that is, communicates itself variously. We could say that the image is not the same image across time. This is demonstrated in a film, *My Silence* (2013), by the Finnish director and visual artist Mika Taanila. Taanila creates a film that is gathered from the excavation of silence within an earlier film. Another way of describing this practice is that he remakes a film that had once existed with dialogue and eliminates speech from his version.

The film that Taanila uses as source material is Louis Malle's *My Dinner with André* (1981), a work famously composed around the fictional occasion of two friends meeting for dinner in a New York restaurant and their sparkling conversation. The two friends are played by the actor and playwright Wallace Shawn and director André Gregory. The dinner is given over to a discussion of art, experience and the priorities that have governed each of their lives. The structure of the film is in two parts, with Gregory's experience dominating the first part of the film and Shawn's the latter. The characters are reminiscent, to all intents and purposes, of Don Quixote and Sancho Panza, with Gregory's exuberant fantastical adventures in dramatically different landscapes deflated by Shawn's modest proposal for a life lived in the detail. Malle's film was a story in which 'nothing happened', where the conventions of action were ignored in the bringing forth of conversation as a dramatic force. Produced as an exercise in scripted dialogue as the gravitational force field of the film, there is little action other than eating and speaking, and no 'development' other than an exchange of

My Silence (Mika Taanila, 2013)

views. *My Dinner with André* received acclaim for its redefinition of the feature film as a conversation; therefore to remove speech from this film, as Mika Taanila does, is seemingly to remove its critical dimension.

What is left of film when language is removed? The answer is not straightforward. The question presupposes that the film *My Silence* is operating with a lack whereas in fact, it is a new experience that refers to a pre-existing film but functions independently of it. It is a different film, one that presents a conversation as two bodies in gesture. As the men sit and dine, their exchange is a series of movements that draws attention to the poise of hands, the angle of a head and the posture of a body during the rituals of eating and drinking. The longer we watch, the more attentive we are to how many fingers are used to hold a glass, the manner in which one of the characters pauses to listen, the direction in which eyes narrow and shift, and the rate at which an eyebrow may rise and fall. All of this activity of communication is in response to the body of the other and words that we cannot hear. Unlike silent cinema in which the body is actively deployed to communicate without the aid of language, *My Silence* extracts gesture from a scene in which the language of the body has been

Film still from *My Silence* (Mika Taanila, 2013)

forgotten in the presence of spoken dialogue. It is a film that requires us to read a script, a plot, a story of encounter through the openness of bodies in gesture, what we might call the chemistry of their alchemical mixing. In addition, *My Silence* is a film of changing patterns of brightness, camera movement and positioning that seems to leap, pull back, or find a new place from which to view this encounter. Its sound track is that of ambience, giving priority to that which is pushed to the background in the presence of the human voice, and the strange warped distortions as an edit takes place to skip over speech. Perhaps most striking of all is the rendering of silence, of the film's ability to bring into being that which is not spoken. In this sense, it is a film that reveals nothing less than the unactualized of speech that resides in and gives shape to every event.

The dynamic of gesture/speech refers back of course to Agamben's essay on the subject where, as we noted earlier in the chapter, cinema resides at the turning point of a mode of human interaction as communicability in bodily gesture towards a pathology of communicative capacity. Gestures, Agamben argues, are prone to misfire in compulsive behavioural tics, and cinema is there to document it. The argument that I have made in relation to Agamben's reading of this occasion follows the implications of this shift further, more directly pursuant of how this continues to manifest in cinema as a new dependency on dialogue. Cinema in turn becomes part of an apparatus that puts into play the concept of a truth lodged within the subject, substantiating the organic life of the body as a site of meaningful interiority. Outside of the cinema, the body becomes the location of a biopolitical enquiry concerned to establish certain truths, whilst within cinema, the individual is a subject who is compelled to speak a truth, to express what would otherwise remain hidden. Cinematic production, as already noted, comes to be defined by scripts and screenplays. The potential of the body to 'speak' gesturally is increasingly sublimated to the demands of this regime, and perhaps this is why Louis Malle's *My Dinner with André*, some fifty years after the coming of sound, garners attention for foregrounding language, for making it visible as a mode capable of essayistic conversation rather than pure expressionism. Mika Taanila's film pivots again on this same point, playing it differently; the essayistic conversation is the centric version of cinema. *My Silence* is the cast of an ex-centric cinema in which 'language' is the lost gesture of bodies.

We might also come to ask what is left of the human when language is removed. Or to put it within Agamben's locution, if the question of language is related to the question of what it means to be human, *My Silence* stages a strange reversal of becoming human. The falling into language has not occurred or has been erased, and so the acquisition of humanness and the mark that distinguishes the human from his own animality is no longer visible. The silence we 'hear' is not exactly 'silent', for the noises of the technical process, of sound warped and blunted, prevail. *My Silence* mixes thoroughly a non-linguistic human language of gesture with the language of machines, revealing a capacity to communicate as though a linguistic turn had never taken place, releasing the human from the state of *in-fans*.[20] What is transmitted by the image and sound sequences twenty-two years after their recording is the significance of the interval between speech. Like the black leader between images rarely seen, the silence between words is rarely heard or constituted as a meaningful space. It is in this sense a cast around words.

Ex-centric cinema as aggregate

That cinema is an aggregate form invokes a sense of materiality, yet it is important to note here that an aggregate is not only the chemical nature of the matter involved. It also refers to the practices, relationships and inhabitations that cohere with and through the aggregate. Cinema is a case in point and its moments of rapid transition and marked obsolescence attract a swarm of commentary until our relationships are once again habituated when material form stabilizes once more. Yet an enlivened attention to cinema as aggregate combining different types and qualities of matter and a range of practices is historically consistent in the work of engineers, inventors, amateurs, assistants and artists. In Simon Starling's work about the Berlin metalwork factory, *Wilhelm Noack oHG* (2006), it is not entirely clear who is doing the making of things; indeed the imagination of engineers, amateurs and assistants may well be at work. In this installation, the definition of cinema is redirected away from the relationship of viewer to screen, diverted towards the object of projection. Starling makes a film about the factory and its making of things, filmed as though by assistants operating a camera at the height of a small child and with the same gleeful appetite to see into and around things. And yet, in the room where the film is screened, its purpose seems to be only to direct us to the object that throws this image.

The experience of 'cinema' here, one could say, is an inversion of the conventions of following the beam of light onto the screen. Rather, tracing the beam of light back towards its source leads to the object in the room, the projector as spiral staircase, a thing that is nothing less than theatrical in its laced platforms of moving film. In remaking the idea of the projector through the historical tropes and practices of the metalwork factory, the artists with their assistants profane this machine and return it to the sphere of common use. The sacred magic of cinema secured through the veiling of the apparatus and its material form is decompressed in play. The ritual of cinema continues, but its meaning or myth is emptied out. What enthrals here is the combination of the materials of a celluloid loop, pulleys, metal arms, and a motor, into a highly charged yet elegantly functioning system.

This category of ex-centricity may also be thought in terms of a diversion of practical effect, or where the diversionary nature of activity draws attention to the materials to hand. The materiality of a commodity such as a camera, like the image as spectacle, is obscured for us by its spectacular sheen, by its becoming-image in a system of circulation. The various materials that constitute a DVD or camera only become apparent to us when the spectacle is less glaring, when the lustre has worn thin and the commodity becomes once again a temporary composition of matter, albeit on the way to the scrap heap. 'A look at the world of toys', writes Agamben in the essay 'Playland', 'shows that children, humanity's little scrap-dealers, will play with whatever junk comes their way, and that play thereby preserves profane objects and behaviour that has ceased to exist'.[21] In play, children re-imagine the possibility of a thing, in the process suspending the object's use value in the world and its relationship to an end. The thing as toy takes on a new mantle that is related to temporality no less. The distortion of economic and practical purpose in play situates the toy at the cusp of the 'once' and 'no longer', at the differential margin between the thing as it was in its context of use and the thing as it is now relieved of the pressure of purpose; the object becomes in play the enactment of ritual in which the meaning of the ritual (or myth) is lost. There is, writes Agamben, an inverse relation between the sacred and play. In making an object sacred, meaning is conferred on the object endowed by the ritual in which the thing is removed from the everyday and relocated to a separate sphere. The inverse performed in play is then the use of an object, in this case by children, for means that are not specified in advance. In so doing, the object is returned to common use, stripped of its pre-existing meaning, a process that Agamben names profanation. Part of the machine of sacrifice, whose task it is to separate the sacred from the profane, the practice of profanation, according to Agamben, can be put to work in the domain of law, nature, culture and economics. Jessica Whyte writes that there is a distinction in Agamben's work between 'profanation' and 'use' that is worth attending to. For profanation returns an object to common use but not to a previous utilitarian mode. She writes, 'Agamben rejects every attempt to return to an earlier use, and seeks instead to retrieve uses that were not able to be, uses that were prohibited by the rigid inscription of things in particular spheres, and by compulsory relations between means and ends.'[22] The profanation of cinema which is another term for its re-purposing, I would contend, runs in several directions away from centric cinema and diverges from Agamben in its attentiveness to material form.

The re-purposing of objects has a relationship to another figure argues Agamben in the essay 'In Playland': the bricoleur. Drawing on the work of Lévi-Strauss and myth, bricolage practises the assembly of an object from 'crumbs' and 'scraps' belonging to other structural wholes or groups. Recombining entities to produce a new form is to transform the meaning of a signified into signifier. What is of significance here is the extraction of objects from their historical context and the consequent transformation of our sense of time. The practice of bricolage is closely related to that of quotation, a process that is at the centre of Benjamin's later work in the Arcades Project. Towards the end of

Agamben's *Man Without Content* (1994), he cites Benjamin in this description of the potent force of quotation:

> The particular power of quotations arises, according to Benjamin, not from their ability to transmit that past and allow the reader to relive it but, on the contrary, from their capacity to 'make a clean sweep, to expel from the context, to destroy'... an alienating power that constitutes its unmistakable aggressive force.[23]

Following this logic, the bricoleur is also like the collector who removes the object from its historical context to create a new paradigm in which the continuum of the past is broken down into ruins and rubble. Hence the valorization of humanity's little scrap-dealers who make hay in their sorting and sifting of the past as mere 'things' whose chronological anchors have been lost. The process of sorting materials is the process of realigning temporal relations. The axis of diachrony (the meaning of a thing across time, in the trajectory of its lifespan activated in play) is brought up against synchrony (its meaning understood in the moment without recourse to its mutable form over time). 'If ritual is therefore a machine for transforming diachrony into synchrony', Agamben writes, 'play, conversely, is a machine for transforming synchrony into diachrony'.[24] If we convert this formula into the domain of ex-centricity, centric cinema is the ritual standardization of time, and play conversely is the re-purposing of cinema as unstable signifiers of time.

Ex-centric cinema as impotentiality

The parsing of the term 'potentiality' includes within its twists and turns the incomplete in cinema. It has a long legacy that embraces Eisenstein's plans to make a film of Marx's *Capital*, Deren's footage of Haiti and Fassbinder's idea for a film called *Cocaine*, in which everything is covered in a layer of hoar frost. Orson Welles will not finish the film *Don Quixote* (along with many other projects), just as Pier Paolo Pasolini some ten years earlier did not finish the screenplay of *St Paul*, a similarly monumental work that began its life in late May 1968 (commensurate with the student riots that Pasolini was so critical of) and gestated over the next six years.[25] At the end of *The Decameron* (1971), Pasolini addresses the viewer with this question: 'Why create a work when it is so beautiful simply to dream of one?'[26] The unfinished is an idea aligned with the concept that takes precedence later in Agamben's work, of potentiality. The incomplete, as he establishes in *Stanzas*, must be viewed from the perspective not only of the finished work, but of all of the possible iterations of a work that are not foreclosed by an ending.

This iteration of ex-centric cinema takes place, paradoxically, in the *not taking place* of cinema, recasting the relations between potentiality and actualization. Perhaps more significantly, impotentiality leads to a political and ethical position deriving from the non-realization of a deed, the complexity of which we will come to. Ex-centric cinema as the exercise of impotentiality is not simply an idea unactualized but a rereading of the term 'potentiality' that calls into question the revering of the executed act and the task undertaken; indeed impotentiality provides a critique of the championing of the act over thought. It is related, as Leland de la Durantaye notes, to *in-fans*, decreation and the *inoperative* in Agamben's work – terms that mark a threshold between doing and not doing as a site of multiple meanings.[27]

The decision to not act upon a potential becomes the actualization of impotentiality. Charlie Chaplin's exercising of his capacity to not play the part of the Tramp after the introduction into cinema of sound and speech is an actualization of impotentiality. The character had been created by Chaplin in 1914, an accidental outcome of his preparations for the filming of *Mabel's Strange Predicament* (directed by Mabel Normand), although the first film to be released starring the Tramp was *Kid Auto Races at Venice* (1914). According to Chaplin, the character emerged out of Chaplin's choice of clothing which he had selected through a principle of contradiction: a tight jacket, loose trousers, small hat and large boots.[28] The evolution of the figure over a number of films generated a character that was transferable to different contexts and with different emphases across the films. The Tramp was typically a character at sea in the modern world, at times envisaged as a vagrant and at others, a down-on-his-luck character who escaped through chance or sly manoeuvring. His last appearance was in the film *Modern Times* (1936), in which his indefatigable optimism radiates in the various worlds of the factory, the prison and the department store. The film was made without speech, with the only exception to this being the Tramp's song, which appears towards the end of the film when he is put on the spot to entertain a crowd of diners in a crowded restaurant and has lost the words to the song. His response is to improvise by singing emphatically, and with presence, a ballad composed of a nonsense language. Even with cinematic sound, the Tramp is a figure maintained without language. Chaplin prefers to not let him speak and after this film, to not perform.

The Tramp has a future that remains impotential and in so doing travels into the future as the past that we never had. This problematizes the binary potential-actual and takes us further away from the neat categories of having occurred and not having occurred, of being and not being. Ultimately it encroaches on the binary of living dead. That is, the acts that remain impotential are something like ghosts that reside with us in the present but remain in a separate and not entirely legible world. Here is Major Harry Larkins who stands up after Muybridge shoots him at point-blank range and walks away, and the Egyptian actress Soad Hosni who flutters to the ground from the high-rise apartment only to find her feet as she touches down. Ghosts are like children, Agamben writes, in that both are unstable signifiers that bring discontinuity into the world of synchronic regulation. Ghosts and children are both incomplete and impotential in different ways. Conversely we find that adults and the dead are aligned in their sharing of the sign of stability. What is needed to mediate these two worlds and binary conditions is the ritual that assures the passage from one to the other. The strangeness of ghosts and children is in their ability to reside in the categories of the between.

The impotential of ex-centric cinema comprises all that has been thought in relation to cinema and that remains at the level of thought, and it also includes the possible configurations of cinema that remain unthought residing metaphorically in a great warehouse of unmade cinema. In this sense, impotentiality maintains a deep relationship with the archaeological as an enquiry into the contingencies of events that occurred and correspondingly those that did not occur, with what are mainly the immaterial manifestations of a cinema that never came to pass. Some material traces of cinema's impotentiality however may be discerned. We might list here a number of the thousands of patents that were registered in the last decade of the nineteenth century for mechanical and technical processes that never materialized. Impotentiality is the practice of the assistants, the actions of those who wandered away from the task, who lost concentration or who fell asleep in the room next to their masters with their heads resting upon a newly formed plan. The exercise of impotentiality resides mostly, however, without material form. It encompasses the will exercised by the models who attended Muybridge's studio, inquisitive about the new photographic method, but who left when they discovered that they must remove their clothing.

Across Agamben's work, as we have come to see in the course of this book, the terms 'potentiality' and 'impotentiality' are key to his framework as it has developed and in recent years the terms have acquired a particularly political resonance. Potentiality, that is, has emerged as a dominant concept that is used to support political moments of actualization of, for example, forms of exploitative labour or natural resources. He writes, 'I think that the concept of potentiality has never ceased to function in the life and history of humanity, most notably in that part of humanity that has grown and developed its potency [*potenza*] to the point of imposing its power over the whole planet.'[29] In his treatment of potentiality, Agamben invokes Aristotle, tracing this term through his works beginning with *De Anima* where Aristotle speculates about what happens to human sensibility when it is not stimulated; do the senses exist only as potential or as an impotential? It is worth following this question as Agamben pursues it through other of Aristotle's works, to obtain a clearer sense of what is at issue. In a further speculative passage, Aristotle distinguishes between the potential that is generic from that which belongs to someone, and it is the latter that interests him the most; the generic potential of a human to be kind, for example, is distinguished from the specific potential of a poet who has the potential to write poems or the architect who has the ability to design houses even when they are not involved in these activities. In this context, potentiality exists both as the potential to do something (actualization) and the potential to not do this or that.

The matter would appear to be straightforward that when potentiality is realized it ceases to be potentiality. But Agamben, after Aristotle, takes this back to the point prior to actualization. A potential to do something is both potentiality and impotentiality, always containing within it the two entities. When a potentiality is actualized, he asks, what happens to impotentiality? In a rereading of one of Aristotle's most complex statements, Agamben argues that when a task is actualized, it retains its own force of impotentiality as a *potential intact*. The line that Agamben fruitfully reinterprets appears in *Metaphysics* and runs thus: 'A thing is said to be potential if, when the act of which it is said to be potential is realized, there will be nothing impotential.'[30] This statement, according to Agamben, has been interpreted as the exhaustion of impotentiality in the moment of an act's realization of the potential; that is, the statement has been understood as a description of the moment in which potentiality is converted through action into actuality, leaving no residue. On the contrary, writes Agamben, for there lies another meaning if we read carefully. In this re-interpretation, Agamben asserts the opposite that when potential becomes actualized, it leaves in place impotentiality, the possibility of not acting. This is not abolished or exhausted by the realization of writing a poem, for example, but remains with the poet as the possibility of not writing. To retain a relationship with impotentiality is to sustain a relationship with one's privation. 'Beings that exist in the mode of potentiality *are capable of their own impotentiality*', he writes, continuing, 'and only in this way do they become potential'.[31] As we follow the movement of thought from potential to impotential, we find that we arrive at the place that is by now familiar in Agamben's work, where the distinction between seemingly opposite terms is rubbed out. By exercising impotentiality, by preferring not to, a being exercises its potentiality thereby erasing or at least significantly blurring the line between the two terms. It remains to be asked what the implications are both for the political, and for cinema, of this claiming of impotentiality.

Are films dead letters?

The figure who inspires Agamben's account of potentiality and who appears in many essays and footnotes across the years (in *Idea of Prose* 1985, *The Coming Community* 1990, and *Potentialities* in 1999) is the titular character of *Bartleby, the Scrivener: A Story of Wall Street* by Herman Melville. Bartleby (the story runs), who holds a bureaucratic position as a copier of legal text in a law firm, decides one day to activate his impotentiality by choosing to not write. His refrain, when asked, is the simple statement 'I prefer not to.' His capacity to copy remains intact; he retains the potential to write documents of law as before, but his preference is to not do so. Bartleby's choice is to exercise impotentiality, the capacity to not do. The story of the scrivener of Wall Street is a significant text not only for Agamben, but for other writers and philosophers, notably Gilles Deleuze who wrote an essay on Bartleby, 'Bartleby, or the Formula'.[32] Deleuze's essay is instructive here as it announces Bartleby as a heroic figure of resistance who, in declining the 'invitation' to work for no apparent reason, exercises a practice of disobedience that is difficult to define. Bartleby's preference therefore is not open to recuperation by the state as it fails to register within recognizable categories of dissent. This is a reading that gathers momentum in various manifestations from Hardt and Negri as the beginning of liberatory politics[33] to William Watkin's account of Agamben and Bartleby, as the exercise of indifference.[34] That Bartleby's discontinuation of work takes place in Wall Street, the finance district of New York, is not without significance, and the fact that Bartleby is a scribe of the law is equally meaningful. The preference exercised by Bartleby is a refusal of acts of repetition (copying), of a reproduction of the law (command). What Bartleby refuses then is not only the practice of an alienated form of labour, but his part in the circulation of words, texts and communications.

As Leland de la Durantaye notes, Agamben reads Bartleby's suspended pen as an ancient gesture that he refuses to interpret through psychology.[35] Bartleby has no internal motive. His refusal is of an attachment to the world of work and of law and, as the story unfolds, even to living his life. As Jessica Whyte argues, 'Eschewing the decision between yes and no, creation and destruction', Bartleby conducts 'an experiment in either what can be or not be – an experiment in potentiality itself, which requires the overturning of the principle of the irrevocability of the past'.[36] In this state of suspension, which exists as the liminal site between being and non-being, the polarities of the human subject as wilful subject on the one part and nihilistically attenuated subject on the other are refuted. To claim Bartleby's artful practice as civil disobedience, as Deleuze does, would seem to attribute a strategic consciousness to the act that is lacking from Bartleby's gradual decline and demise. Rather, Bartleby's refusal in Agamben's reading is closer to a Benjaminian messianism, as Whyte notes, where redemption is of a past that never came to be rather than a claim to influence the future. By refusing to write, Bartleby declines to write over the past that never came to be. Indeed, to reconfigure the relationship between the past and the present is a more true account of Bartleby's withdrawal from the world than that of political dissidence.

The significance of Bartleby for cinema resides in the back-story that Melville provides for Bartleby, which comes on the final page of the story. Here the narrator offers up 'one little item of rumor' which is that prior to his life as a scrivener, Bartleby worked in the Dead Letter Office in Washington, handling the mail that never reached its destination[37] as the addressee had died. The letters, these emblems of communication or communicative capacity, do not reach their destination. It is a situation that resonates with an office mentioned earlier. The patents office for film and cinema equipment was in many ways a dead letters office. The communication within the patent did not necessarily reach actualization. Each patent that may have taken the interpretation of cinema elsewhere, narrowing or multiplying its form, was a letter never delivered. We might say that there is some semblance between the Dead Letter Office in which there amassed texts that retain their potentiality in their state of impotentiality and the unactualized of cinema. Cinema's unrealized films and technical set-ups, that is, are only communications that have not yet reached their destination and may never do so. They are dead letters that have yet to be read, blurring the reality of their existence.

Ex-centric cinema retains possibility in multiple ways: dormant in the apparatus and texts that exist, as unfinished projects that refuse closure, and as the experiment without truth, which is another way of describing the relation between potentiality and impotentiality. Such an experiment returns us to history, where the work of potentiality finally takes its full effect. For the past is, as Benjamin wrote and Agamben paraphrases, recalled as possibility in our return to it: 'Remembrance restores possibility to the past', writes Agamben, 'making what happened incomplete and completing what never was',[38] that is, their becoming possible again. 'Bartleby calls the past into question, re-calling it – not simply to redeem what was, to make it exist again but, more precisely, to consign it once again to potentiality, to the indifferent truth of the tautology',[39] he writes. If the work of ex-centric cinema as a practice is to continue to consign to potentiality all that has been foreclosed, it is a labour that insists on the continuing incompleteness of all cinema. It is possible after this excursus into the ex-centric to articulate its signature of incompletion in this way: what is revelatory is not that incomplete cinema tells us something of potentiality, but that potentiality speaks to us of the incompleteness of all cinema.

Playout

The setting is a garden, and in the garden is a shed of some large proportion. The building, despite its ramshackle exterior, is watertight, and to the side is a small window that has been covered with a cloth pinned carelessly. The floor, if we were to obtain a view of the underside of the shed, is bowed by the weight of a Steinbeck editing desk. At the desk sits a large man whose proportions contribute to the further bowing of the floor. He attends to the machine mostly in the evenings. As the sun is setting he appears in his shirtsleeves and braces, a cigar clenched between his teeth as he strolls down the dusty path towards the shed. At the door he stops to extinguish the cigar before he goes inside, pulls the drape across the window and begins to edit a section of film. It is a film that he has shot on several continents over many years and he labours here to create a consistency across these parts. He finds as he sets the reels onto the desk that he becomes distracted by a detail, a button on a girl's dress that appears to be in place in this shot but is missing in the next. He winds the film forwards and backwards through the rollers in an attempt to identify the exact moment in which the girl's button is lost. He manages with gleeful pleasure to locate the frame in which it last appears, but then there is a gap before the girl is in frame again with the button missing. Despite having this wealth of material to hand that documents each take, he cannot know what happened to this small object which is now lost. The absent thing perplexes him and he wonders if he should reframe the shot so that the absence is less obvious, or cut it all together. Welles needs to ask his friend and editing companion, Mauro Bonanni, his view on the matter. It is late, he is tired and his neck aches. *It will wait until tomorrow*, he thinks as he leans back and inhales the night air.

Notes

1. Akira Mizuno Lippit, *Ex-cinema: From a Theory of Experimental Film and Video* (Berkeley, Los Angeles, CA and London: University of California Press, 2012), 42.
2. Giorgio Agamben, 'Judgment Day', in *Profanations*, trans. Jeff Fort (New York: Zone Books, 2007), 23–28, 24.
3. 'Form-of-Life' is a phrase that comes from an essay of the same name and is Agamben's term for the condition in which bare life could not be separated out to a zone of exclusion, but is a profane life. It was published in English translation as the first essay in the collection *Means Without End: Notes on Politics*, trans. Vincenzo Binetti and Cesare Casarino (Minneapolis and London: University of Minnesota Press, 1996).
4. Lisa Cartwright, *Screening the Body: Tracing Medicine's Visual Culture* (Minneapolis and London: University of Minnesota Press, 1995).
5. The Bradford company Appleton and Co provide an example of this crossover. Having filmed Queen Victoria's Diamond Jubilee and projected this to a large audience in Yorkshire, Appleton also performed demonstrations of the X-ray and advertised his services with the imaging technology. See *The Invisible Light: The Journal of Radiology History and Heritage Charitable Trust*, Adrian Thomas, 13 May 2001.
6. J. Duffin and C.R. Hayter, 'Baring the Sole. The Rise and Fall of the Shoe-Fitting Fluoroscope', *Isis: An International Review Devoted to the History of Science and Its Cultural Influences*, 91:2 (2000): 260–282.
7. Akira Mizuno Lippit, *Atomic Light (Shadow Optics)* (Minneapolis and London: University of Minnesota Press, 2005), 5.
8. Walter Benjamin, 'The Work of Art in the Age of Mechanical Reproduction', in *Illuminations*, trans. Harry Zorn, ed. and introduced by Hannah Arendt (London: Pimlico edition, 1999), 227.

9   Ibid.
10 George Didi-Huberman, *Invention of Hysteria: Charcot and the Photographic Iconography of the Salpêtrière*, trans. Alisa Hardtz (Cambridge, MA and London, England: MIT Press, 1982), 279.
11 Charles Musser, 'Moving Towards Fictional Narratives', in *The Silent Cinema Reader*, 88. Musser notes that the studio was located on 41 East 21st Street, New York City.
12 Benjamin Noys, 'Film-of-Life: Agamben's Profanation of the Image', in *Cinema and Agamben Ethics, Biopolitics and the Moving Image*, eds H. Gustafsson and A. Grønstad (New York, London, New Delhi and Sydney: Bloomsbury Academic, 2014), 92–93.
13 For a fuller account of Warburg's hesitancy with regard to naming his practice, see Leland de la Durantaye's chapter 'A General Science of the Human', in *Giorgio Agamben: A Critical Introduction* (Stanford, CA: Stanford University Press, 2009), 56–80.
14 Giorgio Agamben, 'Warburg and the Nameless Science', in *Potentialities*', in *Potentialities: Collected Essays in Philosophy*, ed. and trans. Daniel Heller-Roazen (Stanford, CA: Stanford University Press, 1999), 91.
15 Ibid., 90.
16 Lippit, *Ex-cinema*.
17 Ibid., 3.
18 Jonathan Walley, 'The Material of Film and the Idea of Cinema: Contrasting Practices in Sixties and Seventies Avant-Garde Film', *October*, 103 (Winter 2003): 23.
19 Giorgio Agamben, *The Coming Community*, trans. by Michael Hardt (Minneapolis and London: University of Minnesota Press, 1993), 8.
20 It is worth noting a further related work by Taanila that pursues the direction of this thought. It is called *My Silence 2*, an ironic reference perhaps to the prevalence of franchise sequel films in contemporary cinema where characters are carried over from one story setting to another. In the sequel to *My Silence*, however, Taanila removes story altogether, and the matter of film. The sequel consists of the script from Louis Malle's film printed onto A4 sheets of white paper each pinned at equidistance from each other on the wall of a gallery. The adaptation that Taanila has made is to remove all of the dialogue. What remains are the names of characters, scene directions and the title. In this second version, it is as though Taanila forces us to think a cinema without words, a cinema only of names.
21 Giorgio Agamben, 'In Playland', in *Infancy and History*, trans. Liz Heron (London and New York: Verso, 1999), 70.
22 Jessica Whyte, *Catastrophe and Redemption: The Political Thought of Giorgio Agamben* (New York: Suny Press State University of New York, 2013), 137.

23 Agamben, *Man without Content*, trans. Georgia Albert (Stanford, CA: Stanford University Press, 1994), 104.
24 Agamben, 'In Playland', 74.
25 Agamben in *il fuoco e il racconto* (Collana: Figure, 2014) reflects on Pasolini's unfinished novel *Petrolio*.
26 Pasolini cited in Leland de la Durantaye, *Giorgio Agamben: A Critical Introduction*, 21.
27 Ibid., 22.
28 Charlie Chaplin, *Autobiography* (London: Penguin Books, 1964), 154.
29 Giorgio Agamben, 'On Potentiality', in *Potentialities: Collected Essays in Philosophy*, ed. and trans. Daniel Heller-Roazen (Stanford, CA: Stanford University Press, 1999), 177.
30 Agamben, 'On Potentiality', 177.
31 Ibid., 182, italics in the original.
32 Gilles Deleuze, 'Bartleby, or the Formula', in *Essays Critical and Clinical*, trans. Daniel W. Smith and Michael A. Greco (Minneapolis: Minnesota University Press, 1997). The volume included a text by Agamben on Bartleby alongside Deleuze's essay.
33 Antonio Negri and Michael Hardt, *Empire* (Cambridge, MA and London, UK: Harvard University Press, 2000), 204 and 446 (n.1).
34 William Watkins, *Agamben and Indifference: A Critical Overview* (London and New York: Rowman and Littlefield International, 2014), chapters 7 and 8.
35 Leland de la Durantaye, *Giorgio Agamben: A Critical Introduction*, 166.
36 Whyte, *Catastrophe and Redemption*, 112.
37 Herman Melville, *Bartleby the Scrivener: A Story of Wall Street* (originally published anonymously in two parts, both in editions of Putnam's Magazine: 1853), 41.
38 Giorgio Agamben, 'Bartleby, or On Contingency' in *Potentialities: Collected Essays in Philosophy*, ed. and trans. Daniel Heller-Roazen (Stanford, CA: Stanford University Press, 1999) 243–274.
39 Ibid.

Bibliography

Note: Works by Agamben are cited with the English translation first followed by the publication date and title of the original text in Italian.

Agamben, G. (1993a) *The Coming Community*, trans. Michael Hardt, Minneapolis: University of Minnesota Press; *La communità che viene*, Giulio Einaudi, 1990.
Agamben, G. (1993b) *Stanzas: Word and Phantasm in Western Culture*, trans. Ronald L. Martinez, Minneapolis: University of Minnesota Press, 1993; *Stanze: La Parola e il fantasma nella cultura occidentale*, Giulio Einuadi, Turin, 1977.
Agamben, G. (1993c) *Infancy and History: Essays on the Destruction of Experience*, London: Verso; *Infanzia et storia*, Giulio Einuadi, 1978.
Agamben, G. (1995) *The Idea of Prose*, trans. Michael Sullivan and Sam Whitsitt, Albany: SUNY Press; *Idea della prosa*, Giangiacomo Feltrinelli, Milano, 1985.
Agamben, G. (1998) *Homo Sacer: Sovereign Power and Bare Life*, trans. Daniel Heller-Roazen, Stanford: Stanford University Press; *Homo sacer: Il potere sovrano e la nuda vita*, Giulio Einuadi, 1995.
Agamben, G. (1999a) *The Man without Content*, trans. Georgia Albert, Stanford: Stanford University Press; *L'uomo senza contenuto*, Quodlibet, 1970.
Agamben, G. (1999b) *The End of the Poem: Studies in Poetics*, trans. Daniel Heller-Roazen, Stanford: Stanford University Press; *Categorie Italiane: Studi di poetica*, Marsilio Editori, 1996.
Agamben, G. (1999c) *Potentialities: Collected Essays in Philosophy*, ed. and trans. Daniel Heller-Roazen, Stanford: Stanford University Press. (This publication has no direct equivalent in Italian.)
Agamben, G. (1999d) *Remnants of Auschwitz*, trans. Daniel Heller-Roazen, New York: Zone Books, 1999; *Quel che resta di Auschwitz*, Torino: Bollati Boringhieri, 1998.
Agamben, G. (2000) *Means without End: Notes on Politics*, trans. Vincenzo Binetti and Cesare Casarino, Minneapolis: University of Minnesota Press; *Mezzi sensa fine*, Bollati Boringhieri, 1996.
Agamben, G. (2002) 'Difference and Repetition: On Guy Debord's Films', in Tom McDonough (ed.), *Guy Debord and the Situationist International: Texts and Documents*, Cambridge, MA, and Cambridge: an October Book for MIT Press, pp. 313–320.
Agamben, G. (2004) *The Open: Man and Animal*, trans. Kevin Attell, Stanford: Stanford University Press; *L'aperto: L'uomo e l'animale*, Torino Bollati Boringhieri, 2002.

Agamben, G. (2005a) *State of Exception*, trans. Kevin Attell, Chicago: The University of Chicago Press; *Il Stato eccezione*, Bollati Boringhieri, 2003.

Agamben, G. (2005b) *The Time That Remains: A Commentary on the Letter to the Romans*, trans. Patricia Dailey, Stanford: Stanford University Press; *Il tempo che resta: Un commento alla Lettera ai Romani*, 2000.

Agamben, G. (2007) *Profanations*, trans. Jeff Fort, New York: Zone Books; *Profanazioni*, Roma: Nottetempo 2005.

Agamben, G. (2009a) *The Signature of All Things: On Method*, trans. Luca D'Isanto and Kevin Attell, New York: Zone Books; *Signatura rerum: sul metodo*, Torino: Bollati Boringhieri, 2008.

Agamben, G. (2009b) *What Is an Apparatus? And Other Essays*, trans. David Kishik and Stefan Pedatella, Stanford: Stanford University Press. The essays in this collection were published separately in Italian.

Agamben, G. (2011a) *The Sacrament of Language: An Archaeology of the Oath*, trans. Adam Kotsko, London, New York and Delhi: Polity; *Il sacramento del linguaggio: Archeologia del giuramento*, Roma and Bari: Laterza, 2008.

Agamben, G. (2011b) *The Kingdom and the Glory: For a Theological Genealogy of Economy and Government*, trans. Lorenzo Chiesa with Matteo Mandarini, Stanford: Stanford University Press; *Il regno e la gloria: Per una genealogia teologca dell'economia e del governo*, Milano: Neri Pozza, 2007.

Agamben, G. (2011c) *Nudities*, trans. David Kishik and Stefan Pedatella, Stanford: Stanford University Press; *Nudità*, Roma: Nottetempo, 2009.

Agamben, G. (2013a) *The Highest Poverty: Monastic Rules and Form-of-Life*, trans. Adam Kotsko, Stanford: Stanford University Press; *Altissima Povertà: Regola e forma di vita nel monachesimo*, Milano: Neri Pozza, 2011.

Agamben G. (2013b) *Nymphs*, trans. Amanda Minervini, London, New York and Calcutta: Seagull Books; *Ninfe*, Torino: Bollati Boringhieri, 2007.

Agamben, G. (2013c) *Opus Dei: An Archaeology of Duty*, trans. Adam Kotsko, Stanford: Stanford University Press; *Opus Dei: Archeologia dell'ufficio*, Bollati Boringhieri, 2012.

Agamben, G. (2014a) *The Unspeakable Girl: The Myth and Mystery of Kore*, trans. Leland de la Durantaye and Annie Julia Wyman, London, New York and Calcutta: Seagull Books; *La ragazza indicibile: Mito e mistero di Kore*, Milano: Electa, 2010.

Agamben, G. (2014b) 'For an Ethics of the Cinema', trans. John V. Garner and Colin Williamson, p. 24, in Gustafsson and Grønstad (eds), *Cinema and Agamben: Ethics, Biopolitics and the Moving Image*, New York, London, New Delhi and Sydney: Bloomsbury Academic, pp. 19–24.

Agamben, G. (2014c) 'Cinema and History: On Jean-Luc Godard', trans. John V. Garner and Colin Williamson, p. 24, in Gustafsson and Grønstad, pp. 25–26. 'Face au cinema et à l'Histoire: à propos de Jean-Luc Godard', *Le Monde*, New York, London, New Delhi and Sydney: Bloomsbury Academic, 6 October 1995 (I: x–xi).

Allen, R. (1985) 'The Movies in Vaudeville: Historical Context of the Movies as Popular Entertainment', in Tino Balio (ed.), *The American Film Industry*, Second Edition. Madison: University of Wisconsin Press, pp. 57–82.

Allen, W.S. (December 2008) 'Melancholy and Parapraxis: Rewriting History in Benjamin and Kafka', *MLN*, 123/5 (Comparative Literature Issue), pp. 1068–1087.

Andrew, D. (2010) *What Cinema Is!* Malden, MA and Oxford: Wiley-Blackwell, p. 19.

Arendt, H. (1970) 'Introduction' in *Illuminations*, trans. Harry Zorn, London: Pimlico, pp. 7–60.

Auerbach, J. (2007) *Body Shots: Early Cinema's Incarnations*, Berkeley, LA, London: University of California Press.

Bálász, B. (1972) *Theory of the Film: Character and Growth of a New Art*, trans. Edith Bone, New York: Arno Press.

Barad, K. (2007) *Meeting the Universe Halfway: Quantum Physics and the Entanglement of Matter and Meaning*, Durham and London: Duke University Press.

Barnes, J. (1988) *The Beginnings of the Cinema in England 1894–1901: Volume 1*, Exeter: Exeter University Press.

Bart, B.F. (1967) *Flaubert*, Syracuse: Syracuse University Press.

Barthes, R. (1977) *Roland Barthes by Roland Barthes*, trans. Richard Howard, New York: Hill and Wang.

Bazin, A. (1967) 'The Myth of Total Cinema', in *What Is Cinema? Volume 1*, Essays selected and trans. Hugh Gray, Berkeley and Los Angeles: University of California Press, pp. 17–26.

Benjamin, W. (1973) *Illuminations*, ed. Hannah Arendt, trans. Harry Zorn, London: Fontana.

Benjamin, W. (1999) 'A State Monopoly on Pornography', in Marcus Bullock and Michael W. Jennings (eds), *Walter Benjamin: Selected Writings*, Part 1 1927–1930, trans. Rodney Livingston and others. Michael W. Jennings, Howard Eiland and Gary Smith, Cambridge, MA, and London: The Belknap Press of Harvard University Press, pp. 72–74.

Benjamin, W. (2003) *The Origins of German Tragic Drama*, trans. John Osborn, London and New York: Verso.

Benjamin, W. (2006) *A Berlin Childhood around 1900*, trans. Howard Eiland Cambridge, MA and London: Belknap Press.

Blanchot, M. (2000) *The Unavowable Community*, trans. Pierre Joris, Barrytown: Station Hill Press.

Braun, M. (1984) 'Muybridge's Scientific Fictions', *Studies in Visual Communication*, 10, pp. 2–21.

Braun, M. (2010) *Eadweard Muybridge (Critical Lives)*, London: Reaktion Books.

Brown, E. (2005) 'Racialising the Virile Body: Eadweard Muybridge's Locomotion Studies 1883–1887', *Gender and History*, 17/3, pp. 627–656.

Bryant, L., Smicek, N. and Harman, G. (eds) (2011), *The Speculative Turn: Continental Materialism and Realism*, Melbourne: re.press.

Bull, L. (unpublished paper) 'Recent Developments in High-Speed Cinematography', presented on 30 May 1924 to The Royal Institution of Great Britain. *Royal Institution Library Holdings*, 245 (1924–5), pp. 2–4.

Calarco, M. (2008) *Zoographies: The Question of the Animal from Heidegger to Derrida*, New York: Columbia University Press.

Cartwright, L. (1995) *Screening the Body: Tracing Medicine's Visual Culture*, Minneapolis and London: University of Minnesota Press.

Caygill, H. (January/February 2015) 'Pier Paolo Pasolini, *St Paul: A Screenplay*', *Radical Philosophy: A Journal of Socialist and Feminist Philosophy*, 189, pp. 49–51.

Chapman, C. (1964) *My Autobiography*, London: Penguin Books.

Clemens, J. (2008) 'The Role of the Shifter and the Problem of Reference', in Clemens, Heron and Murray (eds), *The Work of Giorgio Agamben: Law, Literature, Life*, Edinburgh: Edinburgh University Press, pp. 43–65.

Clemens, J., Heron, N. and Murray, A., (eds) (2008) 'The Enigma of Giorgio Agamben', Introduction to *The Work of Giorgio Agamben: Law, Literature, Life*, Edinburgh: Edinburgh University Press.

Connor, S. (2008) 'Pregnable of Eye: X-Rays, Vision and Magic', http://www.stevenconnor.com/xray/ (accessed 12 March 2013).

Connor, S. (2010) *The Matter of Air: Science and the Art of the Ethereal*, London: Reaktion Books.

Crary, J. (1989) 'Spectacle, Attention, Counter-Memory', in *October*, Vol. 50, Autumn, pp. 96–107.

Crary, J. (2001) *Suspensions of Perception: Attention, Spectacle, and Modern Culture*, Cambridge: MIT Press.

Crary, J. (2013) *24/7: Late Capitalism and the Ends of Sleep*, London: Verso.

De la Durantaye, L. (2009) *Giorgio Agamben: A Critical Introduction*, Stanford: Stanford University Press.

De la Durantaye, L. (2012) 'On Method, the Messiah, Anarchy and Theocracy', in Giorgio Agamben (ed.), *The Church and The Kingdom*, trans. Leland de la Durantaye, London, NY and Calcutta: Seagull Books.

De la Durantaye, L. (Spring 2013) *Bidoun* #28, http://www.bidoun.org/magazine/28-interviews/giorgio-agamben-with-leland-de-la-durantaye/ (accessed 19 September 2014).

Dean, J. (2009) *Democracy and Other Neoliberal Fantasies: Communicative Capitalism and Left Politics*, London and Durham: Duke University Press.

Dean, J. (2014) 'Enclosing the Subject', *Journal of Political Theory*, Sage: December 1, DOI: 10.1177/0090591714560377, pp. 1–31.

DeLanda, M. (2000) *A Thousand Years of Nonlinear History*, New York: Swerve Editions.

Deleuze, G. (1983) *Cinema 1: The Movement Image*, trans. Hugh Tomlinson and Barbara Habberjam, London: Athlone Press.
Deleuze, G. (1997) 'Bartleby, or the Formula', in *Essays Critical and Clinical*, trans. Daniel W. Smith and Michael A. Greco, Minneapolis: Minnesota University Press.
Deleuze, G. and Guattari, F. (1975) *Kafka: Toward a Minor Literature*, trans. Dana Polan, Minneapolis and London: University of Minnesota Press.
Dickey, C. (2007) *The Public Domain Review: A Project of the Open Knowledge Foundation*, http://publicdomainreview.org/2013/03/07/the-redemption-of-saint-anthony/ (accessed 15 August 2014).
Didi-Huberman, G. (1982) *Invention of Hysteria: Charcot and the Photographic Iconography of the Salpêtrière*, trans. Alisa Hardtz, Cambridge, MA and London: MIT Press.
Dixon, L. (2003) *Bosch*, London and New York: Phaidon Press Limited.
Doane, M.A. (2003) 'The Close-Up: Scale and Detail in the Cinema', *Differences: A Journal of Feminist Cultural Studies*, 14/3, Brown University, pp. 89–111.
Duffin J. and Hayter, C.R. (2000) 'Baring the Sole. The Rise and Fall of the Shoe-Fitting Fluoroscope', *Isis: An International Review Devoted to the History of Science and Its Cultural Influences*, 91/2, pp. 260–282.
Epstein, J. (Spring 1977) 'Magnification and Other Writings', trans. Stuart Liebman, *October*, Vol. 3, pp. 9–25.
Esposito, R. (2008) *Bios: Biopolitics and Philosophy*, trans. Timothy Campbell, Minneapolis: University of Minnesota Press.
Flaubert, G. (2005) *Bouvard and Pécuchet*, trans. and introduced by Mark Polizzotti, Illinois: Dalkey Archive Press.
Fleming, P. (April 2000) 'The Crisis of Art: Max Kommerell and Jean Paul's Gestures', *MLN*, 115/3, pp. 519–543.
Foucault, M. (1961) *Histoire de la folie à l'âge classique – Folie et déraison*, Paris: Plon; *Naissance de la clinique – une archéologie du regard médical* (Paris: PUF, 1963), and *Raymond Roussel* (Paris: Gallimard, 1963). FN 28, C1.
Foucault, M. (1966) *The Order of Things: An Archaeology of the Human Sciences*, London and New York: Routledge.
Foucault, M. (1976) *History of Sexuality, Volume 1: An Introduction*, trans. R. Hurley, London: Penguin.
Foucault, M. (1977a) *Discipline and Punish: The Birth of the Prison*, trans. Alan Sheridam, New York: Vintage.
Foucault, M. (1977b) 'Nietzsche, Genealogy, History', in *Language, Counter-memory, Practice: Selected Essays and Interviews*, trans. D. Bouchar and S. Simon, Ithaca: Cornell University Press, pp. 139–164.
Gelley, A. (2007) 'Epigones in the House of Language: Benjamin on Kraus', *Partial Answers*, 5/1, John Hopkins University Press, pp. 17–32.
Gunning, T. (1997) 'From the Kaleidoscope to the X-Ray: Urban Spectatorship, Poe, Benjamin, and Traffic in Souls (1913)', *Wide Angle*, 19/4, pp. 25–61.

Gustafsson, H. (2014) 'Remnants of Palestine, or, Archaeology after Auschwitz', in Gustafsson, H. and Grønstad, A. (eds), *Cinema and Agamben: Ethics, Biopolitics and the Moving Image*, New York, London, New Delhi and Sydney: Bloomsbury Academic, pp. 207–230.

Haas, R.B. (1976) *Muybridge: Man in Motion*, Berkeley, Los Angeles, CA and London: University of California Press.

Haraway, D. (2008) *When Species Meet*, Minneapolis and London: University of Minnesota Press.

Hardt, M. and Negri, A. (2000) *Empire*, Cambridge, MA and London: Harvard University Press.

Harman, G. (2011) *The Quadruple Object*, Winchester, UK and Washington, DC: Zone Books.

Heidegger, M. (1995) *The Fundamental Concepts of Metaphysics: World, Finitude, Solitude*, trans. William McNeill and Nicholas Walker, Bloomington: Indiana University Press.

Highman, C. (1985) *Orson Welles: The Rise and Fall of an American Genius*, London: St Martin's Press.

Humphreys, S. (2006) 'Legalizing Lawlessness: On Giorgio Agamben's State of Exception', *The European Journal of International Law*, 17/3, pp. 677–687.

James, D.E. (2005) *The Most Typical Avant-Garde: History and Geography of Minor Cinemas in Los Angeles*, Berkeley, Los Angeles, CA and London: University of California Press.

Janicot, C. (1995) *Anthologie du cinéma invisible: 100 scénarios pour 100 ans de cinema*, Paris: Jean-Michel Place.

Kafka, F. (1973) *The Great Wall of China and Other Short Works*, trans. Malcolm Pasley, London: Penguin Books.

Kearton, R. and Kearton, C. (1898) *With Nature and a Camera; Being the Adventures and Observations of a Field Naturalist and an Animal Photographer*, London: Cassell and Co.

Keller, S. (2014) *Maya Deren: Incomplete Control*, New York: Columbia University Press.

Khalip, J. and Mitchell, R. (eds) (2011) *Releasing the Image: From Literature to New Media*, Stanford: Stanford University Press.

Kluitenberg, E. (2007). *The Book of Imaginary Media. Excavating the Dream of the Ultimate Communications Medium*. Rotterdam: NAi Publishers.

Kracauer, S. (1995) *The Mass Ornament: Weimer Essays*, trans., edited and introduced by Thomas Levin, Cambridge, MA and London: Harvard University Press.

Kouvaros, G. (2008) '"We Do Not Die Twice": Realism and Cinema', in James Donald and Michael Renov (eds), *The Sage Handbook of Film Studies*, London, New York and Delhi: Sage Publications, pp. 376–390.

Leslie, E. (2000) *Walter Benjamin: Overpowering Conformism*, London: Pluto Press.

Levi, P. (2012) *Cinema by Other Means*, Oxford: Oxford University Press.

Levin, T. (2002) 'Dismantling the Spectacle: The Cinema of Guy Debord', in Tom McDonough (ed.), *Guy Debord and the Situationist International: Texts and Documents*, Cambridge, MA and Cambridge: An October Book for MIT Press, pp. 321–454.

Levitt, D. (2008) 'Notes on Media and Biopolitics', in Justin Clemens, Nicholas Heron and Alex Murray (eds), *The Work of Giorgio Agamben: Law, Literature, Life*, Edinburgh: Edinburgh University Press, pp. 193–211.

Lingis, A. (1994) *The Community of Those Who Have Nothing in Common*, Bloomington and Indianapolis: Indiana University Press.

Lippit, A.M. (2000) *Electric Animal: Toward a Rhetoric of Wildlife*, Minneapolis and London: University of Minnesota Press.

Lippit, A.M. (2005) *Atomic Light (Shadow Optics)*, Minneapolis and London: University of Minnesota Press.

Lippit, A.M. (2012) *Ex-Cinema: From A Theory of Experimental Film and Video*, Berkeley, Los Angeles, London: University of California Press.

Lundemo, T. (2014) 'Montage and the Dark Margin of the Archive', in Henrik Gustafsson and Asbjørn Grønstad (eds), *Cinema and Agamben: Ethics, Biopolitics and the Moving Image*, New York, London, New Delhi and Sydney: Bloomsbury, pp. 191–206.

Marey, E.J. (1873) *La Machine Animale*, Book Three, New York 549 and 551, Broadway: Appleton and Company.

Marks, L.U. (2010) *Enfoldment and Infinity: An Islamic Genealogy of New Media Art*, Cambridge, MA, and London: MIT Press.

Marks, L.U. (2015) *Hanan al-Cinema: Affections for the Moving Image*, Cambridge, MA and London: MIT Press.

Mavor, C. (2007) *Reading Boyishly: Roland Barthes, J.M. Barrie, Jacques Henri Lartigue, Marcel Proust, and D.W. Winnicott*, Durham and London: Duke University Press.

Marx, K. (1887 [1867]). *Capital Volume 1.* trans. Samuel Moore and Edward Aveling, ed. Frederick Engels, Moscow: Progress Publishers.

McCrea, C. (2009) 'Giorgio Agamben', in Felicity Colman (ed.), *Film, Theory and Philosophy: The Key Thinkers*, Durham: Acumen, pp. 349–57.

McDonough, T. (ed.) (2002), *Guy Debord and the Situationist International*, Cambridge, MA, and Cambridge: An October Book for MIT Press.

McLuhan, M. and Fiore, Q. (1967) *The Medium Is the Massage: An Inventory of Effects*, New York: Bantam Books.

Melville, H. (1853) 'Bartleby the Scrivener: A Story of Wall Street', originally published anonymously in two parts, both in editions of Putnam's Magazine.

Mesnard, P. and Cahan, C. (2001) *Giorgio Agamben à l'épreuve d'Auschwitz*, Paris: Editions Kimé.

Metz, C. (1974) *Film Language: A Semiotics of the Cinema*, trans. Michael Taylor. New York: Oxford University Press.

Michaud, P.A. (2007) *Aby Warburg and the Image in Motion*, trans. Sophie Hawkes, New York: Zone Books.
Mills, C. (2008) *The Philosophy of Agamben*. Durham: Acumen Publishing Limited.
Morvan, C. (1988) *When Old Technologies Were New*, New York and Oxford: Oxford University Press.
Mullarkey, J. (2006) *Postcontinental Philosophy: An Outline*, London and New York: Continuum.
Mullarkey, J. (December 2012) 'The Tragedy of the Object: Democracy of Vision and the Terrorism of Things in Bazin's Cinematic Realism', *Angelaki: Journal of the Theoretical Humanities*, 17/4, pp. 39–59.
Murray, A. (2010) *Giorgio Agamben*, London and New York: Routledge.
Musser, C. (1996) 'Pre-classical American Cinema: Its Changing Modes of Film Production', in Richard Abel (ed.), *Silent Film*, London: Athlone, pp. 85–108.
Musser, C. (2004) 'Moving towards Fictional Narratives', in Grieveson L. and Kramer, P. (eds), *The Silent Cinema Reader*, London and New York: Routledge, pp. 97–102.
Nagib, L. (2011) *World Cinema and the Ethics of Realism*, New York: Continuum.
Nancy, J.L. (1991) *The Inoperative Community*, ed. Peter Connor, trans. Peter Connor and Lisa Garbus, Minneapolis: Minnesota University Press.
Neely, S. (2009) '"Ploughing a Lonely Furrow": Margaret Tait and Professional Filmmaking Practices of 1950s Scotland', in Ian Craven (ed.), *Movies on Home Ground: Explorations in Amateur Cinema*, Newcastle: Cambridge Scholars Press, pp. 67–89.
Negri, A. and Hardt, M. (2000) *Empire*, Cambridge, MA and London: Harvard University Press.
Nietzsche, F. (2001) *The Gay Science*, ed. Bernard Williams, trans. Josefine Nauckhoff, Cambridge: Cambridge University Press.
Nietzsche, F. (2003) *Thus Spoke Zarathustra: A Book for Everyone and No One*, trans. and introduced by R.J. Hollingdale, London: Penguin Books.
Noys, B. (2013) 'Film-of-Life: Agamben's Profanation of the Image', in Gustafsson, H. and Grønstad, A. (eds), *Cinema and Agamben: Ethics, Biopolitics and the Moving Image*, New York, London, New Delhi and Sydney: Bloomsbury Academic, pp. 89–102.
Owenby, C. (2013) 'The Abandonment of Modernity: Bare Life and the Camp in *Homo Sacer* and *Hotel Rwanda*', *disClosure: A Journal of Social Theory*, 4/22, Special Edition 'Security', pp. 17–22.
Parikka, J. (2010) *Insect Media: An Archaeology of Animals and Technology*, Minneapolis and London: University of Minnesota Press.
Pick, A. (Winter 2006) 'Review: Agamben's *The Open*', *Bryn Mawr Review of Comparative Literature*, 5/2, pp. 45–46.
Pick, A. (2011) *Creaturely Poetics: Animality and Vulnerability in Literature and Film*, New York: Colombia University Press.
Rilke, R. (2001) *Duino Elegies*, trans. Edward Snow, New York: North Point Press.

Robinson, D. (2008) 'John Barnes: Authority on the Early Days of Film Who with His Brother Created an Unparalleled Cinema Collection', in *The Independent Obituaries*, 30 June.

Röntgen, W. (1896) 'A New Kind of Rays', trans. Arthur Stanton, *Nature*, 53, 274–276.

Rosen, P. (2001) *Change Mummified: Cinema, Historicity, Theory*, Minneapolis: University of Minnesota Press.

Rosenbaum, J. (2007) *Discovering Orson Welles*, Berkeley, Los Angeles, CA and London: University of California Press.

Ross, A. (Winter 2008) ' "Introduction" to Special Edition the Agamben Effect', *South Atlantic Quarterly*, 107/1, pp. 1–14.

Salt, B. (1982) *Film Style and Technology: History and Analysis*, London: Starword Books.

Saxton, L. (2008) *Haunted Images: Film, Ethics, Testimony and the Holocaust*, London and New York: Wallflower Press.

Santner, E.L. (2011) *The Royal Remains: The People's Two Bodies and the Endgames of Sovereignty*, Chicago and London: University of Chicago Press.

Schivelbusch, W. (1983) *The Industrialization of Light in the Nineteenth Century*, Berkeley, Los Angeles, CA and London: University of California Press.

Sebald, W.G. (2014) *A Place in the Country*, London: Penguin.

Serres, M. with Bruno Latour (1995) *Conversations on Science, Culture and Time*, trans. Roxanne Lapidus, Ann Arbor: University of Michigan Press.

Shand, R. and Craven, I. (eds) (2013) *Small-Gauge Storytelling: Discovering the Amateur Fiction Film*, Edinburgh: Edinburgh University Press.

Sheridan, A. (2003) *Michel Foucault: The Will to Truth*, London and New York: Routledge.

Shütz, A. (2008) 'The Fading Memory of *Homo Non Sacer*', in Clemens, Heron and Murray (eds), *The Work of Giorgio Agamben: Law, Literature, Life*, Edinburgh: Edinburgh University Press, pp. 114–131.

Sleigh, C. (2011) 'The Insects', in Tim Boon (ed.), *Secrets of Nature*, London: BFI, p. 5.

Solnit, R. (2003) *River of Shadows: Eadweard Muybridge and the Technological Wild West*, New York: Penguin Books.

Stainton, A. (Autumn 1988) 'Don Quixote: Orson Welles's Secret', *Sight and Sound*, 253–260.

Stallybrass, P. and White, A. (1986) *The Politics and Poetics of Transgression*, Ithaca: Cornell University Press.

Stewart, G. (2013) 'Counterfactual, Potential, Virtual: Toward a Philosophical Cinematics', in Gustafsson, H. and Grønstad, A. (eds), *Cinema and Agamben: Ethics, Biopolitics and the Moving Image*, New York, London, New Delhi and Sydney: Bloomsbury Academic, pp. 161–190.

Stewart, S. (1993) *On Longing: Narratives of the Miniature, the Gigantic, the Souvenir, the Collection*, Durham and London: Duke University Press.

Thomson, D. (1996) *Rosebud: The Story of Orson Welles*, New York: Alfred A. Knopf.

Trahair, L. (2007) *The Comedy of Philosophy: Sense and Nonsense in Early Cinematic Slapstick*, Albany: State University of New York Press.

Väliaho, P. (2010) *Mapping the Moving Image: Gesture, Thought and Cinema Circa 1900*, Amsterdam: Amsterdam University Press.

Vasari, G. (1996). *Lives of the Painters, Sculptors and Architects*, trans. Gaston du C. de Vere. Ed. David Ekserdjian, 2 Vols, London: David Campbell.

Walley, J. (2003) 'The Material of Film and the Idea of Cinema: Contrasting Practices in Sixties and Seventies Avant-Garde Film', *October*, 103 (Winter), pp. 16–29.

Walser, R. (2007) *The Assistant*, trans. Susan Bernofsky, New York: New Directions Books.

Warner, M. (2006) *Phantasmagoria: Spirit Visions, Metaphors, and Media into the Twenty-First Century*, Oxford: Oxford University Press.

Watkins, W. (2012) *Agamben and Indifference: A Critical Overview*, London and New York: Rowman and Littlefield International.

Weiss, D. and Fischli, P. (2006) 'The Odd Couple', *Frieze Magazine*, 102.

Welles Feder, C. (2009) *In My Father's Shadow: A Daughter Remembers Orson Welles*, Edinburgh and London: Mainstream Publishing.

Westphal, C. (1870) 'Contrary Sexual Feeling', *Archiv für Psychiatrie und Nervenkrankeiten*, 2, Berlin: 73–108.

Whyte, J. (2013) *Catastrophe and Redemption: The Political Thought of Giorgio Agamben*, New York: SUNY Press State University of New York.

Williams, S.J. (2014) 'Silence, Gesture, Revelation: The Ethics and Aesthetics of Montage in Godard and Agamben', in Gustafsson, H. and Grønstad, A. (eds), *Cinema and Agamben: Ethics, Biopolitics and the Moving Image*, New York, London, New Delhi and Sydney: Bloomsbury Academic, pp. 27–54.

Zielinski, S. (2005) *Deep Time of the Media: Toward an Archaeology of Hearing and Seeing by Technical Means*, trans. Gloria Custance, Cambridge, MA: MIT Press.

Zimmerman, P. (2008) 'Morphing History into Histories: From Amateur Film to the Archive of the Future', in *Mining the Home Movie: Excavations in Histories and Memories*, Karen L. Ishizuka and Patricia R. Zimmerman (eds), Berkeley, Los Angeles, CA and London: University of California Press, pp. 275–288.

Index

Note: Page references with letter 'n' followed by locators denote note numbers.

abstract art 139
abstraction 106, 107, 111–12, 140, 161
accident 147, 169
Acres, Birt 182–6, 190, 202 n.45
actuality 5, 16, 135, 182, 215, 218, 228
actualization 26, 193, 205, 219, 221, 226, 228, 230
Adorno, Theodor W. 35
advertising 2, 65, 95 n.23, 105–6, 112, 115, 116, 182, 185, 187, 202 n.42, 232 n.5
aesthetics 7, 8, 9, 25, 56 n.70, 65, 111, 206, 211
After Finitude (Meillassoux) 12
after-image. *See Nachleben* (afterlife)
Agamben, Giorgio
  'Bartleby, or On Contingency' 203 n.66
  'Benjamin and the Demonic' 51
  Coming Community, The 15, 35, 87, 95 n.23, 102, 104, 105, 115, 229
  'Difference and Repetition: On Guy Debord's Films' 7, 104
  'Dim Stockings' 106–9, 111–12, 115
  'Example' 35
  'Face, The' 116, 128 n.43
  'Genius' 168 n.60
  Homo Sacer 5, 6, 8, 10, 17 n.9, 26, 37, 59, 81
  Idea of Prose, The 85, 114, 229
  Infancy and History: Essays on the Destruction of Experience 6–7, 19 n.30, 32, 33, 35, 39
  'In Playland' 54 n.41, 194–5, 223–5
  'In Praise of Profanation' 127 n.29
  'Judgment Day' 211
  'Kommerell, or on Gesture' 84, 86
  'Last Chapter in the History of the World, The' 21
  Man without Content 56 n.70, 225
  'Marginal Notes' 103–4, 107
  'Marx; or, The Universal Exposition' 106
  Means without End 98 n.75, 103–4, 116, 232 n.3
  'Notes on Gesture' 6, 63, 65, 67, 215
  Nymphs 45–6
  'On Gesture' 58, 84
  Open, The 10, 16, 148, 150, 156, 158, 164
  Opus Dei: An Archaeology of Duty 35
  Potentialities 35, 51, 84, 217, 229
  Profanations 32, 116–17, 168 n.60, 175
  'Project for a Review' 35
  Remnants of Auschwitz 8, 26, 55 n.55
  Sacrament of Language: An Archaeology of the Oath, The 35
  'Shekinah' 104
  Signature of All Things: On Method, The 1, 26–7, 35, 37, 40, 105
  'Six Most Beautiful Minutes in the History of Cinema, The' 7, 14, 32–5
  Stanzas 35, 48, 68, 106, 178, 226
  'Time and History: Critique of the Instant and the Continuum' 19 n.30
  'Umwelt' 131, 148–9
  Unspeakable Girl: The Myth and Mystery of Kore, The 49
  What Is an Apparatus? 17 n.5, 35
  'What Is the Contemporary?' 4, 17 n.5
  'Without classes' 87
agency 3, 119, 138, 140, 144, 169, 174
aggregate 5, 161, 217–18, 222–5
air 145–6
Alhambra Theatre 161
alienation 58, 102, 103, 107, 109, 119, 121, 225, 230
allegory 34, 109
Allen, William S. 179

Index

amateur/amateurism 3, 16, 55 n.63, 87, 135, 137, 155, 169–70, 180–6, 188, 189, 190, 193, 194, 201 n.32, 204 n.73, 223
  characteristics of 181
  origin of term and definition of 179–80
  terminological trauma 181–2
Amateur Photographer magazine 180, 185
ambiguity 37–8, 65–6, 75, 76, 119
American Cinematographer 181–2
anachronism 4
analogy 13, 26, 34, 37, 38, 46, 114, 213
ancient art 68
Andersson, Harriet 116, 117
Andrew, Dudley 147
aniconism 9
animal/animality 4, 10–13, 16, 38, 46–7, 50, 60–1, 70, 76, 85, 94 n.5, 131, 139–40, 145, 148, 149–53, 155–6, 158, 160, 163, 164, 165, 174, 175, 183, 214–16, 217, 218, 222
animalitas 153
'Animal Locomotion: An Electrophotographic Investigation of Consecutive Phases of Animal Movements' (Muybridge) 60
anthropocentrism 6, 10, 15, 135
anthropogenesis 160
anthropological machine 10, 131–2, 149, 153, 158–9, 164, 214, 217
anthropology 10, 50, 61, 68, 111, 158, 195–6, 217
anthropometry 61, 214–15
anxiety 44, 83, 152, 157, 163, 213
aphorism 189
apparatus 10, 14–15, 23, 33, 36, 60, 63, 79, 80, 82, 86, 87, 91, 102, 106, 109, 110, 116, 118, 123, 124, 127 n.29, 135, 136, 138, 141, 144, 145, 155, 159, 161, 165, 179, 182, 184, 185, 190, 199, 205, 214, 215, 222, 223, 231
Appleton and Co 232 n.5
Arabic-Islamic arts 9
Arcades Project (Benjamin) 27, 224
archaeology/archaeological method 1–2, 6–13, 14, 21–56, 58, 60, 79, 89, 170, 180, 188, 197, 218, 227
  criticism of 7–8, 26–7
  and Foucauldian concepts 2, 35–41
  key features of 23–7
  vs. geological archaeology 22
  vs. media archaeology 8–10, 218
Archaeology of Knowledge, The (Foucault) 36
archive 2, 3, 8, 16, 25, 42, 71, 99 n.91, 186, 194, 197
Aristotle 10, 16, 25, 228
art 2, 9, 48, 68, 85, 95 n.7, 99 n.98, 110, 119, 139, 155, 161, 165, 166 n.23, 182, 183, 189, 217, 219
art history 27, 39, 62, 217
As Seen Through a Telescope (Smith, George Albert) 209–10, 212
assimilation 6, 119
Assistant, The (Walser) 187–8
assistants 16, 49, 51, 89, 105, 137, 169, 170, 171, 174–80, 182, 183, 187–8, 189–90, 193, 194, 196, 197, 199, 223, 227
Attack on a China Mission (Williamson) 75
audience 3, 15, 30, 31, 33, 34, 47, 60, 83, 106, 109, 112, 141, 160, 163, 165 n.2, 197, 232 n.5
Auer, Mischa 28
Auerbach, Jonathan 73
autonomy 5, 15, 67, 181, 211
avant-garde 7, 124, 181, 201 n.32

Balázs, Béla 97 n.54, 161
ballad 226
ballet 91, 93, 160
Barad, Karen 3–4
bare life 8, 10–11, 36, 59, 158, 206, 212, 214, 215, 232 n.3
Barthes, Roland 180, 194
Bartleby 25–6, 52 n.7, 105, 189, 203 n.66, 229–30, 231, 234 n.32
'Bartleby, or the Formula'(Deleuze) 229
Bataille, Georges 104
Bazin, André 13, 20 n.40, 169, 218
bee 138, 139, 141, 148, 151, 163
Belloc, Auguste 129 n.47
belonging 15, 46, 67, 102, 105, 108, 112, 174, 188

Benjamin, Walter 2, 8–9, 11, 16, 22, 25, 27, 32, 34, 35, 37–8, 45–6, 50, 51, 54 n.41, 56 n.66, 58–9, 66, 68–9, 84, 89, 94 n.2, 103, 111–12, 117, 122–3, 143–4, 155, 164, 165, 170, 175–9, 183, 188, 193, 200 n.13, 200 n.20, 201 n.21, 203 n.66, 211, 213, 224–5, 230, 231
Benning, Sadie 204 n.73
Bergman, Ingmar 116, 117
Berlin Childhood, A (Benjamin) 177
Berlin Wall, fall of 15, 104
Bernds, Edward 167 n.46
Bertha, Anna 78, 79
BFI library 186
Bible 11, 145
Big Swallow, The (Williamson) 71–3, 75
binary divisions 5
biography(ies) 29, 45, 49, 52 n.10, 69, 88, 107, 112, 153, 177, 201 n.21
biopolitics 6, 7, 12, 14, 36, 37, 59, 60, 66, 70, 72, 79, 80–4, 87, 93, 222
  definition of 81
biosemiotics 131
bios/zoe distinction 10, 59, 81, 206, 210
Birtac camera/projector 16, 184–6
Blackburn, Douglas 183
Black Maria Studio 57, 89–91, 99 n.90, 160
Blanchot, Maurice 104, 105
Blechyenden, Frederick 183
body, the
  codification of 76, 77
  concept of 206–11
  detached from its materiality 112–13, 115–16, 214–15
  emancipation of 112–13
  fingerprints as signature of 74
  fragmentation of 212–13, 216
  gesture and 57–99, 215, 216, 222
  imaging of (*See* X-ray)
  interiority of 211–15, 222
  language and 85–7, 88, 90
  naked 60–4, 91–2, 94–5 n.7, 114, 115, 120, 121
  'seeing through' 78–80
body image 112–13, 115
Boët, Nathalie 129 n.48
Böhm 38

Bois de Boulogne Park, Paris 28
Bonanni, Mauro 30, 43, 48, 232
boredom 4, 116, 152, 170
Bosch, Hieronymus 160, 193, 203 n.55
Bouilhet, Louis 191
Boulevard du temple (Daguerre) 206–7, 211
bourgeoisie 14, 63, 65, 71, 73, 77, 87, 180
Bouvard and Pécuchet (Flaubert) 188–90, 192–3, 194, 202 n.50
box camera 16, 184
Brakhage, Stan 201 n.32
Braquehais, Bruno 129 n.47
Brassier, Ray 12
Braun, Marta 62, 95 n.7
Brecht, Bertolt 180
Breughel the Younger 193
bricolage/bricoleur 24, 54 n.41, 194, 199, 224–5
Brod, Max 201 n.21
Brown, Elspeth 62
Brown, Richard 186
Brundle, Seth 157
Bull, Lucien 3, 132, 133–8, 141, 142, 143, 155, 158, 159, 160, 161, 164, 165, 165 n.3
Buñuel, Louis 196

Cahan, Claudine 55 n.55
Calarco, Matthew 11, 152
camera 3, 92. *See also specific cameras*
camp 8, 10, 26, 36, 42, 82, 113, 131, 189
Cannes Film Festival 49
Capital (Marx) 225
capitalism 103, 104, 105, 115, 121, 181
captivation 4, 16, 65, 150–3, 156, 159, 164, 165
Carroll, Lewis 142
Cartwright, Lisa 78, 211
causality 22, 101, 174
Cavett, Dick 45
celluloid 23, 103, 124, 125, 164, 197, 218, 223
censorship 129 n.45
centric cinema 206, 214–17, 222, 224, 225
Cervantes, Miguel de 41, 44
chance 169, 213
Chaplin, Charlie 86, 88, 226

characters 2, 6, 9, 12, 16, 28, 29, 32, 44, 51, 60, 71, 73, 75, 76, 77, 89, 105–6, 107, 115, 116, 147, 172, 173, 177, 188–9, 192, 215, 216, 219, 220, 226, 229, 233 n.20
Charcot, Jean Martin 73
children 30, 31, 33, 44, 60, 170, 175, 176, 193–6, 197, 203 n.66, 204 n.73, 223–4, 227
Chimes at Midnight (Welles) 49
choreography 121, 143
chronophotography 3, 65, 69, 137
cinema
    concealedness of 164–5
    definitions of 4, 47–8, 197, 205–6, 223
    forms of 181, 186
    as laboratory 4, 16, 30, 89, 91, 131–68
cinema muto 71, 73, 111
cinema *qua* cinema 23, 66
cinema studies 6, 168 n.50
cinematograph/cinematography 64, 135, 182, 184, 211
cinematographer/cinegrapher/cinegraphist 72, 182
Citizen Kane (Welles) 21–2, 28
class 75, 77, 87–8, 108, 114, 115, 127 n.29, 180, 181
classical cinema 110
Clemens, Justin 37
clichés 15, 101, 123, 216
Closet (Whiteread) 1
Cocaine (Fassbinder) 225
co-evolution 9
collaborations 3, 53 n.17, 99 n.90, 160, 182, 183
collodion 160
comedy 86, 87, 115, 172, 189, 193, 212, 215
coming community 102, 103–6, 108
Comments on the Society of the Spectacle (Debord) 110
commodification 7, 83, 95 n.23, 102, 106, 107, 112, 113, 120, 123, 171, 179
commodity 15, 25, 48, 50, 65–6, 83, 102–3, 106–8, 111, 113, 114, 115, 116, 118, 120, 123, 124, 141, 178, 223
commonality 105, 106, 108

communicability 7, 14, 32, 59, 70, 84–8, 93, 107, 124, 211, 216, 221
communism 102, 104, 105, 115
communitas 71, 82–4
Community of Those Who Have Nothing in Common, The (Lingis) 104
Connor, Steven 78–9, 145–6, 166 n.23
contingency 36, 68–9, 75, 87, 88, 93, 103, 151, 160, 169, 174, 177, 207, 215, 216, 218, 227
'Contrary sexual sensations' (Westphal) 74–5
Copernicus 205
copying 26, 42, 45, 46, 170, 171, 182, 183, 186, 187, 188, 189–90, 193, 203 n.55, 203 n.66, 229–30
copyright 181
Cornell, Joseph 37
Crary, Jonathan 83, 110, 111, 113, 127 n.20, 203 n.59
creative criticism 35
critical animal studies 10, 12, 139
Crosland, Alan 73, 127 n.20
culture 19 n.30, 50, 56 n.70, 68, 71, 83, 102, 107, 109, 110, 111, 123, 143, 170, 172, 181, 205, 217, 224
Curse of the Fly (Sharp) 167 n.46

Dageurrotype 160
Daguerre, Louis 206–7, 211
dance *(chorea)* 57, 63, 64, 86, 88, 89, 90–4, 99 n.98, 106, 112, 210
Darger, Henry 55 n.63
Darwin, Charles 74
Dasein 16, 152
deactivation 51, 102, 115, 127 n.29, 171, 190, 196, 199
Dean, Jodi 15, 19 n.44
De Anima (Aristotle) 228
Debord, Guy 7, 15, 34, 48, 66, 103–4, 106, 107, 108, 109–10, 116, 158, 216
Decameron, The (Pasolini) 225
deconstruction 14, 139
decontextualization 24
decreation 21, 24, 193, 203 n.66, 226
deep time 9, 13
de la Durantaye, Leland 6, 26, 96 n.32, 104, 105, 115, 170, 226, 230

DeLanda, Manuel 13
Delattre, Eugene 202 n.50
Deleuze, Gilles 40, 65, 161, 229, 230, 234 n.32
de Lysses, Chloë 113–14, 118, 119, 120, 121, 129 n.43, 129 n.48
Demeny, George 169
Deren, Maya 25, 181, 201 n.32, 225
Derrida, Jacques 38, 40
desire 3, 7, 15, 33, 47, 49, 65, 66, 76, 77, 78, 87, 102, 104, 106, 107, 118, 121, 145, 160, 161, 171, 173, 177, 188, 190, 192, 211
diachrony 24, 37, 54 n.41, 196, 225
Dickey, Colin 191
Dickson, William 89, 90, 91, 99 n.90, 160, 183
'Dickson Experimental Sound Film, The' 90–1
Dictionary of Accepted Ideas 189, 190
Didi-Huberman, Georges 73, 214
diegetic elements 57, 60, 103
digital art 9
digital video 24, 31, 103, 125, 218
dimension 9, 25, 28, 40, 69, 79, 125
Dim Stockings 106–9, 115
discourses 3, 5, 10, 11, 12, 33, 39, 59, 60, 71, 74, 77, 79, 108, 122, 129 n.45, 189, 190, 191, 192, 213
Discreet Charm of the Bourgeoisie, The (Buñuel) 196
distribution 108, 125, 138, 216
divine, nature as 143–4
divo 123
Doane, Mary Ann 161
documentary 44, 47, 53 n.18, 129 n.45, 161, 181, 186
d'Olivier, Louis-Camille 129 n.47
Don Juan (Crosland) 127 n.20
Don Quixote
  in Foucault's account 41–2, 192
  in Kafka's short story 51
Don Quixote (Welles) 7, 14, 22, 28–35, 42–5, 48, 49, 53 n.13, 124, 191, 195, 225
doubles/doubling 17, 170, 173, 183, 185, 187, 190–1, 192, 193, 196, 206
Doyle, Conan 39

dreams 191–2
du Camp, Maxime 191
Duino Elegies (Rilke) 152
Duncan, Francis Martin 161
DVD 103, 223
dynamis 7, 46, 68–9, 70, 88, 93
dynamograms 46

Eastern Europe 104, 115
Edison, Thomas 57, 83, 89, 90, 91, 99 n.90, 160, 169, 182, 183, 190, 215
Edison Company 215
editing 28, 29, 43, 49, 76, 106, 174, 221, 231, 232
Eisenstein 225
Electric Animal (Lippit) 12
electricity 12, 68, 70, 77
Elliot and Son 182, 186
emotion 4, 46, 60, 76, 77, 188, 211, 215, 216
encryptions 67–71
Enfoldment and Infinity (Marks) 9
engineers 11, 223
engram 67–71, 72, 93, 122
enigma 15, 59, 77, 79, 97 n.54, 210
Enlightenment 38, 39, 40
entomology 11, 141, 145
Epler, Blanche 62
Epstein, Jean 76–7, 143, 161
erotics/eroticization 62, 115, 118, 120, 121, 122, 128–9 n.43, 209, 212
eschatology 6, 11, 114, 115, 211
Esposito, Roberto 71, 82–3, 84
eternal return 51, 193, 203 n.66
ethics 6, 8, 59, 63, 65, 87, 93, 102, 123, 125, 179, 226
ethos 82
Études cliniques et physiologiques sur la marche (Tourette) 64, 95 n.13
Étude sur une affection nerveuse caractérisée par l'incoordination motrice accompagnée d'écholalie et de coprolalie (Tourette) 64
evidence, notion of 39–40, 64, 75, 116
example 105–6, 108, 118–26
ex-centric cinema
  as aggregate 222–5
  centric *vs.* 205–34

definitions of 1, 2, 217–18
form of 3
as impotentiality 225–9
as a methodology 4–5
sites of 3
as transmission 219–22
exchange/exchange value 22, 35, 60, 107–8, 113, 117, 119, 121, 129 n.43, 178, 181, 219–20
ex-cinema 218
exhibition/exhibition value (*Ausstellungswert*) 93, 103, 106–7, 110, 117–18, 120, 121, 123, 182, 199, 215, 216
experience 2, 84
and knowledge 32–3, 39
experimental film 90, 145, 169, 182, 218

Fabre, Jean-Henri 141
face/facial expression 30, 50, 76, 88, 91, 116, 117, 118, 119, 120, 124, 128–9 n.43, 161
failure 8, 27, 47, 84, 87, 107, 119, 129 n.45, 177, 186, 189, 192, 200 n.20
falsification 37, 116
'Fantasia in the Library' (Foucault) 191–3
fantasy 26, 29, 33, 34, 35, 47, 78, 115, 117, 123, 161, 188, 191–2, 213
fascism 111, 177
Fassbinder, Rainer Werner 225
feature films 28, 127 n.20, 215, 216, 220
Feder, Chris Welles 56 n.68
female figure. *See* girl figure
feminism 129 n.45
Ferrando, Monica 49
fetishism 106–7, 111, 161, 178, 210, 212
F for Fake (Welles) 49
fiction/fictional films 16, 33, 34, 47, 60, 101, 116, 120, 123, 129 n.45, 171, 186, 187, 188, 215, 219
film archaeology 5, 6–13, 26, 218
film history 44, 75, 182
film philosophy 6, 13
film-ruin 34, 48
film still 50, 67, 198, 221
film stock 28, 137, 145, 160, 181, 182, 185, 216
Film Studies 168 n.50

First Auto, The (Del Ruth) 127 n.20
Fischli, Peter 171, 173, 174
Fisher Price camera 204 n.73
Flaubert, Gustave 188, 189, 190–4, 202 n.50
Fleming, Paul 84, 85, 87
fluoroscope 211–12
fly, the 3, 15, 16, 23, 131–68
'Fly, The' (Langelaan) 167 n.46
Fly, The (Neumann) 167 n.46
Fly, The (remade by Cronenberg) 157, 167 n.46
form-of-life 10, 11, 82, 87, 171, 211, 214, 215, 232 n.3
Foucault, Michel 27, 35–9, 41–2, 55 n.45, 59, 71, 73, 74, 80–2, 191, 192–3, 203 n.59, 205
France 55 n.55, 137, 183
Franco, Jess 49
'Franz Kafka: on the Tenth Anniversary of his Death' (Benjamin) 175–8, 179, 200 n.13
French revolution 81
Freud, Sigmund 39, 40, 72–3, 80, 212–13
Fulton, Keith 55 n.54
Fundamental Concepts of Metaphysics: World, Finitude, Solitude, The (Heidegger) 16, 150, 153, 156, 228

gags 71–2, 73, 86, 174
Galton, Francis 74, 214
Gammon, Frank 183
Gassman, Vittorio 173
Gazette des Tribunaux 202 n.50
Gelley, Alexander 129 n.50
genius 32, 168 n.60, 169, 217
genocide 82
gesture 5, 6–8, 14–15, 22, 30, 32, 34, 37, 45–50, 57–99, 107–8, 125, 176–7, 188, 209
authorship and 87
biopolitics *vs.* 80–4
and the body 57–99, 215–16, 220–2
crisis of 57, 58, 59, 85, 87, 210
definition of 68
and image 60–7, 75, 89, 91, 105, 106, 107, 108–9, 123, 211
Jean Paul's three types of 84–5

and language 84–5, 219–22
loss of 63–5, 87, 123
as potentiality 84–8
testing 57, 58
and transmission 67–71, 88–94
ghosts 24, 196, 227
Giagni, Gianfranco 53 n.18
Gilliam, Terry 55 n.54
Ginzburg, Carlo 39
Giorgini, Ciro 53 n.18
girl-figure
   in *Citizen Kane* (Welles) 21–2
   in Darger's painting 55 n.63
   in 'Dim Stockings' (Agamben) 106, 112
   in *Don Quixote* (Welles's incomplete film) 22, 28–32, 34–5, 43–5, 49, 195
   in *F for Fake* (Welles) 48–9
   in Goya's painting 121
   in Manet's painting 121
   in 'Mass Ornament, The' (Kracauer) 112
   in Muybridge's images 62–4, 91–2, 94 n.5
   in Peck's painting 50
   in *Three Disappearances of Soad Hosny, The* (Stephens) 101–2
   in *Unspeakable Girl* (Agamben) 49–50
   in Velázquez's painting 121
   in Warburg's work 24–5, 62
glitch 23, 94, 103, 125, 126, 199
globalization 104
Godard, Jean-Luc 7, 24, 47, 48
Goebbels, Joseph 111
Goya 121
grammar, cinematic 59, 73, 75, 76–7, 80, 82, 188
Grant, Iain Hamilton 12
Great Exhibition 106–7
Greene, William Friese 202 n.45
Gregory, André 219
Grønstad, Asbjørn 6, 18 n.12, 24
grotesque 174, 191, 192, 193
Guantanamo Bay 6
Guattari, Félix 65
gun camera 69
Gunning, Tom 78

Gurney, Edmund 183
Gustafsson, Henrik 6, 8, 18 n.12, 24

Hackney Photographic Society 183–4, 185
Haiti 225
halos 105
Hanan al-Cinema (Marks) 125
happiness 30, 64, 106, 112
Haraway, Donna 145, 166 n.20
Hardt, Michael 108, 229
Harman, Graham 12–13, 20 n.38
Harrington, George 183
Heidegger, Martin 11, 13, 16, 86, 115, 131, 148, 149, 150–3, 155, 156, 164, 214
Heise, William 183
hermeneutics 38, 40
heterogeneity 9, 148, 149, 158, 171
heteronormativity 120
heterosexuality 74, 91–2
Higham, Charles 52 n.10
high-speed cinematography 132, 135–43
Histoire(s) du cinéma (Godard) 24, 47
historiography 23
history 36, 38, 42, 48, 50, 51–2, 54 n.41, 56 n.66, 88, 111, 125, 132, 141, 164, 188, 228, 231
History: A Novel (Morante) 117
history of cinema 1–7, 12, 14, 44, 48, 131, 132, 161, 163, 183, 216
Hitler, Adolf 111
Hollywood 111, 127 n.20
Holocaust 8, 26, 82
home entertainment 181, 185
homosemanticism 41
homosexuality 74–5
Hosny, Soad 101, 103, 124–6
Hotel Rwanda 8
human–animal distinction 4, 10–13, 16, 50, 60, 131–68, 214–17, 222
human consciousness 11, 12
human gait 64, 69
humanism 12
humanitas 131–2, 153, 164
Huston, John 29
hypostasis 123
hysteria 64, 73, 214

iconography 67–8
identity 2, 14, 38, 39, 59, 70–1, 74, 75, 76, 77, 79, 82–3, 87–8, 93, 102, 108, 112, 173, 174, 178, 181, 214, 215
image 4, 5, 7, 14, 15, 21, 23, 24, 27, 30–4, 37, 43–52, 57–99, 101–29, 131–68, 180, 182, 186, 197, 199, 200 n.13, 205–34
immanence 37, 39, 66
immunity/immunization 71, 82–4
impotentiality 17, 25–6, 194, 219, 225–9, 230, 231
improvisation 43, 86, 90, 94, 125, 226
inclusion/exclusion binary 36–7, 81–2, 105, 131, 153
incomplete works 23, 25–52, 230–2
  concept of 50–2, 225–7
  as dead letters 229–31
index 37
indifference 113, 114, 118, 119–20, 152, 229, 231
indigenous film cultures 111
individualism 39, 87–8
industrial culture 12
in-fans 21, 222, 226
infinity 9, 12, 120
In My Father's Shadow (Feder) 56 n.68
inner life 58–60, 86
'Inoperative Community, The' (Nancy) 104
inoperativity 16, 21, 104, 117, 124
insect media 140
Insect Media (Parikka) 11
insects 3–4, 11, 132–68
installation 198, 199, 223
Institut Marey 137
intensity 27, 161
interiority/exteriority distinction 15, 57–99, 131, 163, 211–16, 222
interval 135–6, 141, 142, 156, 157, 164–5, 217, 222
Introduction to Metaphysics?, An (Heidegger) 153
invention and inventors 3, 9, 16, 39, 58, 73, 78, 90, 137, 160, 170, 180–7, 189–90, 193, 197–8, 223
inversion 14, 16, 74, 75, 146, 173, 175, 177, 195, 223

Islamic art 9
Italy 28, 29, 30, 44, 48, 53 n.18

James, David 181, 201 n.32
Jazz Singer, The (Crosland) 73, 127 n.20
Joly 169
Jules et Jim (Truffaut) 147

Kafka, Franz 16, 51, 58, 89, 94 n.2, 170, 174, 175–6, 177, 178, 179, 180, 188, 189, 197, 201 n.21
Kamper, Rose 69
Kearton, Cherry 183
Kearton, Richard 183
Keaton 86
Keller, Sarah 25
Kid Auto Races at Venice (Lehrman) 226
Kinemacolor 183
kinetograph 90, 99 n.90
kinetophone 90
kinetoscope 90, 99 n.90, 182, 190
Kingston Museum 60
kinship 3, 38, 41
Kircher, Athanasius 9
knowledge and experience 32–3, 39
Kodak Company 202 n.42
Kodar, Oja 28, 48–9
Kommerell, Max 84–5, 86, 87
Kouvaros, George 20 n.40
Kracauer, Siegfried 111–12, 129 n.50

Laclau, Ernesto 26
La Machine Animale (Marey) 139
La Maja Desnuda (Goya) 121
language 11, 13, 22, 41, 49–50, 58, 60, 76, 79, 80, 84–7, 88, 91, 103, 105, 111, 115, 122–4, 158, 168 n.50, 173, 175, 196, 213, 219–20, 222, 226
Lanzmann, Claude 26
Larkins, Major Harry 69, 227
La Venus del espejo (Velázquez) 121
law 6, 10, 26, 36, 81, 129 n.45, 178, 196, 213, 224, 230
Leroy 169
Les Cloches de Corneville (Planquette) 57, 94 n.1
Leslie, Esther 144
Levi, Pavle 26, 34

Index

Levin, Thomas 109–10
Lévi-Strauss, Claude 224
Levitt, Deborah 7, 66, 95 n.18
library 192, 193, 194
lighting 163, 223
Lights of New York (Warner Bros) 127 n.20
Lingis, Alphonso 104
Lippit, Akira 12, 16, 72–3, 79, 80, 149, 205, 212, 218
lip-synch 43
lithographic art 139
liturgy 35
Lives of the Painters (Vasari) 146
'Loafer, The' (Macklay) 75
Lost in La Mancha (Fulton and Pepe) 55 n.54
Lumière, Louis 169
Lumière brothers 70, 78, 183
Lundemo, Trond 8

Mabel's Strange Predicament (Normand) 226
Macklay, Arthur 75
magic 79, 84, 89, 145–6, 174, 175, 183, 187, 195, 223
Malaga 44, 53 n.15
Malle, Louis 219, 222, 233 n.20
Manet 121, 129 n.48
Marey, Étienne-Jules 3, 65, 69, 135, 137, 139–40, 155, 158, 160, 169
Marks, Laura U. 9, 125
Marx, Karl 106–7, 108, 123, 178, 225
'Mass Ornament, The' (Kracauer) 112
materialism/materiality 3, 10, 13, 14, 17, 23, 33–4, 42, 49, 78, 83, 85, 86, 90, 91, 93, 103, 107, 112–13, 115, 124, 125, 160, 169–72, 182, 188, 190, 196, 197, 199, 214, 218, 219, 222–5, 227, 232
Maurice, Barthélemy 188, 202 n.50
Maurice Guest (Richardson) 173
Mavor, Carol 142
McCormack, Patty 28–9, 43, 44–5, 49
McCrea, Christian 6
McPhee, John 9
meaning 24, 37, 40, 41, 47, 80, 87, 89, 114, 135, 225, 226

means/mediality 34, 38, 39, 43, 57, 65, 79, 82, 83, 86, 93, 118, 124, 127 n.29, 214, 216, 218, 224
media archaeology. *See* film archaeology
Media Museum 185, 202 n.43
mediation 106, 107, 109
medicine 61, 71, 188, 213
Meillassoux, Quentin 12
Mekas, Jonas 201 n.32
Méliès, Georges 70
melodrama 87, 94 n.3, 164–5, 173–4, 175, 216
Melville, Herman 26, 29, 229, 230
memory 46, 67, 68, 89, 127 n.29, 183
Mesnard, Philippe 55 n.55
messianic/messianism 19 n.30, 25, 35, 170, 175, 177, 230
metaphor 11, 29, 70, 75, 78, 79, 82, 121, 139, 148, 227
metaphysics 10, 79, 85, 123
methodology 4, 26, 36, 37, 74, 170
Metz, Christian 168 n.50
Meurent, Victorine 121, 129 n.48
Mexico 28–9, 44
Michaud, Philippe-Alain 89
microcinematography 141, 143, 156, 161–2, 181
Mills, Catherine 119
mimesis 64, 89, 171, 172, 190
mineral 155, 160, 218
mirror image 183
mise en scène 172
Mneme (Semon) 68
Mnemosyne-Atlas (Warburg) 27, 46, 50
modern art 48
modernism/modernity 8, 12, 36, 40, 59, 64, 78, 83, 111
Modern Times (Chaplin) 226
modus operandi 118
monologue 94 n.3
montage 7, 24, 31, 46, 47, 102, 124, 195, 213
monumental history 5
mood 114, 152
Morante, Elsa 117
Moreau, Jeanne 147
Mori, Paola 48
Morvan, Carolyn 77–8
motion pictures 58, 90, 91, 99 n.90

moving image technologies 57, 58, 60–7, 89–91, 99 n.90, 111, 163, 182
Moving Pictures (Talbot) 186
Mullarkey, John 10–11, 13
Mulvey, Laura 24, 67
Munich Film Museum 49
Münsterberg, Hugo 161
Murch, Walter 99 n.91
Murray, Alex 8, 35
Murray, Thomas E. 183
Muselmann 8, 26, 42
Museum of Modern Art 49
music hall 71, 77
Musser, Charles 99 n.90, 183, 215
Muybridge, Eadweard 51–2, 58, 60–7, 69, 70, 88, 91–3, 94–5 n.7, 94 n.5, 95 n.10, 115, 155, 158, 160, 169, 206, 227
My Dinner with André (Malle) 219–20, 222
My Silence (Taanila) 219–21, 222, 233 n.20
My Silence 2 (Taanila) 233 n.20
mysticism 77
myth 49, 145, 175, 196, 199, 223, 224

Nachleben (afterlife) 46, 68, 96 n.32
Nagib, Lúcia 120
nameless science 35, 217–19
Nancy, Jean-Luc 104, 105
narrative films 4, 7, 62, 86, 110, 161, 170, 173–4, 181
natural history 140, 141, 180
nature 8, 84, 131, 143, 164, 224
Negri, Antonio 26, 108, 229
nervous disorders 64, 68, 69, 74
Neumann, Kurt 167 n.46
New Jersey 57, 89, 91
'New Kind of Rays, A' (Röntgen) 78
new media technologies 7
New Testament 114
New York Metropolitan Museum 166 n.23
Niepce 169
Nietzsche, Friedrich 4, 11, 36, 57, 93–4, 98 n.79, 99 n.98, 203 n.66, 205
'Nietzsche, Genealogy, History' (Foucault) 36
nihilism 87, 230
nomos 8

non-knowledge 21–2
non-relationality 149
Normand, Mabel 226
Northern Photographic Works Limited 183
nothingness 146
Noys, Benjamin 7, 65, 86, 119, 216
nudes 60–4, 91–2, 94–5 n.7, 114, 115, 120, 121

oath 35
objects 12–14, 23, 24, 33, 34, 36, 37, 39, 41, 44, 49, 54 n.41, 55 n.45, 61, 66, 67, 74, 76, 78, 86, 93–4, 112, 117, 121, 122, 125, 133, 135, 136, 141, 145, 148, 149, 157, 161, 162, 171–4, 178, 182, 194, 195–7, 208, 214, 217, 223–5, 232
obscenities 103, 119, 122–3
Odradek 178, 195
O'Grady, Lorraine 129 n.49
Old San Francisco (Crosland) 127 n.20
Olympia (Manet) 121
omnipotence 76
180° stage rule 61, 75
'On Parables' (Kafka) 179
ontology 5, 13, 55 n.45, 70, 93, 152–3, 158, 179, 194, 214, 218
open, the (Heidegger's concept) 148, 150–3, 164
Order of Things: An Archaeology of the Human Sciences, The (Foucault) 35–6, 38, 41
Ownbey, Carolyn 8
ownership 182, 190
Oxford and Cambridge Boat Race, The (Acre) 182

Palestine 8
panopticon 27
Paracelsus 38
paracinema 218
paradigm 8, 9, 14, 15, 16, 22–3, 26, 27, 36, 37, 42, 45, 46, 47–8, 50, 51, 60, 67, 71, 82, 96 n.29, 101, 107, 115, 121, 172, 175, 181, 190, 194, 214, 225
para-text, of parody 171, 172, 179, 183, 193

Parikka, Jussi 11, 139, 140
Paris 28, 78, 106, 112, 137, 170, 188, 206
Parmenides 16, 153
parody 16, 30, 41, 44, 116–17, 123, 170, 171, 172–5, 179, 183, 186–90, 192, 193, 194
    definitions of 172, 187
partnership 13, 90, 116, 183, 190
Pasolini, Pier Paolo 53 n.17, 117, 225, 234 n.25
Passions, The (Viola) 46
patents 3, 90, 181, 182, 185, 187, 190, 227, 230
pathosformel 46
Paul, Jean 84–5, 87
Paul, Robert 182–3, 186, 190
Pauline doctrine 19 n.30, 35
Paxton 107
Payne, Ernest 207–8, 211
Peck, Michael 50
Pepe, Louis 55 n.54
Petrus Christus 166 n.23
phantasm 16, 24, 28, 46, 80, 86
phantasmagoria 191
phenomenology 66, 80, 212
philology 6, 35, 217
philosophical archaeology. *See* archaeology
phonograph 58, 59, 91
photography
    amateur 137, 197
    and cinema 57–99, 102–3, 115–16, 119, 129 n.50, 180, 181, 182, 183–4, 189, 206–8, 210, 211
    documentary 186
    erotic 101–29
    of insects 131–68
    new 211–12, 227
    Polaroid 2
    X-ray (*See* X-ray)
physical realism 120
physiognomy 60, 73, 74, 97 n.54
physiology 46, 59–60, 61, 64, 65, 69, 137
Pick, Anat 12, 19 n.40, 149, 152
plagiarism 192
Planquette, Robert 94 n.1

play 24, 93, 118, 121, 169, 175, 190, 194–6, 199, 223–5
    and ritual 195–6, 224
Playboy magazine 157, 167 n.46
Poe, Edgar Allen 178
Poetics (Scagligero) 172
poetry 117, 152, 228–9
polis 10, 59, 81, 83, 214
politics 5, 6, 8, 65, 81, 93, 108, 125, 188, 196
popular entertainment 73
pornography 15, 65, 103, 112, 113–23, 127 n.29, 129 n.45, 129 n.47
Portrait of a Carthusian (Christus) 166 n.23
positivism 3, 58
posthumanism 10, 153
post-production 43, 44, 62
post-structuralism 12
Potemkin 176
potentiality 5, 8, 9, 14, 16, 21, 23, 48, 49–50, 52, 66, 68, 102, 103, 108–9, 118–19, 151, 160, 178, 206
    gesture as 84–8
    and impotentiality 16–17, 25–6, 194, 225–31
Powell, Michael 210
praxis 6, 34, 88, 89, 108, 190, 218
Pressburger, Emeric 210
profanation 2, 16, 66, 89, 103, 113, 115, 117–18, 120, 122–4, 129 n.47, 171, 177, 193, 194–6, 199, 214, 223, 224, 232 n.3
projectors 16, 23, 92, 160, 183–5, 190, 198–9, 223
propaganda films 111
props 115, 190
prose 51, 85
psyche 80
psychiatry 60
psychoanalysis 12, 80, 212
psychology 14, 52 n.10, 71–7, 78, 87, 211, 230
pure gesture 63–4, 84–7
Pushkin, Alexandr 176

Quadruple Object, The (Harman) 13, 20 n.38
Queen Victoria, Diamond Jubilee 232 n.5
Queneau, Raymond 202 n.50

radio 28, 44
radiography 155
Raff, Norman 183
raison d'être 210
Rang, Florens Christian 164
rapid lanternslide changer 182
realism 10, 12, 13, 20 n.40, 120, 145–6
recitation 20 n.38, 91
recording 5, 8, 24, 43, 47, 57, 60, 67, 69, 70, 77, 82, 88–90, 92, 94, 99 n.91, 123, 124–5, 135, 137, 140, 157, 197, 205, 212, 219, 222
recording cylinders 90, 94, 99 n.91, 139
redemption 7, 11, 51, 65, 66, 175, 177, 230, 231
Red Shoes, The (Powell and Pressburger) 210–11
rehearsal 94, 116, 174
Reiguera, Francisco 28, 29, 31
religion 40, 117, 171, 188, 217
remnant 8, 79, 218
Renaissance 41, 146
repetition 7, 10, 14, 15, 23, 27, 35, 46, 48, 51, 94, 101, 102, 103, 109, 119, 120, 135, 139, 141, 143, 169, 173, 181, 188, 191, 192, 193, 229–30
reproduction 15, 26, 43, 59, 61, 91, 109, 135, 173, 178, 181–2, 189–90, 192, 196, 229–30
rerecording 125
resemblance, signature as 23, 38–40, 41–2
returned look 15, 103, 113–14, 116–23, 128–9 n.43, 128 n.34
Return of the Fly (Bernds) 167 n.46
reverie maps 141
rhapsody 172, 173, 191
Rhapsody (Vidor) 173
rhythm 9, 23, 43, 57, 76, 91, 124, 126, 190
Richardson, Ethel 173
Ricotta (Pasolini) 53 n.17
Riefenstahl, Leni 111
Rilke, Rainer 152
ritual 12, 28, 175, 181, 191, 195–6, 199, 207, 215, 220, 223, 224, 225, 227
Rodman, George Hook 154, 155–6, 159
Rogers and Hammerstein Archive of Recorded Sound, New York 99 n.91
Rome 29, 30, 45, 48, 49, 53 n.17

Röntgen, Wilhelm 78, 205, 207
Röntgen Society 155
Roots of Heaven (Huston) 29
Rosabella: Orson Welles's Years in Italy (Giagni and Giorgini) 53 n.18
Rosenbaum, Jonathan 27, 28, 29, 52 n.10, 53 n.13
Ross, Alison 54 n.37, 59
Ross lens 184
Rostock laboratory 142, 156
Royal Institution of Great Britain 135, 141, 165 n.2
Royal Photographic Society 155
running man, photographic sequences of 60–1, 69

sacred 16, 66, 81, 113, 115, 117, 124, 171, 193, 195, 196, 199, 214, 223, 224
sacrifice 81, 224
Salò (Pasolini) 117
Salon Indien du Grand Café 78
Salt, Barry 75
Sancho Panza 28, 30–2, 44–5, 51, 176, 219
Santner, Eric 81, 98 n.68
Sao Paolo (Pasolini) 53 n.17
satire 172, 188–9, 190, 192
saved night 164, 168 n.60
Saxton, Libby 8, 26, 82
Scagligero, Giulio Cesare 172
schism 32
Schivelbusch, Wolfgang 77
Schlemihl, Peter 94 n.2
Schmidt, Carl 36
Scholem, Gerhard 201 n.21
Schütz, Anton 36
science films 73, 87, 161
screenwriting 173
Sebald, W.G. 188
Second World War 105, 157
secularization 40
semiotics/semantic 38, 40, 58, 85, 135, 155
Semon, Richard 68
sensory effects 4, 11, 84, 140, 143, 148, 150, 163
Serre, Henri 147
Serres, Michel 132
sex and sexuality 2, 74–5, 91–2, 114, 115, 118–22, 129 n.43, 216

Shallow Breath (Whiteread) 1
shame/shamelessness 116, 128–9 n.43, 128 n.34, 177
Sharp, Don 167 n.46
Shaw, Howard 167 n.46
Shawn, Wallace 219
Shoah (Lanzmann) 26
short films 53 n.17, 71–2, 78, 138, 172, 209
shot, cinematic
   aerial 139, 156, 197
   close-up 30, 76, 97 n.54, 111, 119, 132, 143, 161, 168 n.50, 171, 209, 212, 213, 215
   establishing 211
   high-angle 211
   long 29, 76
   medium 76
   point-of-view 47, 75
   reverse angle 75, 76
   shot reverse shot 60, 76
   wide 172
sign and signature 23–4, 32, 38, 39, 40, 41–2, 44, 55 n.45, 66, 106, 107, 112, 118, 119, 121, 143, 151, 177
signature 4, 5, 9, 22, 23–4, 27, 37–42, 44, 45, 47, 55 n.45, 74, 116, 117, 118, 120, 124, 166 n.23, 190, 211, 216, 231
silence 49, 66, 75, 86–7, 219–22
silent film 65, 86–7, 226
Singing Fool, The (Warner Bros) 127 n.20
singularity 23, 24, 26, 37, 39, 42, 45, 84, 88, 101, 102, 104, 105, 108, 110, 112, 113, 123, 143, 172, 173, 174, 179, 192, 193, 195, 210, 211
Situationist International 104, 110
slapstick 135, 215
Sleigh, Charlotte 141
Sloane, Everett 52 n.2
slow film 135
Slowik, Michael 127 n.20
slow motion 4, 43, 141, 143, 200 n.13
Smith, George Albert 183, 209, 210
Smith, Percy 161–2
social dramas 135
Society of the Spectacle, The (Debord) 103–4, 109, 110, 216
Solnit, Rebecca 62, 99 n.92

Sortie des Usines Lumière à Lyon (Lumière brothers) 78
sound film 28, 90, 111, 127 n.20
sound/soundtrack 30, 43, 47, 53 n.13, 57, 83, 90, 91, 94, 99 n.91, 110–11, 125, 127 n.20, 133, 140, 143, 163, 221, 222, 226
sous rature 115
Souvenirs Entomologiques (1879–1907) (Fabre) 141
sovereignty/sovereign 6, 10, 36, 69, 80–2, 214
Spain 29, 44
spark drum camera 3–4, 15, 132, 133–44
spectacle 15, 66, 79, 104, 106, 107–8, 109–13, 123, 124, 191, 197, 199, 216, 223
spiders 149, 155
splitting 185
Stainton, Audrey 29, 42, 43, 44, 45, 53 n.16, 55 n.56
Stalinism 111
Stallybrass, Peter 115
standardization 70, 71, 133, 141, 143, 155, 158, 163, 184, 185, 205, 211, 214, 216, 225
St Anthony 191
Starling, Simon 196–9, 223
'State Monopoly on Pornography, A' (Benjamin) 122
state of exception 6, 10, 36, 153
Stephens, Rania 101–2, 124–5
stereoscopic spark drum camera. *See* spark drum camera
Stewart, Garrett 7, 66
Stewart, Susan 141
stimuli 68, 83
Stirn, Carl 202 n.43
stone(s) 13, 150–3, 160, 164, 214, 218
stoppage 7, 15, 48, 102
'Storyteller, The' (Benjamin) 32
St Paul 53 n.17
St Paul (Pasolini) 225
subjectification 79, 82, 83–4
subjectivity 8, 82, 87, 129 n.49
suffering 8, 64, 114
Summer with Monika (Bergman) 116, 117
supernatural 68, 80, 143

surrealism 111
symbols 14, 68, 71, 73, 89, 214
synchrony 24, 37, 54 n.41, 196, 225, 227

Taanila, Mika 219-22, 233 n.20
tableau image 75-6
Tait, Margaret 204 n.73
Talbot, F.A. 186
talkies 73
Tamiroff, Akim 28
taxonomy 39, 74, 79, 155, 205
Taylor, Elizabeth 173
teleportation 157
telescope 209, 212-13
television 2, 28, 30, 44, 45, 110-11
tempo 76, 101
Temptation (Bosch painting) 193
Temptation of St Anthony, The (Brueghel painting) 193
Temptation of St Anthony, The (Flaubert) 191-4
test 57-60, 90-1, 137, 215
testimony 26, 74, 128 n.34
theatre 28, 60, 106, 161, 176, 191, 197, 215
theology 9, 35, 40, 54 n.32, 112, 114, 123, 164, 188
Thousand Years of Nonlinear History, A (DeLanda) 13
Three Disappearances of Soad Hosny, The (Stephens) 101-2, 124-5
three modalities of history 36
Thus Spoke Zarathustra (Nietzsche) 93, 98 n.79
Tiananmen protest 105, 108-9
ticks 7, 131, 142, 148, 152-3, 156, 167 n.44
time/temporality 3, 6, 8-9, 19 n.30, 24, 47, 68, 132, 135, 141-2, 143, 147, 175, 177-8, 195-6, 211, 219, 224
  and space 40, 46, 75, 89, 106, 141, 148, 161, 178
Tourette, Gilles de la 58, 64, 68, 69, 70, 74, 93
Trahair, Lisa 71
Tramp, the 226-7
transcendentals, of cinema 7, 15, 48, 102-3
transfiguration 114-15, 127 n.26
transmission 5, 8, 9, 11, 14, 27, 32, 38, 46, 47, 50, 56 n.70, 60, 67-71, 83, 84, 88-94, 103, 110, 111, 122, 124-5, 157, 217, 218, 219-22, 225
trauma 2, 40, 101, 181, 212-13
tropes 27, 46, 101, 123, 161, 199, 212, 223
Truffaut, François 147
truth 14-15, 32, 35, 36, 55 n.45, 60, 63, 66, 73, 74, 77, 79-80, 85, 87, 103, 116, 179, 206, 210-11, 212, 222, 231
Two Court Clerks, The (Maurice) 188
typographic man 41-4

Uexküll, Jacob von 131, 142, 148, 149, 150, 151, 152, 155, 156, 159
Umgebung 148
Umwelt 131, 148-9, 150, 153
unavowable 104
Unavowable Community, The (Blanchot) 104
unfinished works. *See* incomplete works
Unger, William 183
University of Freiburg 150
University of Pennsylvania 61, 92, 94 n.5, 95 n.10, 155
'Unseen World, The' (Urban) 161-2
unthought cinema 14, 25, 227
Untimely Meditations (Nietzsche) 36
Urban, Charles 161, 183
use
  concept of 190, 194
  form of 190
  laws of 22, 23, 193
  model of 141
  profanation and 224
  value 22, 24, 107-8, 117, 141, 178, 224
utopia 114, 118, 194

Väliaho, Pasi 7
Vasari, Giorgio 146
vector, the 9, 77, 195
Velázquez 121
VHS 124, 125
Vidor, Charles 173
Viola, Bill 46
visual culture 6, 8
Vitascope 183
voice 43, 44, 59, 74, 85, 86, 90, 94, 123-4, 125, 221
Volk (people) 112

waistcoat camera 202 n.43
Walley, Jonathan 218
Walser, Robert 105–6, 174, 187, 188, 189, 197
waltz 57, 90–1
Warburg, Aby 24, 27, 35, 37, 45–7, 50, 62, 67–8, 70, 80, 84, 89, 122, 217, 233 n.13
Warburg Institute 68
Warner, Marina 79–80, 143
Warner Bros 127 n.20
Watkins, William 9, 37–8
Way Things Go, The (Fischli and Weiss) 171–5
Weiss, David 171, 173, 174, 200 n.8
Welles, Beatrice 45, 48
Welles, Christopher 49
Welles, Orson 14, 21, 22, 27–30, 31, 34, 41, 42–5, 48–9, 52 n.10, 53 n.13, 53 n.16, 53 nn.17–18, 191, 194, 225, 232
Westphal, Carl 74–5, 78
whatever being 15, 102, 123
whatever body 112–13

White, Allon 115
White, James 183
Whiteread, Rachel 1, 2
Whyte, Jessica 66, 224
wildlife photography 183
Wilhelm Noack oHG (Starling) 196–9, 223
Williams, James S. 7–8
Williamson, James 71–2, 75
witnessing 5, 8, 26, 30, 33, 57, 82, 193
'Work of Art in the Age of Mechanical Reproduction, The' (Benjamin) 143

X-ray 15, 73, 77–80, 205, 207–8, 210–13, 232 n.5
X-ray of a foot (Payne) 207–9, 211

YouTube 30

Zielinski, Siegfried 8–9, 11, 170
Zimmerman, Patricia 181
zoe/bios distinction 10, 59, 81, 206, 210
zoopraxiscope 70, 91
Zworykin, Vladimir 110

www.ingramcontent.com/pod-product-compliance
Lightning Source LLC
Chambersburg PA
CBHW062125300426
44115CB00012BA/1819